D1251903

Hometown
⇒ Flavor ⇐

Front cover photos:
(Left) Kim Rosenberry and Judy Warren of Clasen's European Bakery, Middleton.
(Right) The Weber Brothers of Weber's Processing, Cuba City.
Back cover photo:
(Top) Bob Wills of Cedar Grove Cheese, Plain.

Hometown Flavor

A Cook's Tour of Wisconsin's
Butcher Shops, Bakeries,
Cheese Factories,
Other Specialty Markets

Terese Allen

PRAIRIE OAK PRESS
Madison, Wisconsin

First edition, first printing
Copyright © 1998 by Terese Allen

All rights reserved. No part of this publication may be reproduced or transmitted in any form or by any means, electonic or mechanical, including photocopy, recording, or any information storage or retrieval system, without permission in writing from the publisher.

Prairie Oak Press
821 Prospect Place
Madison, WI 53703

Designed and produced by Flying Fish Graphics, Blue Mounds, Wisconsin
Printed in the United States of America by BookCrafters, Chelsea, Michigan
All cover photographs by Brent Nicastro

Library of Congress Cataloging-in-Publication Data

Allen, Terese
    Hometown flavor : a cook's tour of Wisconsin's butcher shops, bakeries,
cheese factories & other specialty markets / Terese Allen.
        —1st ed.
          p. cm.
        Includes bibliographical references and index.
        ISBN 1-879483-42-4 (alk. paper)
1. Cookery, American. 2. Cookery–Wisconsin. 3. Grocery trade—Wisconsin—Guidebooks.
I. Title.
TX715.A4428 1998
641.59775—dc21   98-8212
                                                              CIP

In memory of
My mother Agnes, who filled a green box with hand-written recipes
Grandma Smallo, who fried long Johns and made dandelion wine
Grandma Marlow, who did the dishes
Dad, who loved booyah and cream puffs
and Louie, who carved a painted cornucopia.

With love to
Bev, who clips food articles, sews a tablecloth gift, and shares Friday night fish fry
and Marion, who likes the fun-size best.

Contents

Introduction

What's the one thing you can't be without when you're traveling? For some people it's a map or a special toothbrush, but for me it's the small, sturdy, white-and-blue cooler a friend gave me more than twenty years ago. The cooler is a little battered now and I've lost the ice pack that fit neatly inside the lid, but whenever I'm on one of my frequent road trips in Wisconsin, that ice box is my treasure chest.

Unlike travelers who bring back souvenirs or keepsakes from their trips, I bring back food. Instead of going to gift shops, I go to markets that sell local specialties. Dried cherries from Door County, smoked fish from Bayfield, Swiss cheese from Monroe, spicy bratwurst from Sheboygan, it all gets packed into my trusty cooler. When I get home, I unwrap the packages and soon am savoring the trip all over again.

Buying and cooking with products found at specialty markets gives me a delicious way to experience the great diversity of Wisconsin. When I visit small-scale, top-quality businesses like bakeries, butcher shops, and cheese factories, I get a taste of local flavor. These are the places where I learn about the state's varied ethnic heritage, meet creative, hard-working people, and discover the real character of a community.

Hometown Markets

We live in a time when local flavors and food customs around the country are rapidly diminishing. But not so rapidly in Wisconsin, where family bakeries, country meat markets, prizewinning cheese factories, candy kitchens, and other specialty food sources continue the culinary traditions and specialties of a culturally rich state.

At the advent of a new millennium, and having achieved 150 years of statehood, Wisconsin stands out for the quality and quantity of its community-based food businesses. It's a fitting time to look back at traditions that have shaped the state, and to renew an appreciation for the ones—like cheese- and sausage-making—that have endured through much change. There may be no better place to locate those traditions than in a hometown market.

At Chalet Cheese Co-op, the only factory in the United States that still produces limburger cheese, we experience the state's enduring dairy heritage. Scanning the eclectic sausage selection at Miesfeld's Triangle Market, we understand how many ethnic groups settled here. At Honey Acres near Ashippun, we taste a family tradition that's been around nearly as long as Wisconsin has been a state, and at Polak's Maple Hollow in Merrill, we recognize a treat that dates back even further.

These places provide old-fashioned goodness and remind us of our roots. Still, visiting one of them is not just a walk down memory lane. Specialty markets are where we know we'll get the good stuff. They're where the bacon is leaner and the whitefish is fresher. Where the food is unique.

"You can get the shrink-wrapped cookies anywhere," says baker Kathy Sohr of Kathy's on the Square in Marinette. "Close your eyes, they all taste the same." But they won't taste like the ones at her bakery, where she flavors hand-rolled cookies with real butter and bakes them daily in small batches.

The individual and regional differences that independent food businesses offer make our meals more exciting and our shopping more fun. No standard fare here—we savor a tangy goat's milk cheese, a peppery Polish sausage, an exquisite chocolate cream candy. We watch a cake decorator or a cheesemaker in action.

We know that patronizing local markets is smart shopping for lots of reasons: Food from smaller markets is often more healthful than over-processed, over-stored supermarket fare. It can be more affordable because there's no middleman to hike up prices. For travelers, visiting a cheese factory or a sugarbush is entertaining and educational. Local bakeries, butcher shops, and other food businesses add distinctiveness to communities, and buying from them supports the local economy.

Butcher, Baker, Cheesemaker

One of the best reasons to frequent hometown markets is the people—meat processors, pastry chefs, cheesemakers, candy dippers, fishmongers, maple syrup tappers, and a whole host of other independent food producers. At small markets, we meet creative artists, carriers of traditions, and real characters, people like the Weber brothers, a quartet of fourth-generation meat cutters from Cuba City, and

Herby Radmann, a trout farmer near Menomonie whose slogan is "Eat My Fish!" We get introduced to Randy Krahenbuhl, one of a handful of certified master cheesemakers in the nation, and his wife Shelley, who can reel off imaginative cheese-cooking ideas as fast as an auctioneer calls bids. We get to know Shelli McLimans, a lady butcher, and Sara Weihaupt, a candymaker who is building a local legacy one piece of pecan brittle at a time. We get a look at the lives and labors of folks who enrich our lives and deserve our recognition.

These are people we get to know and learn to trust. They tell us how to cook a pot roast and what to do about E. coli. They listen and respond when we ask them to make organic cheese. They welcome us with smiles, samples to taste, and the kind of service unheard of at the giant stores.

The owners of hometown food businesses enjoy a local reputation—and they earned it the hard way. They follow cut-no-corners recipes—some original, some handed down through generations—and keep hours that would kill most people. They're the little guys, the ones who fight mechanization and know bigger is often not better.

Some are heroes, in a way. Gary Engelke, for instance, creates a welcoming "clubhouse" atmosphere at his Platteville bakery. Meatman Louie Muench III, who as scoutmaster, past president of the United Fund and Jaycees, active member of the Wisconsin Association of Meat Producers, and Grand Knight of the Knights of Columbus, is as community-minded as they come. As food-guide writer Ed Levine said (quoted in a *New York Times* article by Ruth Reichl, November 12, 1997), small merchants have "generosity and spirit [that] restores your faith in humanity. . . They're just so real. They make life better."

What's Cooking

The recipes in this book come from butchers, bakers, cheesemakers, and other small-scale food producers. (There are also many dishes inspired by the products they make.) Collecting the recipes, I wasn't surprised that most people were happy to share their tips and favorite dishes. Folks in the food business are like that.

Sometimes my requests were met with amusement, as in, "Who has time for recipes?" or even slight confusion, as in, "Why would mine be anything special?" Fish merchant Eric Johnson of Port Wing, for example, asked for his finest smoked chub preparation, replies with a shrug and a smile, "All's I do is just take one outside, peel it, and eat it! That's the best way."

For other producers, the culinary side of their business is a source of creative expression, and sometimes a means to share their values. Phil Markgren of the Spooner Bake Shoppe gets a kick out of developing breads that feature cranberries, wild rice, and other "Northwoods" foods. Krista Bleich of Krista's Kitchen in Portage lets her pie fillings reflect the season and uses natural ingredients in many baked goods.

Some of the recipes are family or ethnic specialties, like the kringle from O & H Danish Bakery in Racine and pork-filled tamales from Milwaukee's Mercado El Rey. Others are community favorites little known outside their area, such as peanut squares from a bakery in Algoma called Wautlet's. Still others, including Smoked Whitefish Chowder and Wisconsin Fondue, are inspired by regional products and traditions.

Together, the recipes—whether contributed by producers or inspired by their products—illustrate the spectrum that is Wisconsin cooking, something that's as hard to pin down as "American" cooking itself. It's not about this kind of recipe or that method of preparation, but rather, these regional foodstuffs, those cultural influences. If there's no easy definition, there's a lot of enjoyment in discovering the influences and exploring the range of good food that's available—from Amish farm cooking to upscale urban fare, from labor-intensive heritage dishes to easygoing, everyday foods, from health-conscious choices to no-holds-barred edible celebrations.

If such exploration leads us to enjoy our food more, all the better. In an age of nutrition zealotry, eating disorders, and other food-related madnesses, too many people have forgotten that food is one of life's purest, most dependable pleasures. Food is about nutrition and health. It's also about cultural heritage, social justice, the environment, the economy, and animal rights.

But food is also about enjoyment. Especially, I believe, the food from local markets, which doesn't have to be homemade to be down-home. It doesn't have to be steamed vegetables to be good for us.

And it doesn't have to be foie gras or crème brûlée to have its own eloquence.

It's real food that's really good. It can be venison sausage, or a chocolate malt, or a handful of plump, ruby-red dried cherries. It is accessible and delicious. It's worth having for its own sake.

Hometown Flavor

The businesses featured in this book are small-scale, independent operations that offer specialty foods made on premise. Their products are made from scratch, often using original recipes. Each business markets directly to customers from a retail outlet that's open to the public (some also sell wholesale or via mail order). You'll find no chain stores, supermarkets, or large corporations herein. Many places are family-run, feature ethnic foods or regional ingredients, and are revered by residents as part of local history.

Like my sturdy cooler, small-scale specialty food markets are full of treasures waiting to be savored. They give us the sweet bite of an extra-sharp cheddar, the smoky lushness of country ham, and the crusty tug of whole-grain bread. When we visit hometown meat markets, bake shops, cheese marts, and other retail sources, we renew our pleasure in the products and traditions found close to home. We get service, not shrink-wrap.

When we shop at small markets, we acknowledge the stamina and skills of independent food producers. And we play our own important role in a tradition that helps define and strengthen our communities.

A tradition that gives us real food, real people, and real hometown flavor.

—Please Note

All information about the businesses in this book is subject to change. Travelers should call or write before visiting to get hours, directions, etc. Many places have catalogs or product lists and offer mail order service; again, call for more information.

Acknowledgments

My warm thanks to the butchers, bakers, cheesemakers, and other independent food producers who took time from very busy lives to share their stories and recipes. I'd also like to acknowledge the numerous producers whose businesses did not make it into this book, which was necessarily limited in scope. Bakers, butchers, and other small-scale food merchants are undervalued in our culture. This book features and applauds a relative few, but there are many, many more who deserve recognition and support.

Recipe testing is one of my favorite parts of writing a cookbook, but I'm never quite comfortable until each recipe is reviewed further by another cook. So here's to a cadre of testers: The main heroines are my sister Lucia Allen-Voreis—who, if there is such a thing as a culinary soul mate, is mine—and my niece Claire Reinke, to whom I say, "May you always have pork tenderloin with blueberries and may you never forget the flour in your pie filling." As for the others, you know who you are, and now so will everyone else: Billie Greenwood, Ellen and Al Klimek, Bev Allen, Punky Egan and the bakery students at Madison Area Technical College, Kay Ullmer, Judy Fisher, Susie Regan, Beth Zellner, Jane Kunesh, Vicki Linzmeyer, Susan Starr, Dawn Johnson, Wayne Block, and Efrat Livny.

I'd like to salute a number of folks who listened, motivated me, shared knowledge, gave advice, assisted with "grunt work," or helped in countless other ways to make this book happen: Sarah Minasian of the Wisconsin Milk Marketing Board; writer Jerry Apps; Lois Bergerson; Patrick Gundlach; Cassie Willyard; Judy Johnson, "bookmakers" Jerry Minnich, Kristin Visser, Brent Nicastro, Caroline Beckett, and Frank Sandner; and innumerable friends and family members (the great unnamed).

My final thanks are to Jim Block. For his fun-loving palate. For lending me his laptop. For loading the van. For catching fish and cutting down a Christmas tree. For driving. For the teeny tear of pride in his eye when he finishes a draft I've just handed him. (How's that for unconditional support?) For never letting me run out of things to thank him for.

For the Cook: Quick List of Recipes

Side Dishes

Pasta Dishes

Main Dishes: Meat

Pies, Pastries, Cakes, & Other Desserts

NORTHWEST

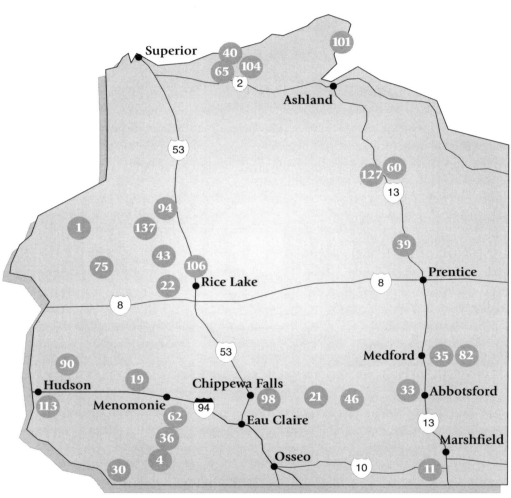

NORTHWEST

NORTHEAST

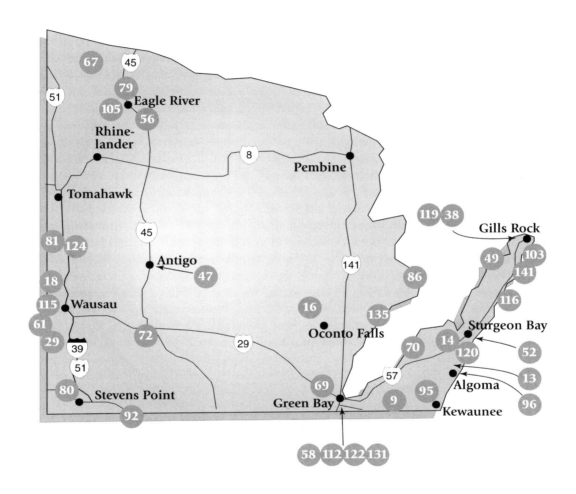

NORTHEAST

SOUTHWEST

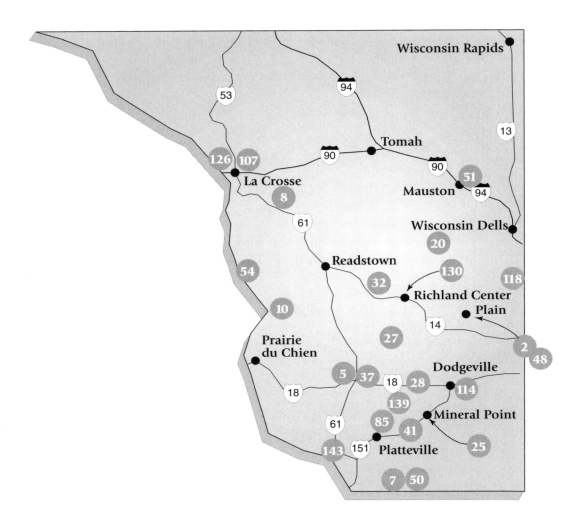

Southwest

SOUTHEAST

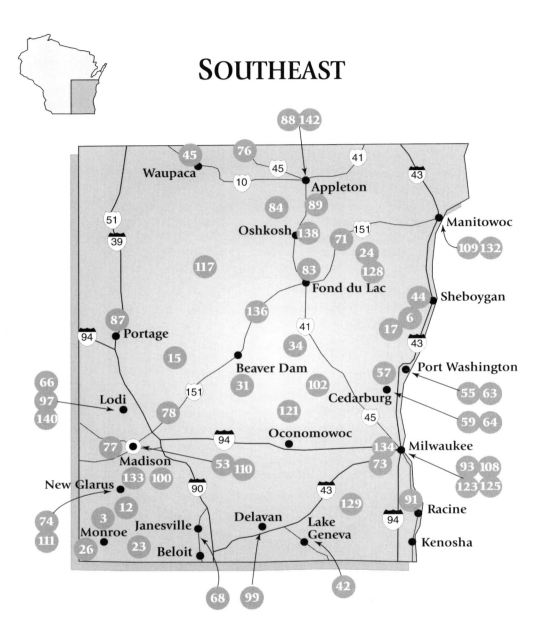

SOUTHEAST

∼1∼

Cheese Factories

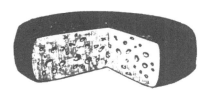

1. Cheese Factories

I remember waiting patiently beside the vat inside the factory for that magical moment when the curd would form. My mouth waters even now to recall the tender squeak of the curds against my teeth, and the warm, milky, heavenly flavor. Sometimes I'd be allowed inside the cool darkness of the curing room, where cheese was stacked high along the shelves in round wooden boxes. Uncle Lester would always ask if I wanted a sample. A taste, to Uncle Lester, meant a quarter-pound slab.

—From "World's Greatest Cheesemaker,"
by Sara Rath in *Wisconsin Sampler*, edited
by Sue E. McCoy (Northword, 1983).

Historical Flavor

Legend has it that the first cheese was made by accident thousands of years ago when an Asian wanderer, carrying milk in the bag-like lining of a sheep's stomach, noticed that some of the liquid clotted into soft, pleasant-tasting chunks. Perhaps that traveler, not realizing that an enzyme in the lining had caused the milk to coagulate, praised the deities for sending such a convenient, nutritious, and delectable new food to the world.

Diners, of course, have been singing the praises of cheese ever since. The ancient Greeks, for example, prayed to a cheese god named Aristaeus, ate cheesecake at weddings, and fed cheese to Olympic athletes in training. In Rome, where cheesemaking was an important industry, citizens particularly relished smoked cheese; wealthier residents built special cheesemaking kitchens, while common folk cured fresh, homemade cheeses in public smokehouses. Second century traders flocked to the city of Hypata to purchase that town's renowned cheese. Both the Greeks and the Romans imported cheese and both used the word for cheese as a term of endearment.

The Old Testament mentions the cheesemaking valley of Tyropœon, an early reference to organized cheesemaking. There's evidence from many quarters that cheese was a staple in numerous ancient civilizations. (However, indigenous peoples of the Americas didn't learn about cheese until the Spaniards introduced them to cows and other domesticated animals.)

Until the Middle Ages, cheeses were of three basic types: simple, fresh varieties not unlike our modern cottage cheese; pressed and aged cheddar-like types; and veined cheeses. Skilled medieval monks went on to develop extra-rich varieties, the forerunners of brie and camembert. Some types of cheese had already been around for hundreds of years and were widely known, such as Roquefort; others went by various local names or had no name at all. Many varieties were readily identified with their country of origin: parmesan and gorgonzola from Italy, and emmental from Switzerland, for example.

By the 1500s, open-air cheese markets were common in large European cities. Cheese stores existed, but unlike bakeries, meat markets, and other small food shops, the product wasn't made on premise.

Manufacturing Cheese

Cheese may have been around since humans first figured out how to milk animals, but cheese factories are a very recent development. Until the middle of the 19th century, most cheesemaking occurred on the farm and involved simple equipment and the milk from a single herd. Some historians have said that the first co-operative cheesemaking operation—using milk

Weekly cheese market, Alkmaar, Netherlands, about 1910.
State Historical Society of Wisconsin WHi (X3)50172

systematically gathered from several herds—operated in the Balkans in the late 1300s. But widespread cheese manufacturing didn't take hold for several more centuries, largely because the cheese needs of the population continued to be met locally.

In 17th-, 18th-, and much of 19th-century England, cheesemaking was still very much a home craft. Men worked the fields while women handled house-related chores which, besides cooking, cleaning, sewing, and vegetable gardening, included milking cows, churning butter, and making cheese. Farm families sold their extra cheese, mostly to wholesalers and at town markets, and maybe directly to passersby. As urban populations grew, however, the demand for milk to drink caused shortages of farmhouse cheese.

One logical solution was to import. Indeed, the cheese-loving British welcomed American cheddar, a cheese they were familiar with and one that traveled particularly well. By the 1880s, much of the imported cheese came from New York State, where home-based cheesemaking had developed into an industry. The quality of this farm cheese was often inconsistent and while it was better than nothing, there still wasn't enough of it.

Demand was greater than supply not just in England, but also in the fast-growing United States and other countries. Fortunately for the cheese industry, the Industrial Revolution had made its mark by this time, bringing advances in dairy husbandry, improved transportation systems, and new industrial technologies. Cheese factories were a "natural," as it were, and indeed, they now began to spring up throughout the cheesemaking world.

The first true cheese factory in the United States was doing business in the early 1850s in Rome, New York. By the mid-1870s, community cheese plants had virtually replaced home-based operations.

In the Eastern states, where farm-based cheesemaking was a centuries-old tradition in many families, dairy farmers and cheesemakers must have been surprised at how quickly the factory system took hold. But what probably really shocked them was what happened next: the just-as-rapid emergence of a young, backwater Midwestern state into the major cheese-producing state of the nation.

Wisconsin: The Big Cheese

Dairy farming, and certainly cheesemaking, weren't much on the minds of Wisconsin's early settlers, not even the ones who came after fur traders and lead miners had led the way in the development of the Wisconsin Territory. Wheat was king to the farmers who moved from the East Coast in the 1830s and who were soon followed by other immigrant groups: Germans, Scandinavians, Irish, Swiss, Dutch, Belgians, Poles, Italians, and many more. They came to take advantage of a lucrative crop that grew readily in the territory's rich soils.

Many of them brought along a cow or two in order to supply meat and milk for their families (and sometimes to provide a little muscle in the field). Many of them also brought old-world cheesemaking skills, which would soon—all too soon for some—come in very handy.

Decreasing yields, bad weather, insect problems, and unpredictable markets caused a serious decline in wheat production within just a few decades. Fortunately,

Wisconsin's natural and human resources were ideal for the development of a sensible alternative—dairying. Those resources included an abundance of land capable of supporting feed crops; a plentiful water supply; a varied and fast-improving transportation system (roads, railroads, and waterways); the dairy heritage of settlers, especially those from New York, Switzerland, and Germany; and last but not least, the forward-thinking agriculturists who were the first to "put it all together."

Dairy farming met with resistance at first—it was harder than growing wheat, and was considered "women's work," to boot—but eventually, inevitably, it took off. And large-scale cheesemaking followed.

Since housewives were responsible for processing excess farm milk into cheese, it's no wonder that the person who opened one of the first cooperative cheese-making operations in the state was a woman. In 1841 Anne Pickett began renting cows from her neighbors near Lake Mills and selling the cheese she made in her kitchen factory. Two brothers are credited with the next breakthroughs. In the late 1850s John J. Smith of Sheboygan County built a structure where he pressed curds from neighboring farms into cheese. But it was difficult to control quality with this system. His brother Hiram Smith then started an operation to collect milk rather than curds.

There were others who made important contributions to the development of cheese factories in Wisconsin, but the person most often credited with first operating a factory as we now know it was Chester Hazen. The small plant he built in 1864 in Ladoga (near Fond du Lac) was a true cheese factory in that it was a building separate from the farm house, it operated separately from other farm operations, the business

Gibbsville Cheese Factory in the early 1900s.   *Photo courtesy of Lee Vantatenhove*

accepted milk (not curds) from neighboring farms, it was a relatively large operation, and Hazen shipped his product out of state. It's likely he also sold cheese directly to his milk patrons and other locals.

Hazen's success was a great impetus for discouraged wheat farmers to jump on the dairy bandwagon. New Yorkers who were making mostly cheddar cheese in the state's eastern counties were joined in southern Wisconsin by limburger-producing Germans and Swiss experts who made Swiss-type cheeses. Soon settlers were emigrating to Wisconsin specifically to make cheese. Eventually, numerous immigrant groups, such as the Italians and the Dutch, popularized their own ethnic cheese specialties. Much later, Wisconsinites even invented brand-new cheeses, including world-famous ones like colby and brick.

But all this was still down the road. In the early years, the cheese factory system met with as much resistance as dairy farming had, and for much the same reasons. Carting milk to the factory twice a day was just more work, and cheesemaking was still considered a domestic (i.e. woman's) task. What's more, Wisconsin cheese was hard to sell. First, who had ever heard of it? And second, quality control remained a problem.

But that's where the forward-thinkers came to the rescue. A group of agriculturists formed the Wisconsin Dairymen's Association to help market cheese out of state and to teach dairy farmers and cheesemakers how to produce better products. One of the organization's founders, William D. Hoard, began publishing a newsletter called *Hoard's Dairyman,* which did much to legitimize cheesemaking as a profession (and eventually became the world's leading dairy publication). Wisconsin cheesemaking was on its way.

Between about 1880 and 1920, cheese factories expanded rapidly throughout many of the eastern and southern counties. They also headed north, where the land had recently been logged over and was ripe for agriculture. Only three sections of Wisconsin didn't become cheesemaking areas: the extreme north, where the climate is severe; the central counties, with their poor, sandy soil; and the southeastern corner of the state, where nearby urban markets drank most of the available milk supply. The cheese industry experienced growing pains, but improvements continued, especially in the areas of quality control and marketing. By 1910, Wisconsin cheeses were winning national and international awards and Wisconsin had become the

Dairy State—the nation's leading cheese producer.

Modern Times

Technology made cheese factories possible, but after the first part of the 20th century, it also changed them forever. Since then cheesemaking has grown far beyond its homecraft origins. Refrigeration, electricity, breeding and feeding improvements, trucks, and new kinds of manufacturing equipment have all helped to make dairying and cheesemaking ever more efficient. So efficient, in fact, that since the 1920s the number of factories has steadily declined while production has continued to rise. In recent years, rising costs, government regulations, standardization, corporate buyouts, and even pollution controls have made it harder and harder for the "little guys" to survive.

With more than two billion pounds produced annually, Wisconsin is still Number One in cheesemaking, but the number of factories has dropped from a high of more than 2800 (1922) to about 150 (1996-1997). Many are highly automated operations that manufacture mild-flavored, standardized cheeses—the kind the American public has come to favor.

But the little guys are still in the picture, too. Small-scale cheesemakers feel the tug of cultural tradition and enjoy their independence. Given the odds, how do they survive? Some of their stories, and thus some of the history of Wisconsin cheesemaking, are told in this chapter. But in a word, the little guys persist—and in some cases flourish—because of specialization. Today's small factories are popular with many diners—old-timers who remember and relish strong-tasting varieties like limburger and aged wheel cheddar; the growing ranks of "foodies" with a taste for adventure and an appreciation for regional distinctions; health-conscious families looking for low-fat and organic cheeses;

and locals who want value and recognize the advantages of buying locally.

Like cheese itself, which is by nature able to please a wide range of tastes, Wisconsin's cheese factories can satisfy whatever the market requires—quality, variety, consistency, value, and uniqueness.

There are also other, relatively new benefits to enjoy at today's cheese factories. Widespread car travel makes them convenient to shoppers. Many operations have observation windows and offer cheesemaking tours, allowing tourists to watch the making of a Wisconsin tradition. Backroads cheese factories are a draw for city dwellers who need a change of pace and a taste of country life.

One curious thing about cheese factories is that, unlike family-run bakeries or butcher shops—which serve mainly local populations—they exist because of demand from farther away. Cheese factories—even some of the smallest and earliest ones—always have sold most of their product wholesale. But while retail sales remain insignificant, financially speaking, that doesn't mean they don't play an important role. Indeed, some factories that produce large amounts of one or two types of cheese for the wholesale market also manufacture smaller amounts of other types strictly to satisfy local demands. A good example is Burnett Dairy Cooperative in northwestern Wisconsin near Grantsburg (see page 8).

Say Cheese

Wisconsin cheese is world famous. Indeed, cheese is not only a state identifier, it is *the* state identifier. The connection to cheese permeates our culture. We honor cheese-making towns like Colby and Monroe. We stand in line for deep-fried curds at cheese festivals. We wear cheese-shaped hats to Packer games and grin proudly at the nickname "cheeseheads." During the holidays, we ship gifts of Wisconsin cheese to faraway relatives and friends. If there were a state appetizer, surely it would be cheese and summer sausage on crackers.

Wisconsin cheese factories are where the past meets the present. They are where we enter the very heart of the state.

—*Please Note*

The featured cheese factories that follow are arranged in alphabetical order by the name of the business. Additional factories are listed in alphabetical order at the end of the chapter. To locate a factory by town name, see page 173. Maps are on pages *xviii-xxv*. All information is subject to change. Travelers should call or write before visiting to get business hours, directions, and other important details.

---

1. Burnett Dairy Cooperative
11631 State Highway 70
Grantsburg, WI 54840
715-689-2748
•

Italian Cheese From Two Wisconsins

When out-of-staters think of Wisconsin they typically have one of two, mutually exclusive visions of the landscape: the rolling, sun-kissed cornfields and brick-red dairy barns of bucolic southern Wisconsin, or the endless snow-covered pine forests and clear lakes of the North woods.

Two Wisconsins do, in fact, co-exist in some northern counties. In sparsely populated Burnett County, near the Minnesota border, for example, you'll encounter eagles, trout streams, and vacation resorts. You'll also find the Burnett Dairy, a cooperative of more than 300 dairy farmers

whose cows graze within a 150-mile radius of the factory.

What's more, cows have been part of the North woods scene for more than a century. The dairy industry in northern Wisconsin harks back to the late 1800s, a time when lumbering had left much of the land barren, a sea of stumps. Rather than grow wheat, which was already declining in the south due to disease and pests, landowners began to buy cows and plant cover crops. They discovered that the area's rich soils, cold temperatures, and abundant waters were particularly suited to dairying.

In 1896, farmers around Grantsburg formed a cooperative and opened the Wood River Creamery in the tiny town of Alpha. Butter was the plant's main product for more than 60 years, until, in 1966, the creamery joined forces with another co-op to form a new one.

"Burnett Dairy was formed expressly to make cheese," says Dale Olson, who was one of the factory's first cheesemakers and is plant manager today. According to Olson, making cheese made sense because "cheese had become more popular and better marketed. Especially Italian cheeses." Indeed, at this time pizza was fast becoming one of America's favorite foods and the demand for Italian cheeses like mozzarella and provolone was growing. The plant eventually added "die-hard Wisconsin cheeses like cheddar and colby" to its line to meet local demand, notes Olson; still, what he calls "pizza cheese" has been the factory's mainstay since day one.

String cheese, which is actually mozzarella in a different form, grew popular in the early 1980s, and is now the factory's best known product, according to Kathleen Larson, who works in the plant office. She describes how string cheese was first made at Burnett Dairy. "After the mozzarella was made, when it was still soft, it would be strung out or stretched by hand," says the slender woman in a measured voice. "It would be put it a salt brine, then pulled out, and then cut. By hand." Now machines do the stretching, brining, and cutting.

Good thing, for today, although the Burnett Dairy is considered a small factory industry-wide, it is a 24-hour operation with about 100 employees, including nearly 10 licensed cheesemakers. In one recent year, the cooperative processed 183 million pounds of milk and sold 21 million pounds of cheese. The cheese, which is packaged under the "Fancy Brand" label, comes in all types and flavors, from cheese curds and low-fat cheddar, to hot pepper string cheese and shredded mozzarella.

String Cheese Slaw
8 servings

It's amusing to pull apart string cheese and see how this popular snack food got its name. But the culinary possibilities for string cheese can also be fun. Kathleen Larson of Burnett Dairy suggests dipping the sticks into a spicy salsa, while I like to slice tiny "coins" of it into a salad. Here's a simple, lighthearted cheese "slaw" that can stand as a side dish or be added to sandwiches. A food processor (to shred the vegetables) speeds its preparation.

    4 ounces string cheese
    4 cups shredded carrots, jícama,
       or celeriac (or use a combination)
    3 tablespoons lemon juice
    1-2 tablespoons olive oil
    pepper to taste

Cut string cheese "cylinders" in half crosswise. "String" the cheese by pulling each piece into strands. Toss with remaining ingredients. Serve as side dish or sandwich filling.

Spinach, Ramps, & Provolone Pie
6-8 servings

Ramps are wild leeks; they have a pungent garlicky smell but mild flavor. Look for them at area farmers' markets in spring. Or substitute 1/2 cup chopped green garlic stems, also available at market stands in spring, or 2 teaspoons minced fresh garlic, for the ramps.

    1 bunch fresh ramps, cleaned (about
       1/4-1/3 pound)
    1 tablespoon butter
    1/2 pound fresh spinach, cleaned
       and stemmed
    salt and pepper
    3 eggs
    1 cup whole milk
    1/4 cup sliced or chopped black olives
    2 tablespoons chopped fresh or
       frozen chives
    2 ounces (about 1 cup) grated
       provolone
    3 tablespoons freshly grated parmesan
    unbaked 9-inch pie crust (for recipes,
       see page 101 and 118)
    2/3 cup finely diced red peppers
       (optional)

Cut ramp leaves off the stems. Coarsely chop ramp stems. Heat butter in large skillet over medium heat. Add ramp stems and saute until tender. Coarsely chop ramp leaves and spinach; add to skillet. Cook over medium-high heat until wilted. Season with salt and pepper to taste. Cool.

Heat oven to 350 degrees. Beat eggs and milk in bowl. Stir in the spinach mixture, olives, chives, and provolone. Season with salt and pepper to taste. Sprinkle parmesan over bottom of pie crust. Gently pour in the egg/spinach mixture. For an optional garnish, sprinkle diced sweet red pepper around outer rim of pie; lightly press sweet pepper bits to partially submerge them. Bake until custard is set in the middle, 45-55 minutes. Let stand 5-10 minutes before slicing.

2. Cedar Grove Cheese
Route 1, Box 72
Valley View Road
Plain, WI 53577
608-546-5284
•

Head for Cheese

For many operators of small cheese factories, the knowledge and love of cheesemaking are passed to them through generations of experience and tradition. Bob Wills, however, wasn't exposed to cheesemaking until he married into the Nachreiner clan. And although he has two degrees, one in law and one in economics, neither one contributed much in the way of a feeling for cheese.

But Bob likes the business of making cheese. He explains that when he worked in the agricultural economics department at the University of Wisconsin, "a lot of the work I did ended up in the trash can. That doesn't happen with the work I do here, does it?"

Indeed it doesn't. Cedar Grove Cheese, which Bob and his wife Beth Nachreiner purchased from his father-in-law Ferdinand (Ferdie) Nachreiner in 1989, is a bustling, almost frantically busy operation that produces a variety of cheeses in demand for their quality and special features.

The factory has been producing cheese since 1900 (the Nachreiners became owners in 1946) and has long been known for being on the cutting edge of cheesemaking. Years before it became common, for example, Cedar Grove milk cans were cleaned by machine. Ferdie Nachreiner was also one of the first cheese factory owners to switch to bulk milk tanks.

Today the Cedar Grove line includes colby, cheddar, monterey jack, butterkase, cheese curds, and farmers cheese. Some varieties come in flavors like pepper, pizza, or garlic/dill, while some are smoked; others are low in fat, and still others are organically produced.

The fact that they carry organic cheese illustrates how Cedar Grove stays on the cutting edge today. All cheese, of course, was once made organically, but now it is considered unconventional to produce food without using synthetic pesticides and fertilizers, without artificial ingredients or preservatives. Besides following these guidelines, Cedar Grove's organic cheese contains only natural, non-animal enzymes and no dyes. Today, as more consumers appreciate the value of organic food, demand for organic cheese is on the rise.

Adding organic cheese to the Cedar Grove line in 1996 led to recognition in a national cheese journal. That year *The Cheese Market News* listed them among the 50 key players in the industry.

On a cloudy spring day, this key player in the industry is as wild as a toy factory two weeks before Christmas. In his office, Bob edges tumbling stacks of books and papers aside to answer an ever-ringing phone. Workers in rubber boots and hair nets are queued up outside his open door, waiting to request a schedule change or address a production problem. Several employees who share the office handle mail orders and patter on computers. And Bob himself is the eye of the storm as he calmly fields a spray of questions, pulls research from a crammed bookshelf, and doodles elaborately while he makes a point. "This is actually standard," he says wryly, referring to the craziness.

If things are a bevy of activity, they are also a reflection of how many talents it takes to be successful in the cheese business today. Intelligence, experience, and education help. So do patience, open-mindedness, and drive. Bob can tell you about the oxidation of fats in cheese as they interact with light. He describes how legal requirements designed to accommodate modern machinery are diminishing the quality of cheese. He understands that his only chance as one of the "little guys" is to make specialty, not commodity, cheese. He is constantly on the alert for new markets and for ways to stay efficient and unique.

Bob is also smart enough to know he isn't doing it alone. He has the benefit of Ferdie's experience and part-time presence. He employs about 30 people, and counting; several are licensed cheesemakers, one of whom is Daniel Hetzel, who has been with the company since 1947. "Dan can tell from the smell in the [production] room what the cows have been eating, how many days we've had the milk, and if anything needs cleaning," says Bob in admiration.

He uses colorful packaging, a company newsletter, and an Internet website to promote products like Squeaks, the Cedar Grove name for cheese curds.

It seems that every aspect of cheese is a fascinating challenge to Bob Wills, for even when it comes to recipe ideas, he comes up with a doozy, "French fries with cheese curds and a tangy, barbecue-like gravy on top." It's something he tried in Quebec. He jokes, "I don't recommend that our customers eat it too often, however. They'd die, I guess, and then we wouldn't have any customers."

At home, Bob and his family of five eat mostly reduced-fat cheese. "We eat so much cheese, we like to watch the fat. And our low-fat line is really good." It's "fabulous," in fact, according to a 1996 issue of *Self Magazine*.

No cheese in Bob Wills's blood? Maybe not, but it's in his head and heart.

Italian Baked Whitefish
3-4 servings

Reduced-fat cheese is a natural complement to Lake Michigan whitefish in a recipe adapted from one by MaryKay Shumway of Teskie Orchards and Fisheries (see page 75). You could substitute other mild-favored fillets like walleye, pike, or cod. Serve with hot pasta and garden vegetables.

    1 cup Italian tomato or marinara sauce
    3 whitefish fillets (about 1 1/2 pounds
       total)
    1 tablespoon olive oil
    1/2 cup shredded low-fat, mild melting
       cheese such as farmers or mozzarella
    2-3 tablespoons freshly grated
       parmesan

Heat broiler. Heat Italian tomato sauce in saucepan over low heat or in microwave oven; keep warm. Cover broiler pan with aluminum foil and brush with a little of the olive oil. Place fish fillets on pan, skin side down, and brush with remaining oil. Broil five inches from flame for 10-12 minutes. Spread warm tomato sauce over fish, sprinkle with the cheeses, and continue to broil until cheese is melted, 2-3 minutes (do not let cheese burn). Serve immediately.

Cheddar Cheese Coins
Makes 75-100 crackers

These savory rounds are a cross between a biscuit and a cracker and can be made with smoked, flavored, or regular cheddar cheese, or a combination of these. The dough comes together easily and may be frozen to make a ready-to-go appetizer for company.

1 cup (2 sticks) unsalted butter, softened

8 ounces sharp cheddar, grated and brought to warm room temperature

8 ounces smoked or flavored cheddar, grated and brought to warm room temperature

2 3/4 cups flour

1 teaspoon baking powder

1/4 teaspoon baking soda

2 teaspoons chili powder

2 cups finely chopped hickory nuts or walnuts

Cream butter and cheeses in large bowl until well blended. Sift flour, baking powder, baking soda, and chili powder into second bowl. Stir sifted mixture into cheese mixture until combined. Mix in nuts until combined. Dough will be soft and pliable. On floured surface, shape dough into 5-6 smooth cylinders about 1 1/2 inches thick. Wrap in wax paper and chill thoroughly (or freeze for later use).

Heat oven to 350 degrees. (If dough is frozen, allow it to thaw 20-30 minutes before slicing.) Slice dough into 1/4-inch-thick rounds and place one inch apart on ungreased baking sheets. Bake 14-16 minutes. Carefully transfer crackers to wire rack and cool. Store airtight.

---

3. Chalet Cheese Co-op
N4858 Highway N
Monroe, WI 53566
608-325-4343
•

The Strong Cheese Survives

The last limburger-producing cheese factory in the United States is a quaint, Alpine-looking building that sits on a rise of an undulating country road outside Monroe. This is the heart of Swiss cheese country, where in the 1920s area factories produced millions of pounds of limburger a year; indeed, according to author Jerry Apps in *Cheese: The Making of a Wisconsin Tradition* (Amherst Press, 1998), they once produced more limburger than Swiss.

Limburger, like liver and lutefisk, is a food people either love, or love to hate. Stories that surround the famously stinky cheese are legend: about the grocer who repeatedly sent back smelly shipments, thinking the cheese had spoiled; about a "Limburger Rebellion" in Green County, when residents threatened to stage a Boston Tea Party over a cheese caravan parked in the sun; and about the Iowa mail carrier who claimed he got sick from the odor of a package he was to deliver, sparking an interstate debate over the worthiness of limburger (it ended in a "sniffing duel" that left limburger victorious on all counts).

Limburger originated in Belgium but is usually associated with the Germans and Swiss, who layer the aged, surface-ripened cheese with dark bread, onions, and horseradish or mustard in a hearty sandwich. A Swiss immigrant named Rudolph Benkert cured the first Green County limburger in his home cellar in 1867. The following year Nicholas Gerber, another Swiss immigrant, established the first

Myron Olson with specially cured cheese boards, Chalet Cheese Co-op, Monroe

limburger factory in the area. Taverns all over the county were soon serving the potent cheese with locally-brewed beer, a combination patrons relished so much that when saloons closed during Prohibition, limburger sales dropped sharply.

These days, it isn't a lack of beer that holds limburger production back, it's changing tastes. Most people prefer the mild cheeses that are more typical of today's streamlined cheese production. But even though we are down to one limburger factory, the Chalet Cheese Co-op, there are still enough limburger lovers to consume close to one million pounds a year, the amount the cooperative produces annually.

And Chalet Cheese is still making limburger the old-fashioned, labor-intensive way. "Each piece of cheese is handled twelve times before it leaves the factory," says Myron Olson, a big, round-faced man with a respect for limburger that shows in the bright gaze of his eyes. He is manager of the cooperative, following in the foot-

steps of the renowned Albert Deppeler, who made limburger and managed the factory for decades before him.

The limburger-making process Myron describes sounds much like other cheeses, at least in the first stages. Special cultures and rennet are added to whole milk, which when thickened is cut with wire knives, stirred and heated to release the liquid whey, pumped into forms, and drained to release more whey.

But then things begin to look different. The cheese is cut into pieces, rolled in salt, and returned to the frames for a brief dry-brining. Soon the individual pieces, which are the size and shape of small bricks, are laid side by side on knot-free pine boards that have been cured specially for this purpose. "You want the bacteria to grow on the boards," says Myron. "This inoculates the cheese and protects it from other bacteria that could grow."

Placed in a cool, ultra-moist cellar, the bricks are wetted daily and brushed with a bacteria-infused solution (called the "smear") twice during their seven-day stay. Eventually the cheese is weighed out and hand-wrapped in parchment and waxed paper. Country Castle, the Chalet Cheese label, goes on about 20 percent of the limburger; the rest is sold wholesale under other labels.

Olson emphasizes the importance of the wooden boards by describing what happened in 1947 when the cooperative, in a joint venture with Kraft Foods, built the current plant and installed new equipment, boards and all. "They wanted to become the most modern, the best limburger factory in the world," says Myron. "But what happened was they got green cheese—it failed. They had to get out the old boards. And these have been used ever since."

Since Chalet Cheese is the source for all domestic limburger sold in the nation, consumers shouldn't find variations from label to label. Except, that is, for the variations that should occur through aging.

"The key to enjoying limburger is knowing the date it was made," notes Myron. "When it is real young, up to one month old, it is very firm, crumbly, and salty, much like feta cheese in taste. At six weeks, it's soft on the corners but still has a hard core that's salty and chalky. The bacteria works from rind to center. At two months, the core is almost gone." He says most people prefer limburger between six weeks and eight weeks old. "From two to three months, the core is gone, it's soft and spreadable, the salt has blended in, and the cheese has a kind of sweet flavor. Older than three months, there's intense smell, intense flavor. It's pungent and almost bitter. If you like it, you're a real limburger lover."

If you like it, you may be an old-timer who has enjoyed limburger all your life, or you may be one of a new breed of gourmet diners that Myron calls "adventure eaters." Either way, you're one of the relatively few consumers today who are helping a strong cheese survive.

Spinach & Brick Cheese Rice Bake
8 or more servings

Limburger is the Chalet Cheese Co-op's most famous product, but it isn't their only one. They also manufacture baby Swiss, smoked baby Swiss, mild brick, and German brick, a surface-ripened cheese sometimes known as beer kase *or* beerkäse *(from the German word* bierkäse, *which means beer cheese). Brick cheese, a Wisconsin original, was developed to have limburger-like qualities, but nowadays it is typically a semi-soft cheese with tiny holes and a mild flavor. Surface-ripened bricks like Chalet Cheese Co-op's, however, do develop pungent flavor with age.*

This is a soothing, rainy-day hot dish especially suitable when you can get fresh spinach from local sources, such as the farmers' market or your own garden. Use a mild dry-rind brick or the stronger washed-rind type.

2 tablespoons olive oil
1 cup finely chopped onion
1 tablespoon minced garlic
1 pound fresh spinach, cleaned, stemmed, and coarsely chopped
1 tablespoon dried dill weed or 2 tablespoons chopped fresh dill
5 cups cooked rice, at room temperature

1 1/2 cups (about 4 ounces) shredded brick cheese
3 eggs, beaten
1/4 cup chopped fresh parsley (optional)
salt and pepper to taste

Heat oven to 350 degrees. Oil a large baking dish. Heat olive oil in large skillet over medium heat. Add onion and garlic; cook, stirring often, until tender. Raise heat to medium-high, add spinach and dried dill (if you're using fresh dill, add it after the spinach has cooked). Cook, stirring often, until spinach is wilted, 5-6 minutes. Raise heat to high and cook off most of the moisture in the pan. Combine spinach with remaining ingredients (including fresh dill, if using). Spread in baking dish. Cover dish and bake until rice is slightly puffed and bubbly around the edges, 30-40 minutes. Serve immediately.

Traditional Limburger Sandwich
Any number of servings

To control the odor of limburger, rinse the rind or cut it off altogether, recommends Myron Olson of Chalet Cheese Co-op. And by all means, store limburger in a glass jar. This will contain the smell without adversely affecting the cheese.

"Limburger is a table cheese," says Myron. While you can include it in any meal ("at breakfast with toast, in a sandwich for lunch, with potatoes for dinner"), you won't often find it listed as an ingredient in recipes.

Myron explains, "It doesn't cook well because when you warm it, the heat intensifies the smell." He does advocate using very young, still-salty, shredded limburger as a pizza topping. Still, if you are a traditionalist, this sandwich is the way to go.

> rye bread (dark or light, pumpernickel, sauerkraut rye, etc.)
>
> mustard (sweet-hot, brown, whole grain, etc.)
>
> sliced limburger (at any age you prefer, rinsed or not, rind-on or rind-off)
>
> thick slices of sweet onion (Vidalia, Walla-Walla, etc.)

Layer the ingredients as you like into a sandwich. Myron Olson prefers sweet-hot mustard on one slice of bread and mayonnaise on the other. Then, as he recommends, "Wash it down with a beer!"

> ## 4. Eau Galle Cheese & Gifts
> **N6765 State Highway 25**
> **Durand, WI 54736**
> **715-283-4211**
> •

First Things First

"Quality first and everything else will come." This was Leo Buhlman's motto. Leo was the Swiss immigrant who founded Eau Galle Cheese Factory in the rolling hills of western Wisconsin. Today his daughter-in-law Carol Buhlman credits this motto with being the reason the plant has survived.

She's been involved with the factory since the mid-1960s, when her new husband John took over management from his father. There used to be a lot of small plants like theirs in the area, says Carol. "I've been here 35 years. I can see the closings, they all have folded. We're small, we have to be special."

The original factory was located in the village of Eau Galle just a few miles northwest of its current country site near Durand. It had been a milk processing plant since the mid-1800s and then, as a cheese plant, produced typical Wisconsin types like Swiss, brick, and cheddar until the 1960s. But, says Carol, when new laws dropped the price of certain imported cheeses, threatening smaller producers with increased competition, Eau Galle starting making Italian cheese, newly in demand at the time.

Today, with the exception of an occasional batch of cheddar or flavored curds, Eau Galle makes only romano and parmesan cheese. And despite moving to larger, more modern quarters in 1986, they are still a small factory relative to many in the state. "We want a quality product, not a quantity product," says Carol.

Parmesan and romano are lower in fat than many cheeses. At Eau Galle, an enormous machine separates the cream from the milk. (Excess cream is sold to Grassland Dairy, where it is churned into butter.) Nearly all the cheese is shipped to special caves and warehouses in South Dakota for 10 to 12 months of aging; some is saved to be aged even longer and sold locally.

While most of the cheese produced at Eau Galle is pre-sold to companies that give the cheese their own label, plenty is reserved for Eau Galle labeling. Some of this is sold to better restaurants and other businesses in the region. A booming mail order business handles more than 1,000 packages on some days in December. As for retail sales at the factory store, low mark-up and one of western Wisconsin's largest gift-and-collectibles shops lure customers from far and wide.

Tomato Wild Rice Soup with Italian Cheese
4-6 servings

Inspired by a recipe from Diet for a Small Planet, *by Frances Moore Lappe (Ballantine, 1982), this soup is exceptionally hearty and nourishing. The colors and textures are appealing—creamy red-orange with chunks of bright carrot and dark grains of wild rice. Bold accents include bits of fresh basil (or pesto) and parmesan cheese. I like it best on the second day.*

2 tablespoons olive oil
1 cup chopped onion
1 cup chopped carrots
2 teaspoons minced garlic
1 1/2 teaspoons dried oregano
2 tablespoons flour
2 pounds tomatoes, seeded
  and chopped*
1 cup cooked wild rice
1/4 cup chopped fresh basil or 2-3
  tablespoons basil pesto
2 cups milk, or more as needed
salt and pepper
freshly grated romano or parmesan

Heat olive oil in pot over medium-low heat. Add onion and carrots; cook, stirring often, 6-8 minutes. Stir in garlic and oregano; cook another minute or two. Stir in flour; cook several minutes, stirring often. Add tomatoes and bring to simmer. Adjust heat to allow mixture to simmer slowly 15 minutes. Stir in wild rice and basil or pesto. Stir in milk; simmer several minutes, and season to taste with salt and pepper. You can thin the soup, if necessary, by adding more milk. Garnish each bowl with grated cheese.

*If it's not tomato season, you may substitute canned tomatoes, with their juices. Or use a combination of 2 1/2 cups tomato juice and 2 tablespoons tomato paste.

Olive, Pepper, & Romano Cheese Stuffing
for Patty Pan Squash, Mushrooms, or Cornish Game Hens
Makes about 3 cups stuffing

Romano, a stronger, more pungent cheese than parmesan, is a good choice for this recipe. Full of vibrant flavors and contrasting textures, this is a stuffing with guts, if you will. It was, in fact, inspired by leftover bits of vegetables and several near-empty jars.

Stuffing:
1 1/2 tablespoons olive oil
1/2 cup finely chopped onion
1/2 cup finely chopped Hungarian
  wax pepper or other mild to
  medium-hot chili pepper
1 cup finely chopped summer squash
  (patty pan,* zucchini, or yellow
  squash)
1 1/2 teaspoons minced garlic
1 teaspoon dried thyme
1/4 cup coarsely chopped pine nuts,
  hickory nuts, or pecans
3 tablespoons chopped fresh parsley
1/4 cup finely chopped black olives
1/4 cup finely chopped green olives
1 cup dried breadcrumbs
1/2 cup freshly grated romano
salt and pepper to taste

Stuffing will fill:
6 patty pan squash, each about
  3 inches wide, or
16 or more large white mushrooms, or
4 Cornish game hens

To make stuffing: Heat olive oil in skillet over medium-low heat. Add onion, and cook slowly until onion is wilted, 5-7 minutes. Stir in chopped chili pepper, summer squash,* garlic, and thyme; saute several minutes longer. Remove from heat and stir in remaining stuffing ingredients. Mixture should hold together loosely (if not, add a little water).

Big wheels at Eau Galle Cheese, Durand

Stuffed Patty Pan Squash: Using a small, sharp knife and starting 1/2 inch from outer top edge of squash, carve into and around the top of each squash. Do not cut all the way through to the bottom. Remove the cut portion (in several pieces, if necessary) and scrape out insides of each squash to form a boat, leaving at least 1/2 inch of flesh all around. Chop squash tops and use this in the filling. Place unfilled squash boats in foil-lined baking pan and bake at 350 degrees 15 minutes. Pack filling into squash cavities and continue to bake until squash is tender and filling is browned, 30-45 minutes. *Makes 6 servings.*

Stuffed Mushrooms: Remove stems from mushrooms (chopped stems may be substituted for summer squash in the filling). Pack filling into mushroom cavities, place on foil-lined baking sheet and bake at 400 degrees about 15 minutes. *Makes 4-6 servings.*

Stuffed Cornish Game Hens: Loosely pack game hens with stuffing, truss lightly, rub all over with softened butter, and sprinkle with salt and pepper. Place in roasting pan; roast at 350 degrees for 60-70 minutes. *Makes 4-8 servings.*

*If you are going to stuff patty pan squash, use the cut-out flesh (see Stuffed Patty Pan Squash, above) in the filling.

5. Fennimore Cheese
1675 Lincoln Ave.
Fennimore, WI 53809
608-822-3777
•

Dream Cheese

Cheesemaker Carl Bahl and his book-keeping wife Nellie realized a family dream when they purchased an old Fennimore landmark, the Peacock Creamery, in 1943. Having managed several creameries in the area, they put years of experience to work building a business that soon became a landmark in its own right. Working alongside them was their son Stephan, who, when his father died in 1964, "pulled up his whey-soaked socks and took over sole operation of the business" (as reported in *Fennimore Then and Now*, Dwight T. Parker Library, 1980). His parents' dream is still Steve's life business. "It takes care of me and I take care of it," he says.

If you're in town it's impossible to miss Fennimore Cheese—a giant fiberglass rat named Igor welcomes tourists from the front of the factory. But it's the Bahl specialties inside that are really worth a visit: Greek feta packed in brine, a low-sodium lacy Swiss, and a sweet, buttery baby Swiss featured in the following recipe.

Bahl Baby Cutlets
8 servings

4 tablespoons butter
8 ounces (about 2 1/2 cups) shredded
    baby Swiss or Swiss cheese
1 tablespoon Dijon mustard
2 tablespoons finely chopped
    green onion
1 tablespoon minced fresh parsley
2 eggs, beaten

2 cups cracker crumbs
additional butter for sauteing
2 teaspoons vinegar and additional
    butter to make sauce (optional)

Melt 4 tablespoons butter in heavy saucepan over low heat. Add cheese and mustard; stir constantly until cheese is melted. Remove from heat; stir in green onion, parsley, eggs, and cracker crumbs. Cool a few minutes. Shape into 8 slightly elongated patties. Melt a little more butter in clean pan, add cutlets, and cook over low heat until light brown on both sides. To make a sauce (optional): Remove cutlets and keep warm. Brown additional butter in pan; add vinegar and cook a few seconds. Pour over cutlets.

---

6. Gibbsville Cheese
W2663 County Highway 00
Sheboygan Falls, WI 53085
920-564-3242
•

Illustrating History

At one time Sheboygan County had more than 200 family-run cheese factories, but today only a handful remain. "Plymouth used to be the cheese center of the world!" claims Leatrice (Lee) Vantatenhove, whose father-in-law, Fred Vantatenhove, bought the Gibbsville Cheese Factory, a few miles east of Plymouth, in 1933. The plant, which had been in operation since 1873, passed from father to son Robert. Today the major stockholder and main cheesemaker is Lee and Bob's son, Phillip.

Lee is a friendly woman who likes to reminisce about the old days. She brings

Proud to be part of Gibbsville Cheese

out a cardboard box and points out how things in the cheese business have changed as she sorts through faded photos and articles that chronicle both family and factory history. "We used to make cheese seven days a week—had to because there were no tanks, no big silos to store the milk. We used to buy directly from our own farmers. Now we get Grade A milk from Dean Foods in Sheboygan."

She displays a picture of the factory site from the early 1900s. It shows a cheesemaker in a hand-cranked car near the two-story wooden structure where he and his family worked and lived. (See page 6.) A later photo shows a Gibbsville driver standing proud in front of a dusty, big-wheeled delivery truck loaded with milk cans. In still another, a picture from 1961, the company's new, modern vehicle advertises Gibbsville's "natural, rindless cheddar cheese" on its shiny, rounded tank.

It's clear that much at the factory has changed through the years. But not everything, says Phillip. The milk still comes from local sources and much of the work is still done by hand. "The bigger plants do it by computer, but we still make cheese the old-fashioned way, like hand-turning," he notes.

Hand-turning is explained in another display of photos that Lee points to on the wall near the factory's observation window. The exhibit explains, "When making cheddar the curds are well drained and then cut into large slabs which are turned over, allowed to set, and then are turned over and piled two high, set again, and are turned over and piled three high, and finally four high. All this time the cheese is compacting and draining, making it a solid product. This process is called cheddaring."

Cheddar cheese is one of Gibbsville's big sellers; colby is the other. Colby cheese is a Wisconsin original developed in Colby, a town several counties removed from the Gibbsville factory. But its popularity made it common at plants throughout the state. "When making colby," reads the exhibit, "as soon as the curds are drained, they are washed with cold water to keep separate, salted, and put into hoops. Colby has little holes in it and is higher in moisture because it doesn't cheddar."

Phillip explains that colby also contains a different enzyme than cheddar; but the big difference is that the curds are put directly into hoops for pressing rather than being cheddared, milled, and then pressed.

And sure enough, she has a photo, shot in 1961, to illustrate curds being packed into small metal hoops that produced one-pound rounds of colby called midget horns. Today, the "hoops" are rectangular and the colby is made into 40-pound blocks.

Old-Fashioned Macaroni Salad
8 servings

When cheese curds are washed, the process removes most of the elements that help a cheese age and dry out a little. Thus, colby, which is by definition a washed cheese, is appreciated more for its mild, "young" flavor, and moist, not crumbly, texture. Kids love the taste and the way its open texture creates a kind of marble effect when you break a piece apart.

Most colby is made in big blocks today, but as a child, I remember taking delight in its unusual cylindrical shape. I'd cut off slices, match them with salami thins, and sandwich these between bread slices. Then I'd cut around the cheese and meat, removing the extra bread to make a perfectly round sandwich. (The crusts were for the birds.)

Here's a classic Wisconsin use for colby, a standard on supper club salad bars throughout the state.

12 ounces macaroni
1 cup finely diced colby cheese
1 cup frozen, thawed peas (uncooked)
1/2 cup finely diced onion
1/2 cup mayonnaise
1-2 tablespoons milk
1 teaspoon sugar
salt and pepper to taste

Boil macaroni in boiling, salted water until tender. Rinse until cool and drain well. Combine with remaining ingredients. Serve chilled.

Packing colby into midget horns, 1961.

Photo courtesy Lee Vantatenhove

7. Gile Cheese Company
Carr Cheese Factory
111 S. Main St.
Cuba City, WI 53807
608-744-3456
•

Cheese to Carry On About

What keeps an independent cheese-maker going? In Wisconsin there were once hundreds like Tim Gile, who with his wife Diane makes cheese—with their own hands and their own recipes—at a third-generation factory on the outskirts of Cuba City. But today the odds are against him; corporate competition, government regulation, and ever-rising production costs have left the Giles among the few family-run factories in the state.

"There's been a lot of times I've wanted to quit," admits Tim, a big man with ruddy cheeks and a boyish look. In fact at one point he did quit, but in all the years since adolescence, which is when he started packaging cheddar for his father, there were only three years when he wasn't involved in cheese-making. Those three years convinced him he pre-ferred being his own boss and they reminded him how much he enjoys the work that "is in his blood."

Small producers like Tim have an espe-cially hard time keeping pace with industry rules and regulations. He gives an example: "In 1992, we had to put in a completely new pasteurization system. It was a huge financial set-back, and one that wasn't going to make us any new money. I thought about closing then."

What kept him from doing so, then as it does now?"I want to keep the tradition going," he says simply.

He means both industry tradition and family tradition. The original Carr Cheese Factory was built in 1921 by a group of farmers, at a time when cooperatives owned the plants and hired the cheese-makers. Tim's grandfather made cheese near Muscoda in western Wisconsin; Tim's father Cletus grew up learning the business firsthand. Cletus and his wife Sally bought the Carr factory (which was named after the landowner on whose property it was built) in 1946, and proceeded to raise 10 children, all of whom took part in the business at one time or another. In 1984 Tim and Diane bought into the family legacy when they took over the operation.

How they endure, given the challenges, isn't quite as simple as why. Tim cites a loyal base of wholesale accounts and the

Tim Gile offers cheddar, colby, Swiss, and specialty items at Gile Cheese Store, Cuba City

success of a downtown factory outlet (the Gile Cheese store) as two main supports. Of course, there are also long, hard hours of work and the skill of generations. And of course there's the cheese. In the old days Cletus manufactured mainly cheddar, and cheddar is still the big seller today. In addition, the Giles produce varieties of Swiss, colby, and monterey jack and their line includes curds, reduced-fat and reduced-sodium types, and smoked or fla-vored cheeses. (They also sell or ship other

Wisconsin specialty products like honey, summer sausage, and cold pack cheese spread). "Our product is consistent," says Tim. "It's not filled with moisture like at some of the big plants."

People notice quality, and Gile cheese is noticeable enough to have won more than 200 awards at state and county fairs, including a recent first place blue ribbon for colby. Clearly, the Gile legacy deserves to carry on.

Chicken Breasts Layered with Swiss Cheese & Stuffing
4 servings

Inspired by a recipe by Diane Gile, this dish is deliciously reminiscent of stuffed roast chicken, but it's easier on the schedule and the waistline.

4 boneless, skinless chicken breasts
 (about 6 ounces each)
4 large, thin slices baby Swiss or Swiss
 cheese (regular or reduced fat)
1 tablespoon butter
1/2 cup finely chopped onion
1 cup finely chopped mushrooms
2 tablespoons chopped fresh parsley or
 1 1/2 teaspoons dried
2 teaspoons chopped fresh rosemary or
 1/2 teaspoon dried
1 teaspoon chopped fresh sage or
 1/4 teaspoon dried
salt and pepper
2 heaping cups dried bread cubes or
 small croutons
1/2-2/3 cup chicken broth or
 white wine

Grease a large baking pan or line it with parchment paper or aluminum foil. Trim chicken breasts of all fat; flatten thickest parts of the meat by pounding it lightly with heel of hand. Lay chicken in pan and top each breast with a slice of cheese. Heat oven to 350 degrees.

Melt butter in skillet. Add onion, mushrooms, and herbs. Cook over medium heat, stirring often, until vegetables are tender, about 10 minutes. Season to taste with salt and pepper. Toss in bread cubes. Stir in enough chicken broth or wine to make a moist stuffing. Cover each chicken breast with a mound of stuffing; flatten and press to fully cover the cheese. Bake until stuffing has browned and chicken is tender, 20-25 minutes.

Diane's Taco Salad Dip
10-12 appetizer servings

When asked what cheese preparations his family most loves, Tim Gile says, "In our house, if [a dish] can accommodate cheese, it gets it." Here's one that accommodates it well, from Tim's wife and co-cheesemaker Diane Gile. If you "like it hot," add a layer of chopped jalapeño peppers to the stack.

1 pound ground beef
1 jar (16 ounces) spicy tomato salsa
1 package (8 ounces) cream cheese
3 cups shredded lettuce
1/2 cup finely chopped green onion
4-8 ounces shredded cheddar
4-8 ounces shredded mozzarella
1 large tomato, finely diced
1 large green pepper, finely diced

Brown ground beef in skillet; drain and cool. Stir in salsa. Spread cream cheese on a 9-by-12-inch sheet pan or similar-sized serving platter. Spread beef mixture over cream cheese. Layer the remaining ingredients on top. Serve as a dip with tortilla chips.

Chili Cheese Cornbread
8 servings

Here's a chili- and cheese-spiked cornbread inspired by a purchase of Tim Gile's aged cheddar. Its deep flavor really comes out in this lightly sweet bread. Serve warm at breakfast with smoky bacon and fresh fruit or as a side bread for any meal.

1 cup (2-3 ounces) shredded
   aged cheddar
1 small can (8.5 ounces) creamed corn
1 egg
3 tablespoons corn oil
1-2 tablespoons minced jalapeño
1 1/4 cups yellow cornmeal
1/4 cup flour
1/4 cup sugar
1 teaspoon baking powder
1/2 teaspoon salt

Grease a 7- or 8-inch cast iron pan; heat in oven set to 375 degrees for 20 minutes. Combine cheddar, corn, egg, corn oil, and jalapeño in large bowl. Whisk remaining ingredients in smaller bowl. Stir dry ingredients into wet ingredients until just combined. Spread batter in heated pan. Bake until toothpick inserted in center comes out clean, 20-25 minutes.

Hill and Valley Cheese, Cashton

8. Hill & Valley Cheese
Route 3, Box 9A
S 0510 County Highway D
Cashton, WI 54619
608-654-5411
•

Fresh as Can Be

Travelers are welcome to stop in at the Hill & Valley cheese plant for a free cheesemaking tour and the chance to purchase factory-fresh products like muenster, monterey jack, colby, and colby jack. But before you pull into the parking lot outside the factory store, where handmade Amish crafts and candies are also sold, take a few moments to pause on the side of the highway. Take as much time as you can, in fact, to enjoy expansive sweeps of farmland that rise like great rounded loaves of bread. Roll down your window and listen to the clop, clop, clop of a horse-drawn buggy as it passes on the blacktop. Take a deep breath to catch the scent of tall, narrow-waisted bundles of hay as they tremble lightly in the wind. Then enter the factory and get a super-fresh taste of creamy Wisconsin goodness.

The Wisconsin Hill & Valley Cheese Cooperative formed in 1982 when a number of Amish families in Wisconsin's Coulee Country realized that the best way to provide a continuing market for their milk, which is collected in traditional metal cans, was to own their own cheese factory. The cooperative bought three acres of land and built a *kase hau*s on County Highway D about 5 miles southeast of Cashton. They contracted with cheesemaker Mike Everhart, who has since incorporated his own business, Hill & Valley Cheese, to hire employees and operate his own cheesemaking and whey processing equipment.

Contract truckers haul milk from about

230 Amish farms within a 40-mile radius of the factory. Here, workers heft the heavy cans one by one and dump the liquid into large vats. All those stops and all that lifting can get expensive, says Kevin Everhart, Mike's brother and the current plant manager. But it's worth it.

"Can milk is *fresh*," Kevin points out. "Ninety percent of it is used quickly, within 18 hours of [the cows being milked]. Bulk milk can be older, pumped four to seven times and held four to five days."

The farmers know it's worth it, too. The Wisconsin Hill & Valley Cheese Cooperative exists to ensure an economic future for Amish milk producers. "We formed the cooperative for the benefit of all the dairy farmers in our community and also for our children," states the organization's handbook. "Our cooperative is only as strong as our mutual effort and spirit. Let us remain strong in our cooperative spirit."

Cheese & Pesto Bread Pudding
4-6 servings

Puffy bread pudding is a thrifty, hearty dish that suits the Amish lifestyle. Though typically a dessert, bread pudding doesn't have to be sweet or heavy. This version layers bread, pesto, spaghetti sauce, and two kinds of cheese for a casserole that actually looks and acts something like a souffle. Serve it hot, straight from the oven, for supper or brunch.

    8-10 slices whole wheat or whole
      grain bread
    1 1/2 cups low-fat milk
    3/4 cup basil pesto
    1 1/2 cups homemade or bottled
      spaghetti sauce
    2 cups (about 6 ounces) grated
      muenster, monterey jack, or
      mozzarella
    2 eggs
    2 tablespoons freshly grated parmesan

Preheat oven to 350 degrees. Grease a 2-quart souffle dish or deep casserole. Pour milk into a shallow pan. Soak 2 or 3 bread slices briefly in the milk and line bottom of the casserole with the soaked bread. Spread 1/4 cup pesto over bread slices. Drizzle 1/2 cup spaghetti sauce over pesto. Top with one-third of the grated muenster cheese (or other choice). Repeat this entire step for a second layer. Now layer on the last of the soaked bread, pesto, and sauce. With a knife or skewer, poke deep holes into the casserole all over. Beat eggs with remaining milk until smooth; pour over casserole. Press layers until the egg mixture has been mostly absorbed. Sprinkle on the remaining muenster cheese (or other choice) as well as the two tablespoons of parmesan. Bake until puffed and bubbly, 50-65 minutes. (If the dish is very full, place aluminum foil underneath it to catch possible drips.) Serve immediately.

9. Krohn Dairy Products
N2915 Highway 163
Luxemburg, WI 54217
920-845-2901
•

Changing With The Times

You can learn a lot about the history of Wisconsin cheesemaking by reading the booklet produced by Krohn Dairy for the occasion of its 100th anniversary in 1992.

The book details how Albert Gruetzmacher built the company's first factory at a time when cheese factories were a familiar sight on the rural Kewaunee Country landscape. Cheesemaking was a seven-days-per-week operation back then (but it was seasonal, so most cheesemakers worked in the logging camps of northern Wisconsin during the winter months). In those days, cheesemakers had to control the heat under wooden cheese vats by pulling logs in and out of the fire. Farmers delivered their milk by horse and wagon, and cheesemakers like Charles Krohn, grandfather of the present owners and the man who bought the factory from the Gruetzmachers, were community-minded men who passed on their hard-earned skills to their children.

Factory-owned milk-hauling trucks started showing up on the scene during the Depression, about the time Charles Krohn's son Leo graduated from high school and chose cheesemaking over college. As Leo gained experience, state standards were changing and by 1945 the Krohns found themselves building a new plant to keep pace. By this time, first- and second-generation cheesemakers like Charles Krohn were dying off, and with increasing changes in the industry, smaller cheese factories began to die out, too. Many cheesemakers of the next generation, including Leo, were now buying out neighboring plants and expanding their operations.

As farmers shifted from cans to bulk coolers, Leo responded by purchasing his first bulk milk truck, and the company began picking up milk from some of the farmers. By 1960 he had also added bulk storage facilities that allowed him to close the factory on Sundays.

Until this time, the company had produced mostly cheddar, but now Leo also took note of the growing popularity of Italian cheeses, particularly mozzarella, an ingredient in a new American food craze—pizza. Soon he joined this new wave of cheesemaking and was producing as much mozzarella as cheddar.

When Leo had a heart attack in 1971, the next generation took over; his daughter Jean, son-in-law Arlie Doell, and sons Roger and Carl are the owners and opera-

tors today. And the improvements continue, as they must for any plant that wants to stay viable. In 1988, for example, the Krohns built a waste water treatment plant to meet new Department of Natural Resources standards.

At the end of the 20th century, Krohn Dairy makes mostly mozzarella and provolone and is one of the largest independent Italian cheese plants in the state. And the future looks bright—Jean and Arlie Doell's son Patrick works at the factory, representing a fourth generation that is extraordinarily rare nowadays.

Grilled Eggplant Stacks
6 servings

You can use smoked, flavored, or regular mozzarella cheese for this recipe, adapted from one in American Country Cheese *by Laura Chenel and Linda Siegfried (Aris Books, 1989). Cook the tomatoes and eggplants on a grill for woodsy outdoor flavor.*

2 medium eggplants, about 1 1/2 pounds total
approximately 3 tablespoons olive oil
1 1/2 pounds medium-size ripe tomatoes
1 large onion, cut in half and thinly sliced
2 teaspoons minced garlic
2 tablespoons chopped fresh basil or rosemary (or 2 teaspoons dried)
salt and pepper to taste
6 ounces mozzarella, cut into 1/4-inch slices
freshly grated hard cheese like romano, asiago, or parmesan

Heat charcoal grill to hot temperature. Meanwhile, cut eggplants into 1/2-inch rounds, salt them on both sides and place in colander for 15 minutes. Rinse, drain, and pat dry. Rub a drop or two of olive oil over each eggplant side.

When coals are hot, grill tomatoes,

turning often, until skin is lightly blistered. Cool, peel, cut in half, and scoop out the seeds with your fingers. Cut each half into quarters. Heat 2 tablespoons olive oil in large skillet, add onions and garlic, and saute slowly until tender. Stir in tomatoes, basil or rosemary, salt and pepper. Simmer until much of the juice is evaporated, about 10 minutes.

Meanwhile, grill eggplant slices on one side about 5 minutes. Turn slices over and top half of them with mozzarella slices. Continue to grill until eggplant is tender and cheese is melted.

On serving plates, stack the cheese-covered eggplant slices atop the plain ones. Cover with tomato sauce and sprinkle with grated cheese.

Bowtie Pasta with Roasted Peppers & Provolone

6-8 servings

2 red bell peppers
2 green bell peppers
2 yellow bell peppers (optional)
1 pound bowtie pasta
1 cup diced provolone
1/3 cup chopped green onions
2 tablespoons capers
2 tablespoons balsamic vinegar
2-3 tablespoons olive oil
2-3 tablespoons chopped fresh basil
salt and pepper to taste

Roast peppers over open flame or on hot charcoal grill, turning frequently, until they are evenly blackened. Scrape off blackened skins with sharp knife. Cut peppers open and scrape out seeds and veins. Cut peppers into 1/4-inch slices.

Boil pasta in lots of salted water; drain, rinse under cold water, and let stand to air-dry for a few moments. Toss pasta with peppers and remaining ingredients. Serve at room temperature.

> **10. Mt. Sterling Cheese Co-op/Southwestern Wisconsin Dairy Goat Products Cooperative**
> **P.O. Box 103, 310 Diagonal St.**
> **Mt. Sterling, WI 54645-0103**
> **608-734-3151**
> •

Gourmet Goats

Driving through the countryside around Mt. Sterling can be dangerous. It isn't so much that you have to ride the brake pedal, negotiate sharp curves, and occasionally unpop your ears through the steep hills and valleys. It's the *view* of the hills and valleys, a stunningly beautiful distraction, that's the real problem. On a warm spring day the wooded landscape's many shades of green give pause, and if you happen to be passing through after a light rain, you can almost hear morel mushrooms popping up in the roadside undergrowth. Who can keep her eyes on the concrete knowing fresh morels are nearby? It's no safer in autumn when area apple orchards are in full fruit, draping Mother Nature's glowing slopes like a close-fitting, red-beaded apron.

For all this—no matter what time of year—it's the sight of a nondescript building near a town crossroads that is just as likely to make a traveler veer off the highway. Cheese factories are a delicious lure for tourists, and at the one in tiny Mt. Sterling they will encounter a temptation as tangy and full-flavored as a ripe McIntosh and as rare as the elusive morel.

Goat milk cheese is a local specialty produced at the Mt. Sterling Cheese Factory by members of the Southwestern Wisconsin Dairy Goat Products Cooperative. Incorporated in 1976, the cooperative processes 100 percent natural, BGH-free milk from about three dozen dairy goat farms in Wisconsin, Iowa, and Minnesota.

Goats are friendly creatures

While this is one of only a few goat cheese plants, they don't make the familiar *chevre*, or soft goat cheese; instead they feature hard cheeses like cheddar.

Mt. Sterling's best selling product is their raw milk cheddar, a cheese that has won awards at American Dairy Goat Products Association competitions and the State Fair. Although the cheese is made from unpasteurized milk, a 60-day ripening period meets safety standards and the resulting cheese has an outstanding full flavor. Their sharp cheddar is aged at least one year and they also manufacture a pasteurized, no-salt-added cheddar.

Jack and feta are two other Mt. Sterling cheeses; the jack makes a mild, velvety base for added flavors like jalapeño, chive, dill, onion, or garlic, and the feta is crumbly and very lightly salted, perfect for Mediterranean preparations like *spanakopita*. Perhaps their most unusual—and unusually good—product is whey cream butter, with the distinctive tang of goat's milk and no color added. Morel mushrooms sauteed in this pure white, super creamy butter live up to their reputation as an aphrodisiac.

The irony in all this gourmet fare produced in a exquisite setting is that it comes from goats, which may be the world's least snobbish animals. Lana Oyloe, the cooperative's sales manager and a 23-year veteran of goat farming, says goats are clean, intelligent creatures who like company and are easy to get along with.

"They're curious about you and very social," she says. "You can have a relationship with them like you might a dog or other pet." Indeed, if you visit Tony Gerstner's goat farm, located a few miles from the factory, some of his 300-plus goats will greet you at the gate, surround you inquisitively, and nuzzle close. The animals are as irresistible as the cheese.

Goat Cheddar Chive Biscuits
12 biscuits

Goat's milk butter, extra-sharp goat cheddar cheese, and buttermilk give triple-rich, triple-tangy flavor to homemade biscuits. Fresh chives add a nip of their own. You can help prevent scorching by using a baking pan lined with parchment paper, but even if the bottoms brown, these biscuits retain a soft, fluffy interior.

1 1/4 cups all-purpose flour
1 cup cake flour
3 tablespoons chopped fresh chives or
    2 tablespoons dried
2 teaspoons baking powder
1 teaspoon baking soda
1 teaspoon salt
4 tablespoons goat's milk butter, cut in
    small pieces (or substitute regular
    butter)
1 cup (about 2 ounces) grated extra-
    sharp goat's milk cheddar (or
    substitute regular cheddar cheese)
1 cup buttermilk
additional all-purpose flour for
    forming biscuits

Heat oven to 400 degrees. Line a heavy baking sheet with parchment paper, if available; otherwise leave it ungreased. Mix flours, chives, baking powder, baking soda, and salt in bowl. Cut in butter until pieces are size of sunflower seeds. (You can do this with a pastry cutter or in a food processor using the pulse button.)

Toss in the grated cheddar with your fingers. Stir in buttermilk briefly, just until dough forms into a sticky ball. Using floured hands, lightly roll dough into 12 balls and place on baking sheet at least two inches apart. Bake on highest rack in oven until golden brown, 14-16 minutes. Serve warm.

Fettucine with Greens, Feta Cheese, & Fresh Herbs
4 servings

A fresh-flavored gourmet pasta preparation that comes together in minutes. Feel free to try fresh greens and herbs other than the ones used here.

1 bunch (about 1 pound) young,
  tender mustard greens
10 ounces fresh fettucine, or
  1 pound dried
3 tablespoons goat butter or olive oil
1 tablespoon minced garlic
salt and pepper
2 tablespoons chopped fresh parsley
2 tablespoons chopped fresh basil
  or mint
heaping 1/2 cup (2-3 ounces) goat's
  milk feta (or substitute other feta)
1/3 cup toasted pine nuts or
  hickory nuts

Bring large pot of salted water to boil. Meanwhile, cut stems off the ends of the mustard greens and slice stems in half lengthwise. Cut ribs away from the leaves. Slice leaves into 1/2-inch strips. Reserve stems, ribs, and leaves in separate piles.

Add fettucine to boiling water. Cook until tender, drain, and keep warm.

While pasta is boiling, cook butter over medium heat in large skillet, stirring constantly, until lightly browned, 3-4 minutes.

Add mustard green stems and garlic; cook 1 minute, stirring. Add ribs and cook

1 minute longer. Now stir in leaves and salt and pepper to taste. Cook until wilted, stirring often, 1-3 minutes. If too much liquid accumulates, raise heat to reduce it. Stir in fresh herbs. Toss with warm fettucine, feta cheese, toasted nuts, and additional salt and pepper to taste. Serve immediately.

Grilled Vegetables, Goat Jack, & Rotini Pasta Salad
4-6 servings

In this pasta main dish, diced goat cheese turns soft and creamy without melting or losing its shape, and it clings invitingly to the spiral-shaped pasta. Smoky-sweet grilled onions are a must, but the other vegetables are up for grabs: consider asparagus, eggplant, zucchini, and small, firm tomatoes.

1 medium Vidalia (or other sweet)
  onion, cut into sixths
1 large green pepper, cut into large
  chunks
8 ounces whole mushrooms
2 tablespoons olive oil
salt and pepper
10 ounces rotini pasta
1 jar (6.5 ounces) marinated and
  quartered artichoke hearts (do not
  drain)
2/3 cup (4 ounces) diced goat jack
  cheese
1/2 cup halved large black olives
3 tablespoons chopped fresh chives
2 tablespoons capers

Heat grill. Toss onion, green pepper, and mushrooms with olive oil and salt and pepper to taste. Boil pasta in large pot of salted water; drain and keep warm. Meanwhile, place vegetables in grill basket or on skewers and grill until charred and tender. Toss hot vegetables and pasta with remaining ingredients (including the artichoke liquid); season with additional salt and pepper to taste. Serve warm.

11. Nasonville Dairy
10898 Highway 10 West
Marshfield, WI 54449
715-676-2177
●

Ken Heiman examines a round of feta cheese at Nasonville Dairy

Tackling Feta

Nasonville Dairy is deep in the heart of colby country; in fact, the town that gave colby its name is located only a few miles north of the Nasonville factory, where cheese has been produced since the 1880s. The Heiman family, who has been making cheese here since the 1960s, produce a lot of colby, and a lot of cheddar and monterey jack, two other Wisconsin favorites. But for about eight years now, they've also been producing feta.

"Feta is a whole different cat," says Ken, one of four siblings who are involved in various ways with the business the Heimans have owned since 1985. Their parents, Arnold and Rena Mae, are retired cheesemakers who began training the children when they were very young.

Ken remembers being placed inside a cheese vat to wash down the walls. "I was maybe three years old. I thought it was great fun." Ken is now a prematurely gray man with a droll sense of Wisconsin-style humor and an appetite for challenge. He does much of the administrative work and marketing for the busy plant located at the corner of Highway 10 and County Highway BB; he's also a cheesemaker and a dairy farmer with a milk retail store located on his farm.

Ken traveled to Greece a few years ago to learn more about feta, which is made with goat's milk there. He learned that he couldn't do it the Greek way. "What they want to accomplish in a day, we need to accomplish in an hour," he says with a deadpan glance.

"I never saw so many goats and sheep in my life," he adds. "But they do give a unique flavor to the cheese." Nasonville feta is made from cow's milk, which Ken says produces a more consistent cheese. Since it takes fewer cows than goats to produce the cheese, there are fewer variables to deal with. The Heimans offer three styles of feta: American, which is similar to but not as pronounced in flavor as Greek feta; kosher; and Bulgarian/Romanian, a much tangier, goatier feta. "The Bulgarian and Romanian ladies of New York love this one," says Ken, who jokes that, to him, it tastes "like a dead cat was thrown in it."

Nearly all of Nasonville's feta is shipped out of Wisconsin to Greek and other ethnic markets on the East Coast and in the Far East. It's available at the factory store, which is run by Ken's parents. Ken is working with an Eau Claire salad dressing producer to promote the pairing of Greek dressing and the crumbly white cheese at area restaurants. While feta comes in many sizes, Ken seems most pleased with the 10-pound round developed at Nasonville.

"The Milk Marketing Board will ask me, 'What do you want to tackle next?'" For now it is *kasseri* that Ken wants to take on. Kasseri is used in the flaming cheese dish of Greek fame.

"I like taking a raw product and making something out of it," says Ken, all joking aside. "That's what I really enjoy."

Greek-Style Omelette with Fresh Spinach, Black Olives, & Feta Cheese
Makes 2-4 omelettes

Unlike Humpty Dumpty, who couldn't recover from his fall, eggs are making a comeback these days. More concerned about saturated fat in the overall diet than the cholesterol content in eggs, nutritionists are once again giving the green light to occasional consumption. And cooks everywhere are happy about that. As New York Times food columnist Molly O'Neill has written, "Eggs are too fierce a culinary force, too formidable in the kitchen to do without."

Especially hard to do without would be the omelette, that little black dress of the culinary world. Omelettes are "easy to slip into," fit into any meal, and always look good. As for accessories, a filling of spinach and feta cheese is as classic as matching gold jewelry. If you like a topping on your omelette, consider chopped fresh tomatoes, a light tomato sauce, or additional crumbled feta.

   1 pound fresh spinach
   2 tablespoons bottled Greek dressing
      or homemade vinaigrette flavored
      with oregano
   1/2 cup coarsely chopped black olives
      (use Greek olives, if available)
   6-8 eggs
   2-3 teaspoons olive oil
   4 ounces (about 1 cup) feta cheese,
      crumbled
   pepper

Clean spinach, remove stems, and coarsely chop the leaves. Heat Greek dressing in a skillet, add chopped spinach, and cook over medium heat, stirring often, until wilted. Raise heat to high and cook until nearly all the liquid is evaporated. Turn off heat and stir in black olives. Keep warm.

Make omelettes one at a time in a small, non-stick skillet with sloping sides: Beat two or three eggs in a bowl. Heat a little olive oil over high heat in the skillet. Pour in eggs; they will immediately begin to set on the bottom. With a spatula, pull egg from outer edges of pan towards the center; the uncooked egg will spread and cook. Keep doing this until most of the egg is set—this will only take a moment—then spread any remaining uncooked egg across surface of omelette. Reduce heat to low. The egg will continue to cook as you distribute some of the crumbled feta, spinach filling, and pepper over the surface. Holding a plate with one hand close to pan and shaking pan slightly with your other hand, slip omelette onto a plate, rolling it into either a cigar shape or folding it over into a half-moon. Serve immediately or keep warm while you prepare additional omelettes.

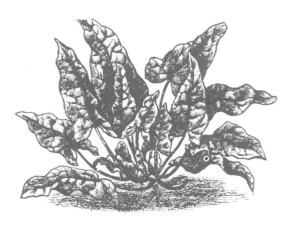

> **12. Prima Käse**
> **W6117 County Highway C**
> **Monticello, WI 53570**
> **608-938-4227**
> •

Small Batches of Big Cheese

Randy and Shelley Krahenbuhl are a husband-and-wife team in the Swiss tradition, manufacturing quality specialty cheeses from their tiny factory near Monticello. Their emmenthaler, for example, is made in giant copper kettles and formed into traditional 45- and 180-pound wheels. Says Shelley, "The Swiss made large wheels because they got taxed by the number of pieces of cheese they made, [not by weight] so it was a way to save money. When they came here to make cheese, the tradition carried on."

Emmenthaler is what Shelley calls "real Swiss," nutty, full-flavored, and a cheese that "develops a real kick on the tongue" as it ages. She claims their company, Prima Käse, is the only one in the United States that still makes this old-style emmenthaler.

Her husband's Swiss heritage and his status as one of a limited number of certified master cheesemakers in the nation are two reasons Prima Käse produces high quality cheese such as gouda, a mild, creamy, meltable cheese, and baby Swiss, a mellow, full-cream Swiss with tiny holes. Randy also follows in the footsteps of other great Wisconsin cheesemakers who

created originals like colby and brick. His sweet-style Swiss, developed while he was a cheesemaker with Swiss Valley Farms, is, as Shelley describes, "not as full-flavored as emmenthaler, not as mild as baby Swiss, creamy like havarti." The couple also sells a hickory-smoked version of their sweet-style Swiss.

Other Prima Käse specialties include edam, similar to but lower in fat than gouda; havarti, a high-fat, ultra-creamy cheese; soft and creamy fontina; and asiago, a hard cheese similar to parmesan. There isn't a pedestrian product in the bunch, but they do make block, or "sandwich" Swiss. "This is our plain Swiss," says Shelley. "It's similar to emmenthaler, but the flavor is less robust, there's no rind, and it's cured in plastic."

Emmenthaler cheese is still made in copper kettles at Prima Käse in Monticello.

One of Shelley's jobs is to poly-coat the gouda. Wearing a bulky sweatshirt, a hair net, and gloves, she hand-wipes a substance that looks like yellow frosting on hundreds of cheese wheels that line the wall in a chilly room. Each cheese gets four coats and it takes each coat six hours to dry. "It's a protective coating that seals in flavor but lets the cheese breathe," says Shelley as she carefully removes specks of coating that have hardened too quickly.

Cheesemaking is clearly hard work, but like her husband, Shelly is uniquely suited to the life. "My grandfather moved here from Germany and my family are restaurateurs," she points out. "That's not a nine-to-five job and neither is this."

Hard work, creativity, training, and tradition are the elements that keep a family business going and produce the highest quality cheeses. "We're really, really small," declares Randy.

And they're really, really good.

Shelley and Randy Krahenbuhl of Prima Käse

Shelley's Suggestions

It's no surprise that Shelley Krahenbuhl, a cheesemaker with a restaurant background, has a lot of creative ideas about how to work specialty cheeses into a culinary repertoire. Recipes? Well, if you had her schedule, you wouldn't have time for recipes, either.

Sweet-style Swiss

-Saute apples with sugar and cinnamon, place in layered phyllo leaves, top with grated sweet-style Swiss, and bake until the cheese is melted.

-Pound a chicken breast flat, line it with cooked broccoli or spinach, add a slice of sweet-style Swiss, and roll it up. Then roll it in egg and Italian breadcrumbs and bake 1/2 hour at 350 degrees.

-Scoop the "meat" from hot, halved baked potatoes and mash them with sour cream. Stir some chopped ham and/or cooked broccoli into the potatoes, scoop them back into the potato shells, and bake until hot. Serve with a white sauce flavored with curry powder and grated sweet-style Swiss cheese.

-Serve with in-season strawberries for a delicious appetizer or dessert.

Asiago

-Brown chicken breasts in butter, add a large splash of marsala wine, and cook gently until chicken is tender. Place chicken on a bed of linguine and top with shredded asiago.

-Make asiago cheese bread: cut a loaf of French bread in half lengthwise, brush it with olive oil and chopped basil, sprinkle with asiago and Swiss and place it under the broiler until bubbly.

Emmenthaler

-Use in Reuben sandwiches and potato dishes like roesti, the buttery Swiss version of grated hash browns.

Gouda

-Cube it and add to quiche with rosemary and bacon.

Roast Root Vegetable Gratin
8 servings

The owners of Prima Käse occasionally set up a stand at the Dane County Farmers' Market in Madison and when they do, I make a beeline for their smoked sweet Swiss cheese. Eating this cheese is as pleasurable as lounging near a crackling fire in a log cabin. I make this dish in late fall, with root vegetables purchased during the final weeks of the market. The cheese and vegetables make a creamy, smoky combination that takes the chill off an on-coming winter. Serve it with a tossed green salad and a full-bodied white wine.

8 cups root vegetables cut into 3/4-inch chunks (use a mixture of carrots, leeks, turnips, and unpeeled potatoes, or any combination you prefer)
2 tablespoons olive oil
1/4 cup white wine
4-5 sprigs fresh rosemary (or 1 teaspoon dried)
1 tablespoon chopped garlic
salt and pepper
2 tablespoons butter
3 tablespoons flour
1 1/2 cups milk (whole or 2%)
1 tablespoon horseradish
1 cup (3-4 ounces) grated smoked sweet Swiss cheese
3 tablespoons dried breadcrumbs

Heat oven to 375 degrees. Spread vegetables in large baking dish, drizzle with olive oil and wine, scatter on the rosemary and garlic, and season to taste with salt and pepper. Cover dish tightly with aluminum foil and bake 30 minutes, then remove foil and continue to roast until vegetables are brown-tipped and tender, 20-35 minutes longer.

Meanwhile, make a white sauce by melting the butter in a saucepan; stir in flour and cook over low heat several minutes. Whisk in milk, bring to simmer, and cook gently 10 minutes, stirring often. Season well with salt and pepper.

If you've used rosemary sprigs, remove them from the vegetables. Stir horseradish into sauce then stir sauce into vegetables. Sprinkle cheese over all and scatter breadcrumbs over cheese. Continue to bake until bubbly and lightly colored, 15-20 minutes.

Wisconsin Fondue
4-6 servings

I'm not much for tricky gadgets and single-use kitchen equipment, but I am glad to have the $1 fondue pot I found at a garage sale years ago. The cheery red enameled pot and long wooden-handled forks make our occasional fondue meals festive. If you substitute a heavy saucepan for the fondue pot, you may need to reheat the cheese sauce once during dinner.

Bock beer gives the fondue Wisconsin flavor and a rich caramel color. Emmenthaler is the classic fondue cheese, but for an unusual touch, use half smoked Swiss and half emmenthaler cheese.

1 pound emmenthaler or Swiss cheese, finely diced
4 tablespoons flour
1 teaspoon minced garlic
1/4 teaspoon salt
2 cups bock beer
2 tablespoons lemon juice
pepper
whole grain or dark rye bread, cut into 1-inch cubes

Mix cheese and flour in bowl. Combine garlic and salt on a cutting board; smash with the flat-edge of a knife until a paste forms. Combine beer and garlic paste in fondue pot. Bring to very low simmer; do not let it boil. Stir in lemon juice. Add a handful of cheese and stir constantly with wooden spoon until melted. Continue to add one handful of cheese at a time, stirring constantly. Do not add more cheese until each handful is melted. After last handful has melted and mixture begins to bubble, stir in pepper to taste. Place fondue pot over burner unit. Serve with cubed bread to dip into the cheese sauce.

---

13. Renard's Cheese
County Highway S
Algoma, WI 54201
920-487-2825
14.
Highway 57
Sturgeon Bay, WI 54235
920-825-7272
•

Wheel of Fortune

Brian Renard, a powerfully built man with a dark mustache and smiling eyes, makes cheese at a three-generation operation in Door County. Brian says he has a special device that helps the family plant compete with the larger companies that are endangering small businesses like his. He calls it the "back-o-matic," pointing behind his broad shoulders. "It bends over the vats day after day," he laughs. At age 32, he's had six knee surgeries, but these were the result of recreational sports, not cheesemaking, he says.

If making cheese the old-fashioned way hasn't hurt Brian physically, it hasn't hurt the reputation of his cheese, either. *Wisconsin Trails* magazine readers have voted Renard's best cheese factory in the state.

"We make what the big guys can't." Brian is talking about wheel-shaped cheddar cheese that is pressed in cheesecloth-

Brian Renard makes wheel-shaped cheddar cheese the old-fashioned way.

lined hoops and is aged in wax. The rounds have quaint names like daisy, midget, flat, and mammoth. "The shape affects taste and texture and they age better in wax," says Brian. "You'll get a better flavor here."

While Renard's produces brick, colby, jack, and many flavored cheeses, the company is best known for aged cheddar. At the factory near Algoma and an outlet outside of Sturgeon Bay, two-year-old cheddar is the company's biggest seller. They regularly stock four-year cheddar and occasionally offer some that is aged five years. These sharp, crumbly aged cheddars explode with flavor and are as rich and satisfying as a classic movie.

Renard's, like so many of the state's small plants, is very much a family affair. Brian's father Howard, whose own father had hauled milk and fished commercially in the area, bought the Algoma factory in 1961; he is "retired" today, meaning he doesn't make cheese anymore but is still involved in sales. Howard's wife Angela and all seven of their children worked at the plant during the family's early years. At one point their eldest son Gary ran the nearby Clover Leaf Factory, but in 1975, when Gary and Howard formed a partnership, that site became a second retail outlet for Renard's. Today, Gary and Brian's wives run the two retail stores and Gary's son Chris is a full-time cheesemaker for the company.

Renard's Cheddar Cheese Soup
4 servings

"I live on good soup, not fine words," said Molière. This cheese soup is better than poetry.

2 tablespoons butter
1/2 cup minced onion
1/2 cup minced sweet pepper
   (green or red)
2 tablespoons flour
1 1/2 cups milk
1 1/2 cups mashed potatoes
1 1/2 to 1 3/4 cups chicken broth
   (homemade or low-salt canned)
1 1/2 cups grated aged cheddar cheese
   (white or yellow)
salt and pepper
2 tablespoons chopped fresh parsley

Heat butter in soup pot. Add onion and sweet pepper; cook over medium-low heat until vegetables are tender. Stir in flour and cook gently 2 minutes. Whisk in milk, mashed potatoes, and chicken broth until smooth. Simmer 10-15 minutes. Remove from heat, let stand 5 minutes, then whisk in grated cheese a little at a time. Season soup with salt and pepper to taste. Stir in parsley. Reheat gently.

> ### 15. Salemville County Cheese Co-op
> **West 4481 Highway GG**
> **Cambria, WI 53923**
> **920-394-3433**
> •

Simply Good

Traversing the plush lands south of Green Lake on a hot, breezy day, I am reminded of a hiking tour I once took through the countryside of southwestern England. In both places, the back roads are free of billboards and the land is quilted with picturesque, family-run farms. Modestly dressed people walk through scented fields rather than speeding by in air-conditioned vehicles. And at a small cheese factory near Cambria in Wisconsin, the gorgonzola is the finest blue cheese I've tasted since the Stiltons of British fame.

The Salemville Cheese Co-op produces just two types of cheese, both veined: blue and the green-veined gorgonzola. Salemville's line of cheese, like the lives of the people who make it, is simple by design. That is, most of the milk suppliers and cheesemakers are Amish. They use only "can" milk, which comes from hand-milked cows and is stored in traditional metal milk cans. The cooperative formed in the 1980s at a time when the local community's time-honored methods of producing cheese were being jeopardized by modern trends.

"We had no choice," says William Schrock, who is sales manager for the co-op. "There used to be no problem shipping can milk, but eventually all the area factories that took can milk were discontinuing cans or were closing their doors." So the community came together to run their own factory.

The first licensed cheesemaker, who was also a major investor, left after a year and a half. "But we decided to continue," says William. They hired another cheesemaker to "babysit production" until Lavern Miller met the requirements for his own license.

Today, Lavern is assisted by his teenage son Wilbur and other community members in producing 60-day-aged blue cheese and 90-day-aged gorgonzola. More than 40 Amish dairy farmers and several "English," or non-Amish, farmers supply the can milk. The building and equipment are leased, but the co-op members own the product. Some of the cheese is private label but most of it is sold under the Salemville Cheese name, distributed by Dan Carter of Mayville. "Ninety percent of our cheese goes to deli counters, not the dairy case," says William, meaning it's good enough to sell in specialty markets. "We're very proud of that."

It's good enough, in fact, to be a national champion. Salemville's gorgonzola, a creamy rich, heavily veined cheese with deep, almost smoky flavor, won first place in the 1997 U.S. Championship sponsored by the Wisconsin Cheesemakers Association.

Blue Cheese Pasta Toss
2 large or 4 small servings

This recipe was inspired by one in Deborah Madison's The Savory Way *(Bantam Books, 1990). I like to vary the pasta shapes and sometimes add bits of cooked asparagus or broccoli at the tossing stage. With a green salad and crusty bread, fine cooking doesn't get any simpler than this.*

1/2 teaspoon minced garlic
3 ounces blue cheese chunks
1 1/2 tablespoons butter
2 teaspoons Dijon mustard
1/2 pound dried pasta
pepper

Bring a large pot of salted water to boil. Place garlic, cheese, butter, and mustard in large, heatproof bowl and place it over the

heating water to partially melt the mixture.

When water boils, remove bowl from top of pot; keep bowl warm. Cook pasta in the boiling water until just tender. Drain briefly and immediately toss pasta with contents of bowl. Add pepper to taste.

Gorgonzola & Tomato Sandwich
Any number of servings

Don't make the mistake of adding any ingredients to this sandwich to "fancy it up." You don't even need pepper. It is perfect as is.

fresh, thick-sliced country-style
    white bread
thick-sliced, vine-ripened, never
    refrigerated tomatoes
thick slices of gorgonzola cheese

Simply layer the tomatoes and cheese between the bread and set to.

Ploughman's Lunch
Any number of servings

Ploughman's lunch is to English pubs as burgers and fries are to American taverns. The British can't get enough of this national specialty, available at nearly every country pub. And while I love a good burger, I'd take a Ploughman's lunch over one any day. Each pub has its own version of the plated assortment, but the basic themes are almost always the same: whole-grain bread, a quality cheese, pickled onions, a small salad of some sort, and some type of chutney or relish. Typically the meal is washed down with a hearty beer or hard cider, a fermented apple cider.

The Wisconsin variations on these themes are endless, but I've suggested a few possibilities to get you going. Say goodbye, burgers.

whole-grain bread (Wild Rice Bread,
　　page 126 or Swedish Limpa,
　　page 102)
wedges of high quality cheese
　　(aged cheddar, gorgonzola, brie,
　　smoked Swiss, etc.)
pickled item (Asparagus Dillys,
　　page 146, or Zucchini and Onion
　　Pickles, page 145)
chutney or relish (Cherry De-Lite Fruit
　　Relish, page 147)
salad: (Old-Fashioned Macaroni Salad,
　　page 19, or Sweet Potato Salad,
　　page 150)
lettuce leaves
beer, hard cider, apple cider, or iced tea

Assemble bread, cheese, pickles, chutney, and salad over lettuce leaves on individual serving plates. Serve with beverage of your choice.

16. Springside Cheese
P.O. Box 142
7989 Arndt Road
Oconto Falls, WI 54154
920-829-6395
•

On an early-winter day traffic is light outside Springside Cheese, located one mile north of tiny Spruce in northeastern Wisconsin. Distant pine trees droop slightly from the melting mounds of snow on their branches. Abandoned stone silos contrast with towering blue modern ones. The snow-spotted fields, lined with neat, undulating rows of corn stumps, look as honorable and forlorn as a military cemetery.

The landscape may appear dormant, but inside the factory life is teeming. Workers decked out in hair nets and boots go at their tasks: one hoses the floor,

another stirs great vats of curds with a pitch fork; others line shiny hoops with cheesecloth, while still more toil in a cheese-wrapping assembly line. Inside the retail store, clerks package orders in holiday gift boxes and wait on a steady stream of customers—a surprisingly steady stream, given the plant's out-of-the way location.

Customers are glad enough to go the extra mile to Springside because the cheese is worth it. The colby, for example, has the sweet taste and slightly marbly texture of old-style longhorn colby; that's because it's still made the old-fashioned way: in round hoops that allow the cheese to cool faster than large blocks. Longhorn colby, smaller and more labor-intensive than block colby, would be extinct by now if it weren't for factories like Springside.

Cheddar, monterey jack, farmers cheese, and fresh curds are the plant's other specialties.

Wayne Hintz purchased Springside Cheese when it was located in a smaller building a few miles north of Spruce. He carves a rare "extra ten minutes" out of his day to relate his story.

"I'm not from a cheesemaking family, really. But my great-grandfather had a small cheese-producing facility on his farm in Sheboygan County. That was in the 1800s, at a time when neighboring farmers would bring a can or so of their excess milk to him. Once or twice a week he'd make cheese. There were no licenses then, you know.

"So my great-grandfather didn't really have a factory, but he made cheese and my family was in dairy farming ever since. I grew up on a farm [north of Pulaski]. I had lots of brothers. Not that there wasn't always plenty of work for everybody, of course, but eventually [it made sense for me to] find work off the farm. So I went to a neighboring cheese plant—it was in Krakow—and worked there all through high school and college. When I had the opportunity I took a full-time job at a

Springside Cheese, Spruce

cheese factory in Elmwood and continued to work part-time at the Krakow plant.

"I got a cheesemaker's license. I wanted to stay in the dairy industry. I worked for the National Farmers Organization in Menasha for three years. For the first year I tested milk, then I managed a receiving plant for two years. By then I wanted to get back to the cheese-making part of it. During the last year there I was looking for a small cheese plant to buy or a cooperative to manage."

Springside has grown steadily since Wayne bought it in 1973. In 1982 he and his wife Licia—"We both play a lot of roles here," says Wayne—built the current plant, which today processes milk from 65 dairy farmers. Being there for area milk producers is one of the couple's stated goals for the plant. Other goals are: "To continue to be an aggressive purchaser of pure quality farm milk in Oconto, Marinette, and Shawano counties; to manufacture only the highest quality cheese; to provide our consumers with the finest variety of cheese at the most economical price; and to provide jobs and an economic base for our agricultural community."

Grilled Colby Cheese Sandwich Du Jour
Any number of servings

There's something about a hot, oozing grilled cheese sandwich that makes me feel like a kid again. Maybe it's the memory of the hefty cast iron griddle that my family would heat over two stove burners on meatless Fridays. The long, black griddle held six or eight grilled cheese sandwiches at a time, and our large family could keep it going for several batches. We rarely put anything but cheese—colby, cheddar, or processed—in our grilled cheese sandwiches, but today I find all kinds of things to tuck inside.

slices of firm white or whole-
   grain bread
softened butter
slices of colby cheese

Fillings:
minced green onion
sliced black or green olives
grilled sweet onion slices
roasted sweet pepper slices
sliced pickled jalapeños
sliced tomatoes
cooked sliced mushrooms
sauteed, chopped zucchini
chopped apples
minced fresh herbs
roasted garlic
chopped, cooked asparagus
fresh tomato salsa
sliced sweet or tart pickles

For each sandwich: Spread two bread slices with softened butter. Make a sandwich, buttered side out, with colby and filling(s) of your choice.

Heat cast iron skillet over medium flame. Grill sandwich(es) on one side until browned; flip carefully and cook, adjusting heat if necessary, until second side is browned and cheese is melted.

More Hometown Cheese Flavor

The cheese factories that follow are arranged in alphabetical order by the name of the business. To locate a cheese factory by town name, see page 173. Maps are on pages *xviii-xxv*. All information is subject to change. Travelers should call or write before visiting to get business hours, directions, and other important details.

Bletsoe's Honey Bee Cheese Factory, Little Chicago

17. Beechwood Cheese Factory Inc.
N1598W County Highway A
Adell, WI 53001
920-994-9306

•

Located just outside the northern Kettle Moraine, this small, old-fashioned factory produces all-natural cheddar-style cheese—a total of 26 varieties—and fresh curds on Saturdays. Visitors can watch production from an observation area.

18. Bletsoe's Honey Bee Cheese Factory
8281 Third Lane
Marathon City, WI 54448
715-443-2526

•

The mailing address is Marathon, but Bletsoe's is actually located about one mile west of Little Chicago on County Highway A. Cheesemakers Bonnie and David Bletsoe and their son Tom make colby, farmers cheese, cheddar, and several kinds of flavored monterey jack. Bonnie personally makes sure area stores are kept stocked with the company's ultra-fresh cheese curds.

19. Cady Cheese
126 Highway 128
Wilson, WI 54027
715-772-4218

•

This family-owned operation offers colby, curds, monterey jack, "Golden Jack," and a variety of flavored cheeses. Tours, cheese samples, and viewing windows available.

20. Carr Valley Cheese Company, Inc.
S3797 County Highway G
La Valle, WI 53941
608-986-2781

•

N4095 Highway 12 and 16
Mauston, WI
608-847-6998

•

Owned and operated by the Cook family's fourth generation cheesemakers, Carr Valley Cheese has been featured in *Saveur*, a gourmet food magazine, and is recognized for its well-crafted cheeses. The aged cheddar is sweet and creamy with a delicious tang and the smoked gouda is reminiscent of premium ham. They also make excellent edam, fontina, havarti, and other varieties; some are smoked or flavored. Watch a cheesemaking video and take a tour at the Mauston location. There's also a retail outlet in Sauk City. For mail order call 800-462-7258.

21. Cloverleaf Cheese, Inc.
W10906 County Highway N
Stanley, WI 54768
715-669-3145

•

Nestled in a quiet rural setting among the dairy farms of western Wisconsin, this company has been manufacturing cheese since 1895. High quality colby, monterey jack, and award-winning aged cheddar are featured; tours are available.

22. Crystal Lake Cheese Factory Blaser's Quality Cheese Products
P. O. Box 36
1858 Highway 63
Comstock, WI 54826
715-822-2437

•

The factory's retail store features Blaser's brick, muenster, and other fine cheeses, plus an upscale variety of Wisconsin specialty foods like mustards, fudge, and premium meats. Call for a mail order catalog.

23. Decatur Dairy, Inc.
W1667 County Highway F
Brodhead, WI 53520
608-897-8661

•

Area farmers provide all the milk for this small, friendly cheese cooperative located in scenic Green County. Featured cheeses are brick, muenster, farmers cheese, and a havarti that was first runner up in a nationwide cheese contest. Watch cheesemaking in action through an observation window.

24. Henning Cheese
20201 Ucker Point Road
Kiel, WI 53042
920-894-3032

•

The Hennings have been manufacturing cheese since 1914. Today they produce cheddar, colby, monterey jack, reduced fat cheeses, string cheese, and "Mozza Whips," a snack cheese that looks like thick spaghetti. Visitors can watch a cheesemaking video or live production through a viewing window.

25. Hook's
320 Commerce St.
Mineral Point, WI 53565
608-987-3259

•

Julie and Tony Hook are a hard-working cheesemaking couple who make world champion colby and 22 other kinds of fine cheese. The factory/retail outlet is located among the galleries and antique shops of historic downtown Mineral Point.

26. Klondike Cheese
P.O. Box 542
W7839 Highway 81
Monroe, WI 53566
608-325-3021

•

A third-generation business that has been manufacturing cheese since 1925. They produce feta, brick, and muenster cheeses in a variety of shapes and sizes. Award-winning Klondike quality has been recognized at both the Wisconsin State Fair and World Cheese Championship competitions.

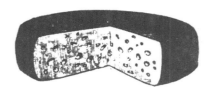

27. Meister Cheese
1050 E. Nebraska St
Muscoda, WI 53573
608-739-3134
•

Monterey jack, colby, and other cheddar-type cheeses are manufactured under the Great Midwest label at this third generation company (with "some of the fourth sprinkled in, too," says family member Vicki Thingvold). Most of the milk comes from Jersey cows. Jersey milk is higher in butterfat and protein than milk that comes from the more common Holstein cow; thus Meister cheeses are very creamy and rich. Their flavored cheeses include pesto jack, salsa jack, peppercorn jack, and a jack cheese flavored with wild morels and leeks (a tribute to Muscoda's signature food, morel mushrooms).

28. Montfort Dairy Products Co.
Box 187
303 East Highway 18
Montfort, WI 53569
608-943-6753
•

Proprietor Woo S. Hong makes high-quality colby, monterey jack, and other cheeses at the tiny plant he built nearly twenty years ago.

29. Mullins Cheese
598 Seagull Drive
Mosinee, WI 54455
715-693-3205
•

The mailing address is Mosinee, but Mullins Cheese is actually located in Knowlton, a tiny town that lies within a sea of corn, potato, and ginseng fields better known as the Golden Sands area of the state. In fact, being the town's only business, Mullins Cheese more or less *is* Knowlton. Brothers Don and Bill Mullins are proud that their large, busy operation is family owned and operated, and that they buy their milk from about 525 dairy farmers in central Wisconsin. Mullins Cheese specializes in colby, cheddar, monterey jack, and a mixture of monterey jack and colby called Jacko.

30. Nelson Cheese Factory
Box 82
Highway 35 South
Nelson, WI 54756
715-673-4725
•

Hubert Greenheck, great-great-grandfather of Edward Greenheck, Nelson's current and fifth generation cheesemaker, was one of many European immigrants who brought a rich dairy heritage from his homeland to southwestern Wisconsin. Today, the Greenheck family gathers milk from dairy farms in the Upper Mississippi Valley to make colby, sharp cheddar, squeaky-fresh cheese curds, and other cheeses.

31. Specialty Cheese Company
Box 425
455 S. River St.
Lowell, WI 53557
920-927-3888
•

This is a small retail outlet for two family-run factories that produce cheese for the country's ethnic minorities. Specialty Cheese makes Mexican, Indian, Arab, and kosher cheeses, in addition to muenster and brick.

32. Springdale Cheese Factory Inc.
Route 1 Box 238
Richland Center, WI 53581
608-538-3213
•

Take Highway 14 west 17 1/2 miles from Richland Center to the second junction with County Highway E. Turn right on

Hooping the curd for cheddar cheese, Plymouth Cheese Factory
State Historical Society of Wisconsin WHi(X3)21913

E and go 1/2 mile north to this small country cheese factory that has small, friendly prices. They produce several types of cheese, but also sell a large variety from all over the state.

33. Suttner's Country Cheese
N14505 Sandhill Ave.
Curtiss, WI 54422
715-223-3338
•

The address above is a mailing address; the factory/store is actually located three miles west of Abbotsford on Highway 29. Father and son Paul and Dennis Suttner make mostly cheddar, colby, and fresh cheese curds.

34. Widmer's Cheese Cellars Inc.
P.O. Box 127
214 West Henni St.
Theresa, WI 53091
920-488-2503
•

Founder John O. Widmer came to America from Switzerland more than 75 years ago and became a Wisconsin cheesemaker. Today, third-generation Widmers offer a Wisconsin original, brick cheese, plus 100 percent natural aged cheddar produced the old-fashioned, handmade way. The business has a retail store with observation windows and offers tours by appointment. Check out their Website at www.widmerscheese.com for unique recipes, company history, and cheesemaking information. For mail orders call 888-878-1107.

2

Butcher Shops
& Fish Markets

2. Butcher Shops & Fish Markets

Butchers wore long white coats to catch the blood and fat that spurted from the sides of fresh meat, and their shop floors were covered with sawdust to absorb the same mixture. Coils of sticky, brown flypaper spiraled down from the ceiling, and kielbasa made on the premises hung in great strings in the front windows. In season, the skinned carcasses of rabbits, deer, and other game hung on barrels in front of the shop. Sulze and pickled pig's feet swam in jars, and tripe, brains, and sweetbreads were displayed on open trays. The friendly butcher offered free liver for regular customers' cats, and made suet available for lard rendering.

—From *Wisconsin: The Way We Were*, Mary A. Shafer (Heartland Press, 1993)

Historical Flavor

The processing of meat and fish has been around for a very long time, going back, no doubt, to when humans first realized cooked flesh tasted much better than raw. Imagine the happy surprise of the cook who discovered that an animal's intestines could be used as edible wraps for bits of meat, thus creating the first sausage. Think of how handy dried meat was for nomadic tribes, and how delighted primitive families must have been to taste smoked fish.

No wonder, then, that as soon as people began to gather and form communities, small, specialized processing services began to crop up. These were the first butcher shops and fish markets; like many of today's ventures, they were family-owned and served locals.

By the time of the ancient Romans only a pampered upper class could afford meat. Still, those infamous over-eaters consumed so much wild boar and stuffed fowl that large-scale packing operations were needed to keep meat markets supplied. Sausages filled with all manner of fish, poultry, animal innards, and exotic spices were particularly popular with the sophisticated diners of Rome.

Like other tradespeople of the time, early butchers organized into guilds to manage production and transportation, but were subject to strict government regulation and control. The Romans, never known for being homebodies, spread their meat-processing skills throughout the territories they conquered. Many of their subjects, notably the Germans, took to sausage-making and meat-preserving like proverbial ducks to water.

The Dark Ages were a dismal time for independent butchers and fishmongers,

what with the lack of vibrant towns and villages, but meat and fish processing continued within the confines of monasteries and lords' manors. During the later medieval period, as European trade and cities began to revive, small processing shops thrived once again. Butchers were especially glad about the increased availability of Eastern spices, which vastly improved the taste and smell of less-than-fresh meat, a necessary evil in an "unrefrigerated" world. Sausage mixtures, called "forc'd-meats," were used in a great variety of dishes. The invention of the printing press in the 1400s brought cookbooks which encouraged the widespread exchange of recipes and food-processing skills.

Newly formed European guilds were free, progressive associations whose existence contributed to the development of democracy. In many countries, butchers' guilds played a leading role both commercially and politically in the struggle against the aristocracy.

The guilds became a powerful force themselves, but as is too often the case with powerful forces, they were responsible for their own share of oppression. Restrictions on membership led to monopoly, which led to high prices and deteriorating quality. Working conditions were abominable and laborers had no civil or economic rights. Naturally, there were worker rebellions, but what really broke up the European guilds was the rise of big merchant capitalists and a powerful, centralized state.

Neither of which, in subsequent centuries, showed much sympathy for the working classes, either.

America the Beautiful

A harrowing transatlantic trip and vast, unfamiliar lands didn't sound so bad to commoners looking to improve their lot in life. Starting in the 1600s, the hunger for religious and economic freedom drew wave after wave of settlers to the Americas. They put a long heritage of meat-processing skills to good use in a country that was rich in wildlife and grazing lands.

Indeed, American pioneers ate a good deal more meat than most people in Europe did. Soon traveling butchers were offering their services to farmers, and family meat markets were part of the street scene in small towns and growing cities.

Native tribes had long been expert at drying, salting, smoking, and other types of meat- and fish-processing. Pemmican was a kind of sausage made of combinations of game, fat, wild rice, corn, herbs, and berries; it was packed into animal skins or formed into cakes and smoked. Indians bartered meats, fish, and other foodstuffs to early immigrants, who could not have survived without them.

The American meat-packing industry began during colonial times. Salted pork and beef were important exports in the early history of the United States. As settlement expanded west during the 1800s, a growing meat industry followed the livestock producers who worked the spacious pastures of the Midwest. The Civil War forced more commerce westward and out of its path; when railroads from the East, South, and West converged in Chicago, that city became the nation's meat-packing center.

Meat Wisconsin

Meanwhile, up in Wisconsin, which achieved statehood in 1848, circumstances were ideal for the development of a notable meat-processing heritage. Lush prairielands and woodlands had quickly become farmlands which easily supported livestock. Wisconsin's frugal rural residents, of course, did their own butchering, but town dwellers depended on local butcher shops to supply them with fresh and processed meats. Livestock processing existed only on a small scale until Milwaukee entrepreneurs and a forward-looking state legislature developed rail connections, which in turn greatly expanded the state's meat-packing trade.

Retail butchers like John Plankinton and Frederick Layton were among Milwaukee's first large-scale meat-packers. They utilized the state's agricultural resources, an improved transportation system, and new refrigeration techniques to give birth to Milwaukee's leading industry. By 1871 Milwaukee as a packing center ranked fourth in the nation. Pork was the mainstay of the trade, but as the century waned, wheat crops declined and dairy farms grew in number. The increasing bovine supply gave rise to more beef processing. Ice harvested from Lake Michigan made meat-packing possible throughout the year.

Milwaukee is no longer a major meat-packing center, but Wisconsin's reputation as land of the bratwurst is certainly intact. Indeed, sausage joins cheese and beer as one of the state's signature foods. And we have 19th-century settlers with a heritage of sausage-making and meat-processing skills to thank for that.

Wherever immigrants settled in Wisconsin, particularly the Germans and particularly in the Milwaukee area, they opened butcher shops which quickly drew crowds hungry for a taste of the old country. Shop-owners made Bavarian bratwurst and braunschweiger, Polish kielbasa, Bohemian jaternice, and dozens of other specialties. Over time, the markets became known for the sausages they prepared from unique, long-held family recipes (some of which are still being used today).

The broad spectrum of ethnic groups that populated Wisconsin added more flavors to the mix: Scandinavian potato sausage, Italian salami, Mexican chorizo, and many more. Some, like Belgian "trippe," remained local favorites; bratwurst, of course, went on to become a state icon. Eventually sausage-makers began creating new types of wurst, flavoring them with regional products like cheese and cherries or drawing on international cuisines and trends. (The latest craze is reduced-fat sausages made from turkey or chicken.) In the end, nothing illustrates Wisconsin's ethnic and agricultural diversity better than its varied and well-loved repertoire of sausages.

Some of the early butchers became top names in the industry. Usinger's of Milwaukee, for example, was started in 1880 by an apprentice sausage-maker from Frankfurt. In 1919, Chicago butcher Oscar Mayer opened a meat-packing plant in Madison which eventually became—and continued for decades as—the company's headquarters.

As the big companies grew, modern transportation and technologies were changing the way people shopped. Like other small-scale specialty food businesses, family-operated meat markets faced powerful new competition: the supermarket.

That so many independent butchers endure is partly due to another Wisconsin legacy—deer hunting. Custom venison processing is big business to many small shops; some work into late spring processing thousands of pounds of venison sausage annually. What's more, one of the busiest days of the year for a Wisconsin butcher is the day before rifle season opens, when camouflage-clothed deer hunters stop on their way out of town to stock up on enough bacon, summer sausage, and brats to last for a week of hunting.

Fish Wisconsin

Commercial fishing and small fish markets have long been part of Wisconsin culture. The first Europeans purchased whitefish, trout, herring, and many other kinds of fish from Woodland Indians living near lakes Superior and Michigan. Nineteenth-century trappers needing work during the fur trade's off-season fished along the southern shores of Lake Superior. Some of this early commercial catch was shipped to the lower lakes and marketed inland, but most of it was sold locally. Eventually, transportation improvements made it possible to ship fish farther east and to the south, and for the Lake Superior fishing industry to thrive.

Hardy fishermen from numerous ethnic backgrounds worked the bountiful fishing grounds along Green Bay and Lake Michigan. Icelanders, Norwegians, Danes, and Swedes in particular affected the Door Peninsula's fishing culture. Scandinavian-inspired foods such as pickled herring, smoked chubs, and fish boil have become identified with the area. At least one authority credits Icelander Gudmund Gudmunder with starting a rich fishing heritage on Washington Island. The immigrant fisherman wrote to his friends back home about the wealth he had found in the waters of Lake Michigan. Fourteen of Gudmunder's countrymen joined him, and while most of the local fishing has given way today to farming and tourism, names like Gunnlaugson and Gudmundsen still dominate on the tiny, secluded island.

Freshwater fishing, especially along the Mississippi River, has also had its place in Wisconsin history. Farmers who hauled in catfish, sturgeon, walleye, and other species during the 1800s either ate it themselves or took it by wagonload to sell in nearby towns. By the 1870s, Mississippi steamboats carried tons of fish south each year.

Today, commercial fishing has dwindled for all kinds of reasons: over-fishing, foreign species, pollution, regulations, and more. But fish will always be a part of the state's culinary heritage. For one thing, sport fishing is as popular as ever; for another, fish farming is on the rise.

Thriving Markets

Butcher shops, fish markets, and smokehouses don't just survive—they thrive—in Wisconsin.

Wherever fishing occurs along the state's waterways, small markets offer the catch of the day, as well as smoked fish and other specialty fish products. Whitefish livers are a delicacy from the fishmongers of Bayfield. Smoked chubs and smoked whitefish spread are Door County favorites. A few markets along the mighty Mississippi offer catfish cheeks, smoked carp, and fresh-from-the-river catfish fillets. Numerous fish farmers sell dressed rainbow trout and packaged smoked trout.

Independent butchers are the keepers of local traditions as well as traditions that are beloved all across the state. Small meat markets supply brats and burgers by the tens of thousands to tail-gaters at Camp Randall, County Stadium, and Lambeau Field. (How fitting, too, that the state's No. 1 football team got its name from the meat-packing industry.) Family retailers assemble trays of summer sausage and cheese for picnics and holiday parties. From T-bones to turkey breast, from venison snack sticks to blood sausage, it's all there at the local butcher shop.

—Please Note

The featured markets that follow are arranged in alphabetical order by the name of the business. Additional markets are listed in alphabetical order at the end of the chapter. To locate a business by town name, see page 173. Or check the maps on pages *xviii-xxv*. All information is subject to change. Travelers should call or write before visiting to get business hours, directions, and other important details.

Tom Armbrust offers quality meats and old-fashioned service from the shop his grandfather built.

---

35. Armbrust Meats
224 S. Main St.
Medford, WI 54451
715-748-3102
•

What'll It Be:
Service or Shrink-Wrap?

When butcher William Armbrust emigrated from Germany, he worked at a number of meat markets in northcentral Wisconsin before buying a shop in Medford and giving it his name. Working and living at the shop, he soon expanded the establishment by erecting a bigger but nearly identical building in the empty lot next door. It's the same shop where his son Robert grew up learning the business, the same one his grandson Tom owns and operates today.

The old Armbrust butcher shop may be intact, but the European-influenced sausages and custom cuts that have been specialties of the house since William's day are on the endangered list now. "Years ago, people went to the grocery store for groceries and came here for meat," says Tom, who, with wire-rim glasses and a trim mustache, looks like he could be from his grandfather's time. "But the everyday traffic isn't here anymore."

The meat cases of his Main Street market are partially filled on a Friday afternoon; there's the natural-casing wieners and summer sausage Armbrust's is best known for and some fresh sausages like bratwurst. There are a number of beef items and fresh chickens. While Tom notes that the area has always been good for pork cuts ("our seasoned rolled pork loin is real popular"), he says the only time his store is really busy is around the holidays, when ham and roasts are in demand. "Most of our regular customers are older; they've been coming for years and years."

Tom has had to cut back on once-popular items like liver sausage and head cheese. He supplements his retail sales with custom work and some wholesale business.

"People want ready-to-cook, ready-to-eat products. They want convenience and packaging. The younger ones, even my generation, don't know much about [good meat]." Tom thinks more and more people prefer self-service to the personal attention available at smaller markets. "I think it makes them a little nervous."

Nevertheless, Armbrust Meats is still around for folks who appreciate good meat and for those who prefer real service to shrink-wrap.

Spareribs with Onions, Apples, & Maple Syrup
4 servings

Traveling near Medford, you can tell you've reached northern Wisconsin by the number of "Maple Syrup for Sale" signs hung near roadside mailboxes. One of the foods these home producers love to match with their liquid gold is pork, another area favorite, especially if it, too, comes from a nearby source like Armbrust Meats. This recipe is inspired by one that was winner in the 1997 Wisconsin Maple Festival cooking contest, held annually in nearby Merrill. Its creator is Merrill resident Mildred Behm, who serves the spareribs over white rice. For best flavor, stew the meat and vegetables in the morning, then reheat and thicken it just before serving. Note: the apple chunks "disappear" as the stew cooks.

        2 tablespoons vegetable oil
        2 pounds spareribs or baby back ribs,
            cut into pieces
        2 medium onions, cut into
            large chunks
        2 medium sweet peppers (red or green),
            cut into chunks
        3 tart apples, peeled and cut into
            large chunks
        1 cup apple cider
        1/3 cup maple syrup
        1/4 cup apple cider vinegar
        4 tablespoons soy sauce
        2 tablespoons cornstarch
        salt and pepper

Heat oil in large, heavy skillet over medium heat. Brown ribs in the hot oil on all sides. Remove meat, add onions and sweet peppers and brown them, turning often. Stir in apple chunks, apple cider, maple syrup, and vinegar. Return meat to the pan, bring to simmer, reduce heat, cover, and cook gently until spareribs are tender, about 1 hour. Combine soy sauce and cornstarch in small bowl; stir into spareribs until thickened. Season with salt and pepper to taste.

36. Bullfrog Fish Farm
**N1321 Bullfrog Road
(566th St.)
Menomonie, WI 54571
715-664-8775**
•

Eat His Fish

Twelve miles south of Menomonie off Highway 25, County Highway Y travels east briefly through a hilly prairieland and across the Dunnville Bridge and Red Cedar Trail. Two miles past the bridge, just before Highway Y hooks to the north, Bullfrog Road drops towards the Chippewa and Red Cedar rivers and makes its graveled way to Herby Radmann's trout farm.

As sunset dims the outlines of the marshy Dunnville Bottoms and the November night-cold descends, it's comforting to step inside Herby's fish barn, where several lengthy, waist-high tanks churn with rainbow trout. Despite the waning sun, the trout catch what light remains, creating a dancing, blue-green glimmer of fish that's as captivating as a hearthside fire.

There is beauty outside and inside at Bullfrog Fish Farm, but for all the natural wonders here the most arresting sight on the property is Herby's office. Or shall we say, his office/kitchen/conference room/ sleeping quarters/observation deck. Herby, who wears a floppy cap and a yard-long braid tucked into a denim jacket, sits in a worn upholstered swivel chair with his life spread around him: Cast iron pans, clipboards, and scribbled notes hang from hooks and tacks that rim the workspace. Open shelves from floor to ceiling hold everything from canned goods and a 20-cup coffee pot to crated bank statements and a boombox. On one side of the room is a rumpled bunk and a reclining retriever named Buddy; on the other, two large windows give a wide-angle view of the outdoor fish ponds and a lightly wooded stretch of the Dunnville State Wildlife Area.

Herby's workplace and living quarters are as intriguingly haphazard and richly integrated as a crazy quilt. Which is much like the man himself.

Herby and Amy Radmann of Bullfrog Fish Farm net fine profits with farm-raised rainbow trout.

Some people might point to Herby's snaking braid, his company's peace-sign logo, even his tongue-in-cheek slogan ("Eat My Fish"), and think "aging hippie removed from reality." But Herby's lifestyle and fun-loving business manner are part of a closely held philosophy about the importance of rural culture and rural economic development.

"I came here from the Twin Cities in '78 and bought land," Herby says in a raspy voice. "I wanted a rural lifestyle. I had come from a truck-farming family and these were my roots." He started Bullfrog Business, a jack-of-all-trades venture that included, he says with a toothy smile, "rubbish removal, painting, carpentry, landscaping, work-along-with-you projects, and marriage counseling." As time passed, he and his wife Vicki raised their two children as well as provided home care for ten children with special needs.

Ten years ago Herby began making plans for a fish farm, then built fish tanks and a dry well himself and eventually worked with two state rural economic development programs to finance the buildings. Today he and his partner, daughter Amy, sell custom-cut rainbow trout, hickory-smoked trout, and smoked trout spread from a small, on-the-farm market and through area grocery stores and fine restaurants. (Their smoked products are also available by mail order.) Open year-round, the farm offers group tours, pond-side fishing, fish cook-outs (dubbed "Hobo Chefing"), and the "Bullfrog Fish School," which gives workshops and presentations.

"We've got to start having some rural pride," says Herby, and he believes workshops and tours are ways to give urban visitors that experience. "We make it fun." The tours, geared for students, business groups, and out-of-state tourists, teach people how fish are raised, give them a chance to catch their own, and typically end with a rousing, round-the-campfire meal of grilled trout. Says Herby: "People come to Wisconsin for cheese, milk, sausage—why not for trout, crappies, blue gills, crawfish?"

He thinks there should be more fish farming in Wisconsin because it's good for families, good for the state. He works closely with state programs to promote his business and the fish farm industry and has a Website to further spread the word. "Gumption, wit, practicality: these are rural qualities I'm trying to develop here. Fish farmers are doers, growers. I want to help 'grow' the industry, the family farm. I want to open up a dialogue about rural culture, rural development."

Herby Radmann may be a self-described "old hippie," but when it comes to living life with purpose, goals, and a little fun, he's a class act. "Yeah, I got lots of class," he says with a big, proud laugh, "and it's all low."

Smoked Fish & Fettucine with Fresh Vegetables
4-6 servings

Take a tip from Herby Radmann and put a little fun in your food. Here's a playful toss of pasta, fresh vegetables, cheese, and "smokin' good fish."

12 ounces fettucine (use herb-flavored, spinach, or plain)
1 pound green beans, cut into 2-inch lengths
2 carrots, thickly cut on the diagonal
3 tomatoes, cut into chunks
1 cup coarsely chopped tender, young spinach leaves
1/4 cup chopped green onion
1 1/2 cups boned, smoked rainbow trout chunks
2 tablespoons olive oil
1/4 cup coarsely grated parmesan cheese
pepper to taste

Boil pasta in large amount of salted water 3 minutes. Add beans and carrots. Boil until pasta is tender. Drain, toss with remaining ingredients, and serve immediately.

Smoky Devils
24 deviled egg halves

A little smoked rainbow trout replaces some of the high-cholesterol yolks in deviled eggs with a savory smolder. Don't use super-fresh eggs or they'll be impossible to peel.

12 eggs
1/2 pound smoked rainbow trout
2 tablespoons minced fresh or frozen chives
5-6 tablespoons mayonnaise
1 1/2 tablespoons Dijon mustard
2 dashes cayenne pepper
pepper to taste

Cover eggs with cold water in saucepan; bring to boil, turn off the heat, cover pan, and let stand 20 minutes. Cool eggs in ice water. Peel and halve. Discard yolks from four of the eggs; place the remaining yolks in bowl. Remove skin and bones from smoked fish. Add to bowl with yolks. Mash yolks, fish, and remaining ingredients with a fork. Fill cooked egg whites with fish mixture.

---

37. The Butcher Shop
4391 Highway 18 East
Fennimore, WI 53809
608-822-6712
•

Champion Couple

At the Wisconsin State Fair, bone-in whole ham is to the annual smoked meat competition as track is to the Olympics. In other words, "Ham is the most noted there," says Shelli McLimans, co-owner

Butcher Shelli McLimans and her husband Rick work side by side at the family business.

with her husband Rick of The Butcher Shop in Fennimore. Having won Grand Champion status for several years, their ham could therefore be considered the Carl Lewis of Wisconsin meats.

"It's what we gloat about," admits Shelli, but not just because of the honor. When the governor auctions a McLimans prizewinner at the State Fair, the top bidder might pay $5000, money that is used to support the state's 4-H Foundation. What's more, the top bidder has been known to donate the ham back to the competition for a re-auctioning that can bring in thousands of dollars more.

Ham isn't the only Butcher Shop product that inspires such unusual behavior. "We have some customers from Chicago who have their own airplane. They've actually flown in to get our bacon," says Shelli. I myself would travel a good distance for their cottage bacon, a thin-sliced smoked cut taken from the shoulder that makes an excellent BLT sandwich. It used to be known as "butt bacon," but the new

name better reflects its quality: cottage bacon is less fatty than bacon, moister than ham, and more affordable than Canadian bacon.

An amber-eyed woman with fine features and a direct, knowledgeable manner, Shelli McLimans doesn't look like the stereotypical butcher. She wears discreet diamond earrings under a white hard hat and wipes slender hands on a blood-spattered apron.

"I hunt. I fish. I trap," she says to explain how she got interested in meat processing. Then with a grin: "I was my dad's son, I guess. In our family, the policy was always, 'you shoot it, you clean it.' So that's how it started."

Shelli studied butchering at the technical college in Fennimore two years after Rick went through the same program; they met several years later at a processing plant in Bloomington. In 1983, the couple pooled their skills and experience and bought a small custom processing business housed in a one-room slaughterhouse. When the building burned in 1986, the McLimans rebuilt it to meet state codes for a retail operation. Since then, their business and their family have grown to include a building addition and their children, Amber and Adam.

The Butcher Shop features summer sausage, landjaeger, beef jerky, dried beef, ham hocks, and ring bologna; in all, they offer up to 35 products, most of which come from recipes Rick has developed over the 20 years he's been in the business. Shelli says that except for "some boxed beef to get through the busy times," all of their pork and beef is raised in Wisconsin, and they butcher it themselves. About one-third of the meat they handle is sold retail, while custom processing still takes up the bulk of their time.

During deer hunting season, Butcher Shop custom smoking is particularly popular in the Fennimore area. A big year like 1996 found the staff processing some 80,000 pounds of venison sausage, which took them well into April of the following year to finish. (The deer meat is frozen until processing time.) Custom-smoked wild turkey is also a local favorite.

What the future may hold for the McLimans is anybody's guess. Says Shelli: "This is a very physical job. You stand on cold cement. Your hands are in cold hamburger. Arthritis is common. There's a lot of heavy lifting. We don't know how long we'll be able to do it." Still, they are rightfully proud of their work and enjoy the "the personal satisfaction of being in business for yourself." Not to mention being the makers of the Carl Lewis of hams.

Red Beans & Rice with Grilled Polish Sausage
6-8 servings

I visited the Butcher Shop in Fennimore not long after my husband and I had taken a trip to New Orleans. With the memory of Louisiana red beans and rice still lingering, we cooked a batch with one of the McLimans' hickory-smoked ham hocks, some peppery Polish sausage, and organic cranberry beans found at our local farmers' market. The dish is as smoky, spicy, and creamy as the sounds of jazz in the French Quarter.

1 pound dried beans (red, kidney, or
　cranberry), covered with water and
　soaked overnight
1 meaty smoked ham hock
2 cups chopped onions
1 1/2 cups chopped green pepper
1 1/2 cups chopped celery
1 tablespoon minced garlic
4 bay leaves
1 teaspoon dried thyme
1 teaspoon dried oregano
1 teaspoon cayenne pepper
1/2 teaspoon white pepper
1/2 teaspoon black pepper
salt

Producing champion sausages and smoked meats takes hard work and professional know-how.

Serve with:
grilled, smoked kielbasa or
　Polish sausage
cooked white rice
chopped green onions

Drain and rinse beans; place in large, heavy pot with ham hock and cover with cold water. Bring to simmer and cook (uncovered), skimming often, 10-15 minutes. Add onions, green pepper, celery, garlic, bay leaves, thyme, oregano, and the three kinds of pepper. Continue to simmer until beans are very tender, 1 1/2-2 1/2 hours. Remove ham hock; let cool.

If beans are still watery, raise heat and boil beans to reduce liquid. To give a creamy texture, use a wooden spoon to mash about 1/3 of the beans against sides of pot. Pull ham off bone, break into chunks, and add to beans. Season to taste with salt.

To serve, place a sausage and some hot rice on a dinner plate. Ladle on beans and sprinkle with chopped green onion.

Scalloped Potatoes & Ham
10 or more servings

Contrary to what you might expect about a couple who toils at a meat market all day, both Rick and Shelli McLimans love to cook at home. In fact, laughs Shelli, "there's usually a fight over who's going to get to make supper." They like the versatility of marinated chicken breasts for everyday cooking, and Shelli says it just wouldn't be Easter without one of their hams. She contributed this old-fashioned favorite.

3-4 cups cubed ham
8 medium potatoes (about 2 1/2 pounds), sliced or cubed
1 container (16 ounces) sour cream
1 can (10 1/2 ounces) cream of celery soup
1/2 cup chopped onion
1/2 cup (about 2 ounces) shredded cheddar cheese
3 tablespoons chopped, cooked bacon

Mix all ingredients, place in buttered baking dish and bake uncovered at 350 degrees until potatoes are tender and bubbly, about 1 1/2 hours.

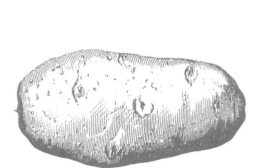

---

38. Charlie's Smokehouse
12731 Highway 42
in Gills Rock
Ellison Bay, WI 54210
920-854-2972
•

Classic Catch

In days gone by, before refrigerators and freezers, smoking fish was a necessity. Native Americans and early settlers preserved their catch by slow-cooking it over a smoldering flame. That the process also yielded sweet-smoked, woodsy flavor was a bonus—one it was easy to get hooked on.

Today it's no longer necessary to "hold the fire," and while we appreciate smoked fish for being ready-to-eat with no added fat, primarily we're addicted to that smoky taste.

Photo (c.1980) courtesy Voight family.

Luckily, one can find all kinds of freshly smoked fish in Wisconsin, including lushly textured whitefish from towns along the shores of Great Lakes Michigan and Superior, delicate, pink-fleshed rainbow trout raised by inland farmers, and imported specialties like Canadian lake trout and Pacific salmon.

"The classic, old-time Wisconsin smoked fish is chub," says Chris Voight of

Charlie's Smokehouse, located at the tip of the Door County peninsula in Gills Rock, where for three generations his family has been brining the local catch and smoking it over maplewood. Small and thin-bodied, smoked chubs (which are in the whitefish family and when fresh are called cisco) are mild-flavored and agreeably oily. It's the most popular fish sold at Charlie's and is Chris's first choice, served simply, with bread and butter. "I also go for the salmon—it's the other extreme, with a stronger flavor and drier texture."

Brothers Eric and Chris Voight, and father Charlie, at Charlie's Smokehouse, Gills Rock.

Chris is aware that family businesses often falter in the third generation and he's determined to beat the odds. He is lean and long-boned and moves with the unhurried grace of someone who enjoys his life and is sure of his future. "I've been helping my dad since I was 11," he says. "My first job was hanging the fish. I had to stand on a big wooden fish box to reach the screens."

Helping each other is still a family affair. Chris's father Charlie assists in the smokehouse when he's not operating his other business, a passenger ferry to Washington Island. Charlie's wife Bonnie and sister Carol work in the retail store and his younger son Eric, who could pass as Chris's twin, deals with fish processing, smoking, and sales. Some of the fish comes from Voight cousins, and even grandfather Leroy, who started the business in 1932 and died in 1974, is present in an historical display just inside the market entrance.

As for Chris, he's the "smoke master," a title he admits to with a modest, joking nod. But genuine expertise is revealed as he details the smoking process: First the fish are gutted and cleaned, then soaked overnight in salted water (this adds flavor, and just how much salt is added to the brine is a trade secret). Then the fish is rinsed in cold water and prepared for smoking; chubs are hung by the tails while chunks of whitefish are placed on screens. A slow fire is started in two large iron pans that sit in the floor of a blackened, double-doored smokehouse. (The Voights have two smokehouses, each four feet wide by eight feet tall). For the first few hours the upper door is kept ajar while the fish dry out, but later the fire is built up into a pyramid and both doors are firmly shut to keep the fire smoldering—but not too hot—during the smoking process.

"It's all real variable," says Chris, meaning the volume of the catch, the amount of brining time, the heat of the fire, the size and type of fish. Even the width of the maplewood makes a difference. The Voights cut their own from a 36-acre family plot, in picturesque view across Garret Bay from the smokehouse. Chris maintains a smokehouse temperature of 175 to 200 degrees and times the smoking to fit the type of fish, tiny chubs taking as little as one and a half hours, trout and salmon taking up to three. "It's mainly color that determines doneness," says Chris.

From the end of June through August, the Voights smoke an average of 300 pounds of fish a day. Retail sales are brisk throughout tourist season, and they also ship mail orders when the weather is cool, from October through April.

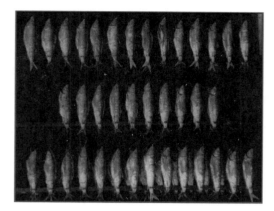

Smoking chubs. Photo courtesy of Voights.

Creamed Smoked Fish on Toasted English Muffins
4-6 servings

A Voight family recipe.

3 tablespoons margarine or butter
3 tablespoons flour
2 cups milk
3 tablespoons chopped fresh chives
   or 4 tablespoons minced onion
2 diced hard-cooked eggs
1 cup boned, flaked smoked fish:
   chubs, whitefish, etc.
salt and pepper
4-6 English muffins

Melt margarine or butter over low heat in heavy saucepan. Stir in flour until smooth and bubbly. Cook, stirring constantly, 5 minutes. Whisk in milk and bring slowly to a boil, stirring often. Stir and cook several minutes. Stir in chives or onions, hard-cooked eggs, and smoked fish; heat through. Add salt and pepper to taste. Mixture may be thinned with additional milk. Toast English muffins; spoon mixture over muffin halves and serve immediately.

Smoked Whitefish Chowder
8 servings

Chowder is comfort food that's easy and satisfying to prepare. If you have extra time, make this one a few hours ahead for full smoky flavor.

3 tablespoons butter
1 cup chopped leeks
1 1/2 cups chopped carrots
2 cans (each 14 1/2 ounces)
   chicken broth
4 cups peeled, chopped potatoes
2 1/2 cups milk
1 cup half-and-half
2 cups fresh or frozen corn kernels
2 cups boned, smoked
   whitefish chunks
salt and pepper to taste
chopped fresh chives or parsley

Melt butter in heavy soup pot; add leeks and carrots and saute until tender. Add chicken broth and potatoes; simmer until potatoes are very tender, about 20 minutes. If desired, mash some of the potatoes against the side of the pan to thicken the broth. Stir in milk, half-and-half, corn, smoked fish, salt, and pepper. Gently simmer 10 minutes. Garnish each bowl with chives or parsley.

39. Country Sausage
Highway 13 South
Phillips, WI 54555
715-339-3631

•

Sausage Spectrum

Country Sausage is the kind of place where braunschweiger and landjaeger are on the pedestrian side of the product line. If you're looking for a real specialty, try their *jiternice*, a Bohemian sausage that is popular at the town's annual Czechoslovakian Festival. Pronounced "YEE-ta-neet-za," the sausage is made with pork heart, tongue, and liver; traditionally the filler is bread or rice, although owner and sausage maker Dennis (Roscoe) Skomaroske uses barley in his.

If jiternice (also spelled jaternice) sounds a bit out there for you, try the Swedish potato sausage. It's a large, plump product that doesn't look delicate, but is: you must simmer it slowly or it will burst. Prepared correctly, its thin skin turns brown, crispy, and fragile; inside it's well-packed and soft-textured. It reminds me a little of the tender cereal-stuffed breakfast sausages of England, but with oh-so-much more flavor.

Roscoe uses only fresh potatoes in his potato sausage. "I have a woman who comes in and does all the peeling for me," he says in a voice as deep as Lake Superior. "I freeze it immediately so it doesn't turn brown." Roscoe's version is good enough to skip the mustard and ketchup, and it makes a full breakfast with toast and seasonal fruit. Or try it in this dinner main dish, served with fluffy mashed potatoes and a cucumber salad.

Swedish Potato Sausage with Braised Red Cabbage
6 servings

2 pounds potato sausage, fresh
   or frozen (if frozen, do not thaw)
small amount vegetable oil
8 cups shredded red cabbage
2 cups chopped, peeled apples
1 cup chopped red onion
1 cup beer or dry red wine
1/2 cup cider vinegar
1/2 teaspoon salt
1 tablespoon honey
coarsely ground pepper to taste

Do not prick or cut sausages. Place them in a pot and cover with cold water. Bring to slow simmer and cook very gently 20 minutes (30 minutes if the sausage is frozen). Do not boil. Drain well and place in large, lightly oiled skillet over low heat. Cook slowly, turning often, until browned on both sides, 15-20 minutes.

Meanwhile, place cabbage, apples, red onion, and beer or red wine in large, non-reactive saucepan. Bring to simmer and cook over medium heat until vegetables become slightly tender, about 10 minutes. Add remaining ingredients and continue to cook, stirring often, until tender, 10-15 minutes. As it cooks, add more liquid (use beer, red wine, or water) if necessary to keep vegetables from sticking.

To serve, mound the cabbage on a large platter. Cut sausage into large pieces and arrange on cabbage.

40. Everett Fisheries
Johnson's Store & Gas Station
Highway 13 & Co. Highway A
Port Wing, WI 54865
715-774-3658
•

Where There's Smoke

If Eric Johnson invites you take a tour of the smokehouse at Everett Fisheries, don't walk in wearing clothes you care about; the merest brush against a wall or rack of smoked fish will leave you with permanent black smears. Six walk-in smokers line the back of the building, each belching dark, dense swells of smoke with a scent so concentrated you could serve it for dinner. Overhead tracks direct rolling racks of smoked chubs, whitefish, trout, herring, and salmon from the smoldering ovens to a cooling room.

Outside, nearby Lake Superior isn't visible from the smokehouse or the Johnson family residence that stands next door, but its presence is felt. The sky here seems higher, wider, and more powerfully lit than it does farther inland. On a sunny September day, pine trees heave slowly in a soft breeze that carries the smell of water. The wind's winter character, however, is the reason the Johnson homestead wasn't built closer to shore. "It's warmer here," says Eric, himself smudged and blackened from cap to fingertips. "And the wind affects the smoking, the fires, too."

Fishing pervades the family line like the smoke that permeates Eric's clothes. "I never knew anything else," he says. Eric operates the business his father Everett started around 1950. His mother is from town, Port Wing, a tiny burgh that lies at the top of Wisconsin about half-way between Bayfield and Superior. His father moved here from Gills Rock to fish a lake even greater than Michigan. "He fished

right up until he passed away in 1978," says Eric. "I have cousins in Door County," he adds, reeling off several well-known names in the fishing industry there. He employs his son Christopher as a full-time fisherman; another son, Jeremie, has a degree in fisheries management.

Everett Fisheries supplies grocery stores and meat markets in northern Wisconsin; Eric makes a weekly drop in the Twin Cities, and his smoked fish also travels to Michigan and the Dakotas. There's also plenty available at the family's combination gas station/grocery store in town during the tourist months of July through September.

Smoked Lake Trout & Rosemary Roast Vegetables with Roast Garlic Vinaigrette
4 servings

Smoked fish fits in to any season of the year, but I like its balance of smoke and salt best in autumn. The fall harvest brings hearty root vegetables that—combined with chunks of smoked lake trout or salmon—make a nourishing main course salad, fitting whether the day is warm or cool.

1 small head garlic
1 1/2 pounds baking potatoes, cut into large chunks
4 medium carrots, peeled and cut into chunks
12 golf-ball-size onions or 4 quartered medium onions, peeled (leave root ends intact)
5 tablespoons olive oil, divided
about 5 tablespoons white wine, divided
1 tablespoon chopped fresh rosemary or 1 1/2 teaspoons dried
salt and pepper
2 small zucchini (about 1/2 pound total), in large chunks
2 tablespoons wine vinegar

1/2 teaspoon sugar
1 1/2 cups boned, smoked lake
    trout chunks
2 medium tomatoes, cut into wedges
1/3 cup coarsely grated parmesan
    cheese

Heat oven to 375 degrees. Slice off and discard top quarter of head of garlic; remove the loose, papery outer skin. Toss garlic head, potatoes, carrots, and onions with 2 tablespoons olive oil in baking dish. Sprinkle on 3 tablespoons white wine, the rosemary, and salt and pepper to taste. Cover tightly and bake 30 minutes. Uncover, add zucchini, and bake until vegetables are tender, about 30 minutes longer. Let vegetables cool while you make the dressing.

Remove garlic head from roasting pan and squeeze roasted garlic from their skins into a small bowl; mash to a paste. Measure pan juices and add enough white wine to them to equal 2 tablespoons. Stir this mixture, the vinegar and sugar into the mashed garlic. Whisk in remaining 3 tablespoons olive oil. Season to taste with salt and pepper.

Arrange roast vegetables, smoked fish and tomatoes on platter. Sprinkle on the dressing and parmesan.

Welcome to Knebel's, Belmont

> **41. Knebel's Processing, Inc.**
> P.O. Box 303, Highway 151
> **Belmont, WI 53510**
> **608-762-5197**
> •

Salami, Salami, Bologna

Although butchering wasn't in his family background, Clarence Knebel thought his home town of Belmont needed a meat locker, so that's what he opened upon his return from World War II. At first Clarence offered slaughtering, cutting, and freezing services only, but when home freezers become popular he made it his goal to fill every one. Thus the retail market was born. Now citizens of the town that was the site of the state's first capitol, plus visitors from Madison to Dubuque, rely on the quality that has become a time-honored tradition at Knebel's.

Partners Nick Galle (Clarence's son-in-law) and Nelson Necollins are the owner-operators today. Renowned for their ham—the business has won so many awards for it they rarely even enter it in contests anymore—the shop also features an array of specialty sausages, lunch loaves, and fresh meats. You can see the quality in the meat cases, in the awards that hang wall-to-wall, and in the faces of the clerks who offer service that goes above and beyond the basics. "People trust us," says Nelson. "They can ask us questions about nitrates or the E. coli scare or anything they need to know. We find out what people want to know about."

Nelson is even willing to share instructions for making old-style meat market ham salad (following page). Without giving away any trade secrets, of course. "Make it the way my grandfather would," he recommends. "Put some good things in it, sample it, then put in more of what you like: a little more sugar, a little more onion, whatever it takes." The sandwich spread can also be made with bologna.

Knebel's-Style Ham Salad
Makes 2 1/2 cups

1 pound boneless ham, well-trimmed
  and cut into 1-inch pieces
1/2 cup sweet pickle relish
1/2 cup mayonnaise
4 tablespoons minced onion
3 tablespoons white vinegar
1/2 teaspoon sugar

Grind ham through meat grinder or in food processor using pulse button. Place in bowl; fold in remaining ingredients. Add more of any of the ingredients to suit your taste. Serve the same day you make it.

---

42. Lake Geneva Country Meats
**Route 3 Highway 50 East
Lake Geneva, WI 53147
414-248-3339 or 414-539-2999**

•

Specialties of the House

Award-winning sausages, smoked meats, and U.S.D.A.-inspected cuts of fresh beef and pork represent the bulk of business at Lake Geneva Country Meats, the butcher shop located on a busy stretch of Highway 50 in the heart of the Lake Geneva tourist area. In the summer, Illinois tourists pack up the market's specialty, cherry bratwurst, for outdoor grilling; during winter they can't get enough of the summer sausage that once achieved Grand Champion status at the

State Fair. In late fall, local hunters drop off their deer for processing, and all year long customers stock their freezers with the company's large-size "bundles" of beef, pork, steak, or sausage.

Shoppers go out of their way to come here because, like other top Wisconsin meat markets, Lake Geneva Country Meats is known for its variety and quality. But this shop also carries something most others do not: a selection of buffalo products.

Bison became part of the line a few years ago when an area buffalo farmer approached the owners about processing his animals. Current manager Jeff Schmalfeldt says, "It took us awhile. At first we sold fresh halves, quarters, and cuts. Then things started picking up and we got into sausage. Now the most popular are ground buffalo and steaks."

At 90 to 92 percent lean, buffalo meat is lower in fat than beef, making it a good choice for health-conscious shoppers. "A lot of women will buy their husbands a steak," says Jeff, and he always tells them the same thing: don't overcook it or it will get dry. "We recommend cooking buffalo medium-rare or medium." In a long-simmered stew or soup, however, bison will be as tender as any other meat.

Their buffalo sausage is 20 percent beef and 80 percent bison, again much leaner than its pork or beef counterparts. Otherwise, recipes used for buffalo sausage are pretty much the same as for their regular sausages.

Lamb is another Lake Geneva Country Meats specialty. It's especially popular with the Chicago and Madison markets, says Jeff. But, he adds, "A lot of people around here like lamb."

Buffalo (or Beef) Mushroom Stew
6-8 servings

Inspired by Native American ingredients, this chunky, fragrant stew is a natural served with these other New World originals: boiled potatoes and maple syrup-sweetened baked squash.

The directions look lengthy, but the dish is really quite easy to make. Experiment with other fresh and dried mushrooms if you like (although there's nothing like the taste of morels you hunted and dried yourself). Beef stew meat may be substituted for the buffalo.

olive oil
2 pounds buffalo (or beef) stew meat
flour seasoned with salt and pepper
1 cup chopped onion
12 ounces (1 1/2 cups) dark beer
3 tablespoons tomato paste
1 teaspoon thyme
1 teaspoon oregano
1 1/2 cups (15-20 medium-size) dried
   morels (or other dried mushrooms)
8 ounces medium-size brown
   mushrooms, ends trimmed
8 ounces medium-size white
   mushrooms, ends trimmed
salt and pepper

Film the bottom of a large, heavy skillet with olive oil. Heat over medium heat. Toss buffalo meat in seasoned flour. Brown the meat in the hot oil, a few pieces at a time (do not crowd the pan or the meat will simmer instead of brown). As pieces are browned, transfer them to a heavy pot. If necessary, add a bit more oil to the skillet with each batch.

When all the meat is browned, add a bit more oil to the skillet and add the chopped onions. Cook, stirring often, until they begin to soften. Transfer onions to the pot with meat. Stir beer, tomato paste, thyme, and oregano into the skillet; bring to simmer, stirring to scrape up any bits on the bottom. Pour beer mixture into pot with meat and onions. Bring to simmer, lower heat, cover, and cook very slowly.

As stew begins to cook, bring 1 cup water to boil and pour it over the dried mushrooms. Place a small plate over the mushrooms to completely immerse them. Let stand until mushrooms are soft, about 5 minutes. Strain the mushroom liquid through cheesecloth or a thick layer of paper towels into a bowl. Remove soaked mushrooms from the cheesecloth, rinse them, and add them to the stew. Now stir the strained liquid and both kinds of fresh mushrooms into stew. (Don't worry if it seems as if there's not enough liquid; the mushrooms will throw off additional liquid as they cook.) Return stew to very slow simmer, partially cover, and continue cooking, stirring occasionally, until meat is very tender and stew is thickened, 1-2 hours. (Alternatively, stew may be cooked in 300-degree oven.) Season to taste with salt and pepper. Although the stew will be rich and flavorful at this point, it will be incredible if you let it chill several hours before reheating and serving.

Chicken Fricassee with Cornmeal Fennel Dumplings
6 servings

Part stew, part saute, chicken fricassee is all comfort food. This one-dish meal gets a subtle anise flavor when you add fennel three ways—bulb, stalk, and feathery leaves.

1 cut-up chicken (about 3 pounds)
flour seasoned with salt and pepper
2 tablespoons butter
2 tablespoons olive oil
4 small carrots, in 2-inch pieces
2 medium leeks (white and pale green
   parts only) in 1-inch pieces
1 medium fennel bulb, halved and
   sliced thick
2 cans (each 14 1/2 ounces) low-salt

chicken broth (or use homemade broth)
1 cup apple cider
pepper

Dumplings:
1 cup all-purpose flour
1/2 cup yellow cornmeal
2 teaspoons baking powder
1/2 teaspoon salt
1 heaping tablespoon minced fennel leaves
3/4 cup half-and-half or milk

Garnish:
1 teaspoon butter
1 cup cubed zucchini
1/4 cup minced fennel stalk
salt and pepper

Rinse chicken pieces and pat dry. Heat half the butter and olive oil in large, heavy pot over medium-high heat. Dredge chicken in seasoned flour. Brown it in batches in the pot, adding a bit more butter and olive oil as required. Remove browned meat to a platter. Add carrots, leeks, and sliced fennel bulb to pot; saute 5 minutes. Stir in chicken broth and apple cider; season with pepper to taste. Arrange chicken in broth, cover, and simmer slowly 20-25 minutes. (If you've used homemade stock, you may need to add salt to taste at this point.)

To make dumplings: Sift flour, cornmeal, baking powder, and salt into a bowl. Stir in minced fennel leaves. Stir in half-and-half until just blended. Drop 8 spoonfuls of batter onto simmering chicken; cover and continue cooking over low heat 15 minutes.

Meanwhile, heat butter in skillet, add zucchini and minced fennel stalk; saute until tender. Season with salt and pepper. Ladle fricassee into wide, shallow bowls; garnish with zucchini.

43. Louie's Finer Meats
P.O. Box 774
Highway 63 North;
2025 Superior Ave.
Cumberland, WI 54829
715-822-4728 or 800-270-4297
•

The Spice of Life

He comes in the night twice each week, after the shop is closed and all is quiet. In a room he calls his "cave," he measures elements with cunning and concentration, filling vessels and marking them with cryptic labels like "20 Germ" and "15 CJ." He smiles with satisfaction, imagining the effect his work will have on many people.

He is Louis Muench III; no, not a mad scientist but a sausage lover and master mixer of spices. The shelves of his tiny office, which looks like a laboratory and smells like an exotic herb garden, are stacked with plastic jars whose contents will season 20 pounds of German sausage, 15 pounds of Cajun sausage, and up to 150 other kinds of sausages and processed meats, products that delight customers of Louie's Finer Meats in Cumberland.

Louie is part of a dynasty that started when his grandfather Louis Muench (rhymes with pinch) immigrated from Bavaria and opened a meat market in Chicago with his brother George. Louis's son, Louie II, was only 16 when his father was killed in a car accident. As a youth he worked in his uncle's business and traveled with his family for summer vacations to the Park Falls area. Later, he moved there to live and to raise his own family. After several years as a meat department manager, Louie II opened his own butcher shop in downtown Cumberland.

One re-location and one expansion later, Louie II's sons Jim and Louie III are his partners and his meat market is known

Louie Muench III, Louie's Finer Meats,
Cumberland

throughout northwestern Wisconsin.

Louie III, the spice mixer, starts with sausage, appropriately enough, as he describes some of the company products:

"Capicolla, an Italian product made with ham, fennel, garlic, paprika, and red pepper. Cotto salami, a semi-dry Italian item that has won more awards than any other product here. Hungarian salami: a [customer] with a thick Hungarian accent couldn't believe it was made in America. Hunter's sausage, flat and dry like jerky, but it's actually a sausage, with meat stuffed into a casing. Minnesota sausage, an all-beef summer sausage flavored with wild rice and blueberries, and Wisconsin's answer to it, Wisconsin summer sausage, made with beef, cheddar cheese, maple syrup, honey, and cranberries...Someone said the only Wisconsin ingredient missing is mosquitos!"

He goes on, listing sausage after sausage and their seasonings: Russian (caraway and dill), Cajun (five kinds of pepper), chorizo (annatto seeds, chili powder, cumin), Greek (oregano), Swedish (potato), Belgian "trippe" (pork and cabbage). Then it's on to several kinds of bacon and jerky and an inventory of smoked, fresh, and frozen meat cuts. All in all, there are some 300 meat products at Louie's.

And what about quality? In a state

which celebrates sausage, there is a great deal of competition for the state and national awards that adorn the walls of many meat markets, Louie's Finer Meats included. Which makes the international awards that also hang here all the more impressive. Entering international contests can mean a lot of red tape, so the Muenchs have done it only once. In 1995, they entered a salami and a summer sausage in the International Meat Trades Fair in Frankfurt, Germany. Up against centuries of European tradition and expertise, both products took gold medals.

As if this kind of quality and selection were not enough, the company also offers venison processing, mail order, and a grocery store full of regional food products. At Louie's Finer Meats, variety is the spice of life and sausage.

Hoppelpoppel
3 servings

Salami travels well so consider packing it into your cooler when you go camping in the North Woods. And with appetite stimulants like coffee, wood smoke, and the heady smell of a new morning you'll need a breakfast as hearty as this German-style hash.

vegetable oil
2/3 cup chopped onions
3 cups cubed, cooked potatoes
1 cup diced salami
3 eggs, beaten and seasoned
    with salt and pepper to taste
grated Swiss cheese

Film bottom of cast iron skillet with oil; heat on Coleman stove or on a grill over a wood fire. Saute onion a few minutes, then add potatoes and salami. Cook, turning occasionally, until potatoes are browned. Pour on eggs and cook until almost set, tilting and shaking pan to distribute eggs. Sprinkle with cheese, let melt, and serve immediately.

Mixed Greens with Grilled Pork Tenderloin & Blueberries

2 large or 4 medium servings

Fruit and meat? It's not another wacky, new wave cooking idea, but a classic combination that dates to the Middle Ages. Here, blueberries complement the flavor of pork and are a sweet counterpoint to a mix of fresh greens, which could include any of the following: red leaf lettuce, bibb lettuce, chicory, arugula, radicchio, watercress, romaine.

6 tablespoons fruit-flavored or
　wine vinegar
2 tablespoon blueberry preserves
juice of 1/2 orange
1 teaspoon minced garlic, mashed to a
　paste with a fork
3 tablespoons olive oil
pepper
1 whole pork tenderloin (about 1
　pound) or 1 pound boneless pork
　loin chops, trimmed of fat
8 cups mixed greens, washed, torn into
　bite-size pieces, and dried in towel
　or salad spinner
4 slender green onions
1 cup fresh blueberries
for garnish: edible flower petals or
　chunks of peeled fresh orange

Combine vinegar, blueberry preserves, orange juice, and garlic in medium bowl. Whisk in olive oil in small stream. Season with pepper to taste. Marinate tenderloin in this mixture 1 hour or longer, turning occasionally. Remove pork; pour marinade into small saucepan, and simmer 10 minutes. Strain and cool.

Prepare grill. If using tenderloin, fold the slender end of the tenderloin over about 3 inches and secure with a toothpick (this will help meat cook evenly). Grill pork to internal temperature of 165 degrees, 6 to 8 minutes per side. Let stand 10 minutes or cool to room temperature. Slice 1/2-inch thick. Toss greens with cooled marinade and divide onto 4 plates; arrange pork over greens. Diagonally slice green onions into 2-inch slivers and sprinkle over pork. Distribute blueberries and preferred garnish over salad

---

44. Miesfeld's Triangle Market
1922 N. 15th St.
Sheboygan, WI 53081
920-452-1214
•

Name That Sausage

During the 1996 football season, when the Green Bay Packers rose like a phoenix to Super Bowl fame after a 30-year hiatus, Wisconsin was suddenly in the national limelight. Even the state's signature meat, the humble bratwurst, got special attention in a New York Times article. And since Sheboygan is the bratwurst capital of Wisconsin, it's appropriate that Chuck Miesfeld, whose family meat market has been producing brats there for three generations, was pictured in the article with a display of his prize-winning sausage.

There was just one problem, however. The caption identified the photographed meat as bratwurst, but as any Wisconsinite worth his or her mustard could tell, it was, in fact, summer sausage.

Chuck Miesfeld knows his bratwurst.

The hoots could be heard throughout Packerland as locals reveled in the mighty newspaper's slip. Chuck Miesfeld, however, was more gracious: "I won't say anything bad about the *New York Times*," he said with a big smile. Indeed, the inaccuracy was perhaps less sloppy journalism than it was proof of the very local, very special nature of bratwurst's popularity.

Chuck Miesfeld's brats are made from a recipe his grandfather Charles developed when he opened Miesfeld's Triangle Market in 1941. Like his grandad, Chuck uses fresh pork ("never frozen!"), natural hog casings, salt, pepper, and nutmeg. If there's anything else in them, he's not letting on what it is. But compared to others, "our brats are a little spicier," he says.

In addition to the German-influenced standard bratwurst, Miesfeld's offers more than a dozen other varieties of brats, some filled with low-fat chicken or turkey, others flavored with jalapeños, garlic, or even apricots. There's even one called "The Works"—a take-off on Sheboygan's famous brat-eating style—that contains mustard, catsup, pickles, and onions. (All you need to add is the semmel roll, I suppose.)

Still, brats are just part of the story at Miesfeld's. They make more than 35 kinds of sausage (and that's including bratwurst

and all its variations as only one type). There's a smooth-textured braunschweiger made from pork livers, an all-beef rinderwurst, and kranski, a lightly smoked, garlicky Yugoslavian pork sausage that's popular with the Slovenian-American families of Sheboygan. And of course, all types of more familiar ethnic sausages, including a zesty Italian link that has won state awards three times.

No matter what heritage sausage you crave, Miesfeld's probably carries it. And to help you with your selection are several employees who really know what they're talking about, since they've been with the company for more than 30 years. John Wagner, for instance, is a clerk in his 80s who was hired when the meat market opened. John has been selling Miesfeld sausages for nearly 50 years.

I'll bet he knows the difference between bratwurst and summer sausage.

Brat & Wild Rice Side Dish
6 servings

Adapted from the Miesfeld family files, this "side dish" could easily make a main course for a casual supper. I'd also serve it for brunch, for lunch, at a campfire cookout, as a late night snack, etc., etc.

3/4 pound (3 links) bratwurst
1/2 cup chopped onion
1/2 cup chopped celery
2 cups chopped mushrooms
3 cups cooked wild rice
salt and pepper

Remove casings from bratwurst; discard casings and chop the meat. Heat a large, heavy, greased skillet. Saute the meat with onion, celery, and mushrooms until done. Stir in wild rice, and salt and pepper to taste. Heat through.

Penne with Italian Sausage & Roasted Tomato Sauce
8 or more servings

This is a good recipe for end-of-the-harvest tomatoes, the ones that are gathered while still a little green, before the frost hits. I let them ripen in the house and roast them to concentrate the flavor. Then the tomatoes are pureed, simmered with Italian sausage and sauteed mushrooms, and tossed with tube-shaped penne pasta. Don't worry about removing every seed and every bit of skin from the tomatoes; this is a rustic, deeply flavored dish that's well suited for a casual weekend supper in autumn.

8 pounds tomatoes
5-6 cloves garlic, peeled
2 medium onions, peeled and quartered
1 tablespoon fennel seeds
1 tablespoon dried basil
about 2 tablespoons olive oil
1 pound hot Italian sausage links
1 1/2 pounds (about 6 cups) thinly sliced mushrooms
salt and pepper
1 1/4 pounds penne pasta
freshly grated parmesan cheese (optional)

Heat oven to 375 degrees. Core and halve tomatoes; gently remove seeds with your fingers. Place tomatoes cut side down on one or two large baking pans. Scatter garlic, onions, fennel, and basil over tomatoes. Drizzle 1-2 tablespoons of the oil over all. Roast until tomatoes are partially charred and garlic is very tender, about 1 hour.

Meanwhile, heat a tiny amount of olive oil in heavy skillet over medium-low heat; swirl the pan to coat the bottom with hot oil. Add Italian sausages and cook, turning often, until cooked through, about 20 minutes. Drain sausages on paper towels. If necessary, add a bit more oil to the pan. Raise heat, add mushrooms and saute

them, stirring often, until tender, about 10 minutes. Set mushrooms aside. Slice the sausages into thin rounds and set aside.

When tomatoes are done, let them stand until cool enough to handle. Slip off and discard the skins. Puree tomatoes, garlic, onions, and all the pan juices in food processor or blender. Transfer puree to a pot; stir in the mushrooms and sausage.

Bring sauce to simmer and season to taste with salt and pepper. Cook pasta in lots of boiling, salted water. Drain pasta and toss with the sauce (use as much or as little as you want). Serve immediately, with parmesan cheese, if desired.

---

45. Niemuth's Steak & Chop Shop
715 Redfield St.
Waupaca, WI 54981
715-258-2666
•

As You Like It

You have to go out of your way to shop at Niemuth's Steak and Chop Shop, which lies north of downtown Waupaca, but it's worth the trip. For one thing, you can't find cured beef brisket bacon or Grandpa Bob's smoked summer sausage at just any grocery store meat department. It'd be difficult to locate a T-bone to match Niemuth's, and nearly impossible to sight the Polish blood sausage called "kieska" (not to mention sweet blood sausage, a version of kieska which has brown sugar and raisins in it). Niemuth's also regularly carries lamb cuts, which is unusual in this state even for specialty meat markets.

Niemuth's offers all the usual and most of the unusual, but there's another reason customers flock here. Brothers Roger and Robert E. Niemuth are owner/operators who maintain the same standards of service the shop has been known for ever since their father opened it in 1957. "We package it for you," says one staff member. "However you want it: trimmed, tenderized, the thickness, the number per package, however you want your chicken cut up. We've got ladies that want just a quarter pound of something or a single piece of liver. We'll slice your cheese or chunk it. We'll give you samples."

They even offer recipe suggestions. Roger recommends their smoked pork chops with maple syrup as a barbecue sauce. Another idea is marinating beef round in Italian dressing before grilling it.

If regulars know they'll get good service at Niemuth's, they also know who they'll get it from. Some customers have known the brothers since they were small boys.

Retail is their main business, Roger points out. "We try to stay out of wholesale. There's no loyalty there." And from an employee: "It's not like a business atmosphere here. Customers like that. And so do we."

Grilled T-Bone & Garden Vegetables
2 servings

I was once enjoying a grilled T-bone steak with my sister Sue when her honey happened to call. They chatted briefly and when he asked what we were having for dinner and she told him, there was a short pause, after which Susie laughingly told me he had dropped the phone. Indeed, T-bones are such a brazen indulgence these days that the mere mention of one can bring on stunned jealousy. But if you have reason to celebrate—like having a whole summer evening to spend with your sister—then by all means, go for it.

Behind the scenes at Niemuth's Steak and Chop Shop in Waupaca.

Marinade ingredients:
3 tablespoons balsamic vinegar
4 tablespoons olive oil
1 tablespoon brown mustard
garlic powder, onion powder, salt, and pepper to taste

Other ingredients:
1 T-bone steak
6-8 small, partially boiled (or "left over") new potatoes
2 small eggplants, thickly sliced lengthwise
1/2 bunch thick green onions, ends trimmed
2 small zucchini or yellow squash, sliced in half lengthwise

Combine marinade ingredients in a jar; shake well. Use your hands to spread the marinade over all surfaces of the steak and vegetables; let stand at room temperature while you prepare a charcoal fire on an outdoor grill. When coals are medium hot, grill the meat and vegetables, turning often, until tender. (It doesn't matter if some items are done and removed from the grill before the others; this food tastes even better if it isn't piping hot.) If there's any excess marinade from the vegetables, brush it on the food as it cooks. Do let the steak stand at least 10 minutes before cutting into it. Arrange everything on a big platter, get out the steak knives, pour some wine, and dig in.

Lamb, Potato, & Asparagus Stew
6 servings

Thinly sliced potatoes placed at the bottom of the stew pot dissolve as they slow-cook, providing a convenient, low-fat thickener for the broth. Marrow spooned (or sucked) from the small, rounded bone in each lamb shoulder steak make a decidedly non-low-fat but wonderfully succulent treat. If fresh herbs are not available, substitute a smaller amount of dried. Whatever you do, don't skip the lemon; it adds a bright zip to this rich-flavored stew.

1 tablespoon olive oil
2-2 1/2 pounds lamb shoulder steaks
    (bone-in), cut into large,
    equal-sized pieces
10-12 red potatoes (about 2 1/2
    pounds), scrubbed, divided
1 large Vidalia or other sweet onion,
    chopped
salt and pepper
2 tablespoons chopped fresh lemon
    thyme or regular thyme
1 tablespoon chopped fresh sage
2 cups low-salt chicken or lamb stock
1 pound asparagus, chopped into
    large pieces
juice of 1 lemon

Heat oil in heavy stew pot over medium-high heat. Brown lamb in batches without crowding the pot. Remove meat to a platter. Thinly slice about one-third of the potatoes; place in bottom of pot. Spread half the onions over the potatoes; season with salt and pepper. Arrange meat over onions; season with salt, pepper, and the herbs. Cut remaining potatoes in half and arrange over meat. Pour on the stock, cover with foil and a tight lid, and simmer over very low heat until meat is almost falling off the bones, 1 1/2-2 hours. Stir in asparagus and season to taste with salt and pepper. Cook gently until asparagus is barely tender, 5-10 minutes. Press sliced potatoes against sides of pot to thicken the broth. Stir in the lemon juice just before serving.

46. Nolechek's Meats
P.O. Box 599
104 N. Washington St.
Thorp, WI 54771
715-669-5580 or 800-454-5580

Whole Lot of Bacon Goin' On

There's a stretch of Highway 29 in northern Wisconsin that extends like a high wire from Chippewa Falls to Wausau. Perched on the wire is tiny Thorp, where locals and travelers pause during their day to down a slice of homemade pie at the Dairy Bar Cafe or stock up on bacon and brats at Nolechek's meat market. And why not? These are places that offer local flavor as well as a friendly face.

Still, if you're in the mood for a chat,

The Nolechek siblings

don't stop in at Nolechek's on the Friday before the opening of deer hunting season.

The customer lines are five- and six-people deep, filling the store from meat cases to doorway. Burly men in camouflage jackets heave ten-pound boxes of sausage onto their shoulders. A half dozen clerks rush to keep up with the orders that will supply hungry deer hunters for the following week.

The day before hunting season is a maelstrom at Nolechek's, but it isn't the only busy time there. Loyal customers include visitors from as far away as Chicago and the Twin Cities. During the holidays, there is a mountain of mail orders for Nolechek's specialties. Newcomers get drawn in by billboards out on the highway, and of course, there's always a steady supply of area residents who come in for their favorites.

Four Nolechek siblings—Bill, Kelly, Jennifer, and Tracy—operate the business that was originally a locker plant owned by their Bohemian grandfather, W.F. Nolechek. When their father William was fresh out of college with a hotel management degree, W.F. asked him to take over. He did, and stayed on until retirement, when he passed ownership to the current generation.

Nolechek's specialties include a delicious variety: semi-boneless, spiral-sliced ham, summer sausage, prime rib, smoked chickens, spicy snack sticks, beef jerky, pork jerky, turkey jerky, and a list of fresh and smoked sausages that sounds like a European tour. Bill Nolechek says it's hard to pinpoint which is the most popular item, but mentions their sliced bacon, ultra-lean and ultra-thick.

Indeed, on the day before hunting season begins, there's little chat but a lot of bacon flying across the counters at Nolechek's.

Brussels Sprouts with Bacon & Egg Crumbles
4 servings

A crusty topping of breadcrumbs, bacon bits, and chopped hard-cooked eggs really dresses up brussels sprouts, which are actually mini-cabbages. Use the same topping for cauliflower or broccoli.

1 pound brussels sprouts, root-ends
    trimmed
3 strips (each 1 ounce) extra-thick,
    extra lean bacon, chopped into
    1/4-inch-wide pieces
3 tablespoons dried breadcrumbs
1 hard-cooked egg, finely chopped
1 tablespoon butter or
    3 tablespoons beer

Cut brussels sprouts in half lengthwise and blanch in boiling water until barely tender, 4-6 minutes. Drain, immerse sprouts in ice water to cool them quickly, and drain again. Meanwhile, cook bacon in a heavy skillet until crispy. Remove all but 1 tablespoon of fat from pan. Stir breadcrumbs into the bacon in the pan and cook about 1 minute. Turn mixture into a bowl and stir in chopped egg; keep warm.

Wipe out pan, place over medium-high

heat and add butter or beer. Add brussels sprouts and cook, tossing often, until hot. Place brussels sprouts in shallow serving dish, sprinkle with topping, and serve immediately.

Bacon Potato Pudding ("Kugelis")
16 or more servings

"Kugelis" is a favorite with Lithuanian Americans. The dense, robust mixture of grated potatoes, bacon, onions, and eggs can be used to stuff roasts or make sausage, but is more often baked into a kind of savory pudding/side dish. It's plenty hearty to be a main course, however.

Use older, baking-type potatoes like Russets and grate them finely, preferably on a hand grater. (I've also used red potatoes with success.) And use a large, deep, rectangular baking dish for this recipe, which is an adaptation of one from friend Margo Vizgirda of Wheaton, Illinois. Margo serves kugelis with sour cream or gravy on special occasions like Thanksgiving and Christmas and says leftovers can be sliced thickly, sauteed in butter, and served for breakfast or brunch.

1/2 pound bacon, cut into
   narrow strips
1 medium onion
3 eggs
1/2 cup evaporated milk
1 tablespoon salt
pepper to taste
5 pounds potatoes
sour cream

Heat large, heavy skillet over medium heat; add bacon and cook until crispy. Discard all but 3 tablespoons bacon fat.

Heat oven to 500 degrees. Grease a large, deep, rectangular baking dish. Finely grate onion into large bowl. Beat in eggs, evaporated milk, salt, and pepper. Stir in bacon bits and bacon fat.

Peel potatoes, dropping them into cold water as they are peeled to prevent darkening. Working as quickly as possible (again to prevent the potatoes from darkening), finely grate potatoes and stir them into the onion/egg/milk mixture. Press mixture into prepared pan and bake 15 minutes. Reduce heat to 400 and continue to bake until browned and set, about 45 minutes. Cut into squares and serve with sour cream or gravy.

47. Peroutka's
Sausage Shop
206 Highway 64
Antigo, WI 54409
715-623-2227
•

That's What They Come Here For

There are no fresh meat cuts and no mail order available from Peroutka's meat market in Antigo. That's because their niche is processed and smoked products like old-style wieners with natural casings and ham cured with maple sugar. The shop's list of sausages includes the familiar and the exotic—Italian sausage, Polish sausage, mettwurst, sulze—plus smoked meats like pork hocks, roast beef, pork chops, turkey, and chicken.

Owner David Jorgensen uses no premixed spices in his recipes. He learned his craft on the job at a meat market near his hometown of Suamico. He bought Peroutka's in Antigo in 1983.

The previous owner was Bohemian-American, as are many of the local population. Says David: "They like garlic and some of the spicier stuff, so I put lots of garlic in [my sausage]. That's what they come here for. In Suamico and Howard, it was NO garlic. You gotta adjust to the taste of the people.

"Take our liver sausage. We make it the old-fashioned way. First it's cooked, then formulated, then we cook it again. You get more of the good broth flavor. It takes longer, but that's what they come here for. If I had to pay somebody else to do it, we couldn't do it. This is a family shop. A family shop's gotta be run by the family.

"Every place has something different. Me? I can't pick a favorite; I eat it all." Then after a short moment, "I like garlic myself."

Ham Spirals
Any number of servings

Peroutka's maple sugar-cured ham has a mellow smokiness and is very rich but clean-tasting, without any of the "dry-mouth" feeling that comes after eating over-salted ham. The old-time flavor of quality smoked ham brings back memories of church suppers, with piled-high platters and big bowls of potato salad and baked beans. It's good to know this kind of quality can be updated for today's lighter fare. For example, when Peroutka's lean ham is sliced clingingly thin, the meat can be wrapped around all manner of fresh and flavorful ingredients. The following suggestions make quick, wholesome, and attractive snacks or hors d'oeuvres.

• spiral some strips of ham around dilly beans or dilly asparagus (see recipe page 146).

• curl them around wedges of ripe cantaloupe, tart apples or fresh pears.

• gently swipe ham slices with softened cream cheese and roll around whole green onions.

• spread ham with a bit of mustard and wrap it around the top half of breadsticks or long, narrow pretzels.

• sprinkle the meat with chopped fresh

dill and twist it around lengths of peeled, seeded cucumber.

• roll ham up with butcher-thin slices of cheese and secure with toothpicks.

• brush ham lightly with vinaigrette dressing and wind strips around wedges of red bell pepper, kohlrabi, or tomato. Grind fresh pepper over all.

Twice-Baked Potatoes Stuffed with Ham & Winter Greens
8 servings

Twice-baked potatoes are a perennial favorite; here, the whipped potatoes are layered with a savory filling of chopped ham, onions, and lightly sauteed collard greens, making the dish hearty enough to serve as a main course for brunch or supper.

You may substitute other assertive greens like kale, turnip, or mustard greens for the collards, and 3/4 cup cooked, lean bacon could replace the ham.

3 pounds medium Russet potatoes
   (8 total)
2 tablespoons butter or olive oil
1 cup chopped onion
1 cup finely chopped lean ham
1/2 pound collards or other greens,
   thick stems discarded and
   leaves chopped
1/2 teaspoon sugar
salt and pepper
1/4-1/2 cup milk
melted butter

Poke potatoes with a fork and bake in 350-degree oven until very tender, 1 1/4-1 1/2 hours.

Meanwhile, heat butter or olive oil in large skillet, add onions and cook, stirring often, until tender, 5-10 minutes. Stir in ham, chopped greens, sugar, and salt and pepper to taste. Cook over medium-high heat, stirring often, until greens are wilted and tender, 4-6 minutes. Set filling aside.

Remove potatoes from oven and slice off top third of each, to make "boats." Scoop the cooked potato flesh from tops and shells (reserve both tops and shells). Whip hot potatoes with milk and a little melted butter; season to taste with salt and pepper. Spread 2-3 heaping tablespoons whipped potatoes in bottom of each shell. Divide the ham-and-collard filling amongst the shells and top with remaining whipped potatoes, mounding them above top of each shell. Brush the exposed whipped potatoes and reserved tops with melted butter and place the tops at a slant on top of the potatoes. The stuffed potatoes may be held under refrigeration until ready to bake. Bake at 350 degrees until hot, 25-30 minutes.

---

48. Straka Meats, Inc.
Plain, WI 53577
608-546-3301
•

Plain Old-Fashioned Goodness

No street name and number are given on this small-town company's bright yellow brochure; that's because Straka's Meats is easy to find in Plain even though it's not on the highway route through town. Just ask anybody and they'll point out the brown brick building that's right around the corner no matter where you are downtown.

The town and the directions may be "plain," but inside Straka's things are anything but.

The walls are wood-paneled, flanked with wildlife trophies, and a bit dark, all the better to show off a ring of illuminated meat cases and the dozens of framed awards that hang above them. Straka's has a full line of locally raised beef and pork products, smoked and fresh, and their specialty is old-fashioned cuts like pork shoulder roast, pig hocks, and thick slabs of fresh beef liver.

"Places like this are getting to be a thing of the past," says John Straka, who is co-owner with his brother Jim. But there's still a demand for the 300 pounds of head cheese they make every few weeks. Head cheese an old-time luncheon meat made of beef heart, beef tongue, pork parts, vinegar, and natural gelatin. It is mostly popular with older folks, says John.

He does have "a hard time keeping up the bacon," which is so lean there are a few folks who tell him it's too lean. Their ham has won state championships, they're one of the state's leading processors of venison, and Bob Wills of nearby Cedar Grove Cheese (see page 10) proclaims Straka's "the best sausage in the county." Even area pets love Straka's products, especially the big smoked "doggie" bones sold from a wooden barrel in the center of the store.

"Plain" Barbecued Pork
10-14 servings

This Southern-style barbecued pork could hardly be any plainer to make, but if you want to complicate things in a delicious way, serve it with the homemade barbecue sauce on page 145. The point, says cookbook author Betty Fussell, is to "balance the sweet unguent richness of pork with the cutting edge of a sharp sauce." This recipe is adapted from one in her book, I Hear America Cooking *(Viking, 1986.)*

John Straka has a full line of locally raised beef and pork products.

6-8 pounds pork shoulder roast
5 teaspoons salt
1 tablespoon black pepper
hamburger buns
barbecue sauce

Heat oven to 500 degrees. Rub pork roast all over with the salt and pepper. Set on rack in large roasting pan and place in oven for 15 minutes. Lower heat to 250 degrees, cover tightly, and bake until interior temperature of meat reaches 170 degrees, 4-5 hours. As the meat nears doneness, heat a charcoal or hardwood fire in an outdoor grill (one that has a fitted lid). When coals have burned down to medium heat, remove roast from pan and place on one end of the grill, away from the direct heat. Cover grill and smoke the meat 20-30 minutes. Remove the smoked meat, let cool, then remove meat from the bone and chop it fine or shred it. Toast the buns briefly on the grill, and make barbecue sandwiches by layering meat and sauce on the buns—or mix sauce and meat first.

Tomato, Bacon, & Summer Squash Gratin
4 side dish servings

A little bacon goes a long way when you layer it with garden-ripe summer vegetables, fresh herbs, and a crusty breadcrumb-parmesan topping.

4 thick slices bacon, chopped
1 large onion, chopped
1 tablespoon minced garlic
6-8 plum tomatoes, cut lengthwise
    into three slices
1 medium (about 1/2 pound) yellow
    zucchini, cut into thin rounds
salt and pepper
1/4 cup breadcrumbs
1/4 cup grated parmesan cheese
3 tablespoons chopped fresh basil,
    chives, dill, or other fresh herb,
    divided

Cook bacon over medium heat until lightly browned. Reduce heat, add onion and garlic and cook over low heat, stirring often, until onions are limp and rich-colored, 15-20 minutes. Meanwhile heat oven to 350 degrees.

Arrange 4 or 5 tomato slices at an angle against one side of a rounded baking dish, overlapping them a bit. Spread some of the onion mixture along the bottom of the tomatoes, then arrange several squash pieces over the onions, again overlapping them slightly. Repeat these layers until all the vegetables are used up. Sprinkle with salt and pepper to taste. Combine remaining ingredients and sprinkle this over all. Bake until vegetables are tender and top is browned, about 30 minutes.

**49. Teskie Orchards &
Fisheries /Berry Best
Foods Unlimited**

**12266 Highway 42
Ellison Bay, WI 54210
920-854-4443**

•

Berry Best Fish

Only in Door County, land of abundant waters, rich farmlands, and thousands of hungry tourists, is one likely to find a family business that combines fishing, farming, and baking. Of course it takes a large family. At the Teskies' Berry Best Foods roadside market on Highway 42, Fran and Neil Teskie and most of their seven children sell an array of products they catch, grow, process, and cook, including fresh, smoked, and pickled whitefish, whitefish pâté, asparagus, seasonal fruits, and homemade baked goods. The Teskies may handle more details than an airport control tower, but that doesn't keep them from producing the best: witness Fran's cherry pie, which took first place in the county at the 1995 Cherry Blossom Festival. Fran is understandingly hesitant to reveal her pie secrets, but here are other Berry Best Foods specialties from Fran and Neil's daughter Marykay Shumway.

Whitefish Scampi
2-3 servings

2 whitefish fillets (each about
   8 ounces)
2-3 tablespoons butter
1 tablespoon olive oil
1-2 tablespoons minced garlic
2 tablespoons chopped green onion
1 tablespoon chopped fresh parsley
1 tablespoon fresh lemon juice
salt and pepper to taste
for garnish: lemon wedges
   and chopped fresh parsley

Carefully skin whitefish fillets with sharp knife. Cut fish into 2-inch pieces. Melt butter over medium heat in large frying pan. Add olive oil, garlic, green onion, parsley, lemon juice, salt, and pepper. Add fish pieces and cook, stirring frequently, until fish is white, shows no signs of pink or grey, and is just beginning to flake, 7-10 minutes. (Regulate heat to prevent butter from burning.) Serve immediately over rice, pasta, or couscous. Garnish with lemon wedges and chopped parsley.

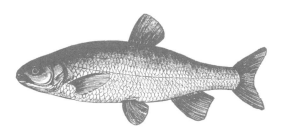

Berry Best
Smoked Fish Pâté
Makes 3 1/2 cups

2 packages (each 8 ounces) cream
   cheese, softened
1 cup boned smoked whitefish
1/2 cup boned smoked chub (take extra
   care to get all the bones out)
1/2 cup finely chopped red onion
1 medium green pepper,
   finely chopped
1 tablespoon lemon pepper
bottled hot pepper sauce to taste

Mix all ingredients and chill thoroughly. (The spread may be packed into a 4-cup mold or bowl lined with plastic wrap, if desired. Unmold unto a platter.) Garnish with chopped fresh parsley, chives, or paprika. Serve with crackers or as a sandwich spread or omelette filling.

50. Weber's Processing
725 N. Jackson St.
Cuba City, WI 53807
608-744-2159

•

Butcher Shop Quartet

The little boy fussed mildly as he stood at the meat counter near his mother. "Can I have some, please, Mommy, please?" he persisted, pointing at eye level to summer sausages that beckoned like giant Lincoln logs from a gleaming glass case. "No," she repeated wearily, then with a placating finality, "Just wait a little bit longer. We're eating at Grandma's; you can have summer sausage there."

The three-year-old didn't miss a beat. "But it won't be Weber's!" he cried.

Good comeback. And one that many Cuba City folks can sympathize with. Around here Weber's is so popular that their ground beef is specified in main dish recipes printed in a local fund-raising cookbook. Pretty much wherever you go throughout the lower left corner of Wisconsin, if you ask where to buy quality meats, "Weber's" is the response.

One good look inside the retail store explains why. A long, rounded display case luxuriously lined with dozens of neatly arranged meat trays extends across the room like a stretch limousine. Chops, steaks, and sausages are stacked three and four deep, all curves facing outward in heavy-lipped grins. The butchers wear white shirts, white aprons, and white paper caps that report Weber ham's "National Grand Champion" status in

restrained letters. Gold plaques and framed testimonies cover the walls. And there isn't a fingerprint, a drop of beef blood in sight.

Weber's meat market is as lush and ordered as a barber shop harmony. It is owned and operated by a quartet of brothers, each with his own voice, or specialty. Leland works with the slaughtering, Reginald, the curing, David, mainly processing, and Norman, the retail store. Unlike a musical ensemble, however, each can hit a full range of notes. "We all step into the others' areas," Lee points out. "You have to in an operation like this."

But that's no problem for a team whose meat processing skills are a family legacy.

Reginald, David, Lee, and Norman Weber harmonize to produce quality meats.

The Webers' great grandfather was a sausage maker and meat cutter in Switzerland, their grandfather processed meat in nearby Belleville, and their father, Otto, built the Cuba City plant more than 50 years ago. The brothers were boys then; they inherited the business as young men when Otto died suddenly in 1962.

Despite much growth since then, Weber's has maintained uncompromising standards of quality. Their secret is a mix of ultra-modern know-how and old-world values. According to Lee, they buy "farm-raised, farm-fed cows and hogs from within a 50-mile radius of the plant." In fact, Weber's meat comes from some of the same local families their father and grandfather dealt with. As for customer service, they preserve butcher shop traditions like wrapping beef products in heavy tan paper, pork and chicken in white. "Yay and behold," says Lee with an old-time style of his own. "The housewife opens her freezer and can tell right off what's she got."

Employees appear as courteous, competent, and proud of their work as the brothers; turnover is low. Scott Werner, for example, is a Weber's veteran of 15 years; others have been there twice as long.

Scott's forte is the beef jerky—a spicy, chewy ready-to-eat smoked stick with no casing. Scott starts with "the leanest beef round." It's ground and then blended with a seasoning that's "specially formulated for Weber's only." He uses the hose of a giant stuffing machine to form the mixture into flat strips across a screened tray. He hands are a blur as he trims the ends off the strips and repeats this until there's enough to smoke a 200-pound batch. "After smoking we cool, cut to size, package, and seal," Scott says, as if it were all one motion.

Although there is a steady stream of locals who frequent Weber's market, their products have found fame in other quarters, too. For more than 15 years, Lee has been handing out beef jerky samples to thousands of shoppers at the Dane County Farmers' Market in Madison. "We get the same customers back and they always get the same thing, week after week." Wholesale accounts supply hospitals, taverns, and school systems throughout southwestern Wisconsin. And Chicago Bears fans who follow their heroes to a summer training camp in Platteville stop at Weber's for bratwurst and smoked beef sticks. Says Lee with a shake of his head: "This place gets so doggoned busy!"

And why not? Everything about the place says, "We know what we're doing and we love doing it." And for the brothers in a butcher shop quartet, the response is music to their ears.

Half & Half Pot Roast
8 servings

A boneless, rolled pork or beef roast makes supper special and easy to prepare (plus there's no waste). If you can't decide which to make, try a Weber's "half and half." The brothers tie seasoned pork loin and sirloin tip together around thick slices of brick cheese. "The cheese disappears as the meat cooks," notes Lee Weber. His bushy auburn eyebrows rise and fall in pleasure as he gives this cooking tip: "After it's roasted, pour a cup of coffee right over the meat—the gravy will be out of this world!" I liked the concept of a hearty liquid to flavor the dish and came up with a variation of my own.

1 tablespoon butter
1 tablespoon olive oil
1 "half and half" roast, about 3 pounds (you may substitute a beef or rolled pork roast)
4 small onions, peeled
1 teaspoon minced garlic
8 medium Russet potatoes, scrubbed and quartered
1/2 cup dark beer
1 bay leaf
salt and pepper to taste
flour

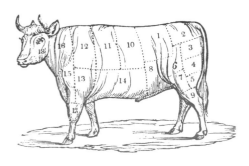

Heat oven to 325 degrees. Heat butter and oil in roasting pan or large Dutch oven over medium-high heat. Brown roast and onions on all sides. Add remaining ingredients except flour. Cover tightly and roast about 1 1/2 hours. (You can use an instant meat thermometer to check for desired doneness. I take the roast out when the pork registers an internal temperature of 160 degrees and find it rises to a safe 165 degrees as the meat stands for several minutes.)

Remove roast and vegetables from pan; keep warm. Mix 2-3 tablespoons flour with 1/2 cup water; stir into liquid in pan and bring to simmer over medium heat. Cook, stirring often, 5-10 minutes. Adjust thickness of gravy by adding more flour/water mixture or plain water. Season with salt and pepper to taste. Be sure to add any juices that accumulate beneath the roast to the gravy.

Slice meat; serve with the vegetables and gravy. Sauteed whole mushrooms and a green salad are good complements.

Carol Weber's Roast Peppered Rib Eye of Beef
10-12 servings

Carol and Reg Weber and family enjoy this knock-out roast each year on Christmas evening. Carol, who serves the roast with potato casserole and cranberry salad, doesn't specify the type of vinegar to use; I tried it with red wine vinegar and loved the results. In the recipe, which was previously published in The Platteville Journal, Carol indicates that "time and temperature settings are suggested guidelines only" and recommends using a meat thermometer to check internal temperature. She notes: "Thermometer will read 140 degrees for rare, 160 degrees for medium and

Weber's store in Cuba City is spotless.

170 degrees for well-done beef." Remember, the roast will continue to cook awhile even after it's been removed from the oven. For medium-rare results, I suggest removing it when the thermometer reads 140 degrees.

boneless rib eye of beef (5-6 pounds)
1/4-1/2 cup coarsely cracked
    black pepper
1/2 teaspoon ground cardamom
1 tablespoon tomato paste
1 teaspoon paprika
1/2 teaspoon garlic powder
1 cup soy sauce
3/4 cup vinegar
1 1/2 tablespoons cornstarch
    mixed with 1/4 cup water

Trim excess fat from beef. Combine pepper and cardamom; rub all over beef, pressing mixture into meat with heal of hand. Place roast in shallow baking dish. Mix tomato paste, paprika, and garlic powder in bowl; gradually whisk in soy sauce, then vinegar. Pour over meat, cover, and refrigerate 8 hours or longer, turning the meat in the marinade occasionally.

Remove meat from marinade (reserve the marinade) and allow meat to stand about 1 hour to bring it to room temperature.

Heat oven to 300 degrees. Wrap meat in foil, place in shallow roasting pan, and place in oven. Roast about 1 1/2 hours if you are aiming for rare or medium-rare meat. Open foil and strain pan drippings into a bowl. Raise oven temperature to 350 degrees and continue to roast the uncovered meat to brown it, and to continue the cooking until desired doneness is reached. The amount of time will depend on how done you want the meat, but plan on at least 20-35 minutes longer for rare or medium-rare meat.

To make gravy, skim excess fat from pan drippings in bowl. Combine 1 cup skimmed pan drippings, 1 cup water, and 1/4-1/2 cup of the marinade in saucepan; bring to boil. (If you get less pan drippings, adjust the amounts of other ingredients, also.) Remove from heat and whisk in cornstarch mixture until smooth. Return to heat and simmer a few minutes until thickened.

Allow roast to stand at room temperature 15 minutes before carving.

Optional ingredients:
1/2 cup chopped marinated artichoke
hearts, plus 2 tablespoons marinade
drained from the jar
2 tablespoons chopped flat-leaf
(Italian) parsley

Heat olive oil in non-stick frying pan over medium-high heat. Dice all the potatoes. Add them to the hot oil and cook, tossing occasionally, until browned and nearly tender, 10-15 minutes. (Adjust heat as needed to prevent scorching.) Reduce heat to medium, add remaining ingredients except optional ones and continue to cook, tossing occasionally, until potatoes are tender, about 15 minutes. Stir in optional ingredients, if desired, and season again as needed with salt and pepper. Serve immediately.

Roast Beef Hash with Russet & Sweet Potatoes
3-4 medium servings

The best part about making roast beef is the leftovers. There's no end to the soup, salad, or sandwich possibilities, and even hash holds creative promise.

3 tablespoons olive oil
4 medium (1 pound) Russet potatoes
1 large (1/2 pound) sweet potato
1-1 1/2 cups diced roast beef
  or pot roast
1 1/2 teaspoons minced garlic
1 teaspoon dried basil
1/2 teaspoon fennel seeds
salt and pepper to taste

51. Wisconsin River Meats
N5320 County Highway HH
Mauston, WI 53948
608-847-7413
•

The House That Venison Built

Wisconsin is nicknamed after 19th-century miners, the "digging badgers" who sometimes lived in the same iron-ore-rich caves they mined. But maybe a better name for the Badger State would be the Deer State, for deer hunting is an age-old tradition practiced by early native tribes, European settlers, and modern families.

John Hamm belongs to one of those families. His deer legacy began with

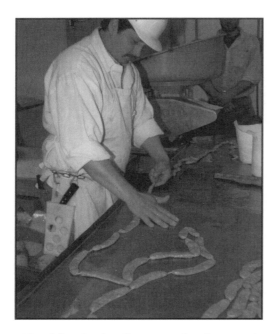

Hand-forming landjaeger, *a dry, fermented sausage. Wisconsin River Meats, Mauston*

German ancestors who brought butchering skills and a love of sausage when they immigrated to Wisconsin. John's grandfather Louis Hamm, like other subsistence farmers who needed to supplement their food supply during the 1930s, hunted in secret because of post-logging conservation laws (which were quickly successful at deer re-population). John writes in *A Sportsmen's Guide to Venison Sausage* (Wisconsin River Publications, 1993):

These farmers had to be able to dress and process these deer in a hurry to avoid detection by the law or waste any meat. These old timers would not tolerate any waste of meat, and they developed really fast and efficient processing methods.

As hunting was legalized, farmers and landowners gathered at deer camps, where they passed on the tradition, teaching their children and grandchildren how to hunt, dress, and process venison.

Grandpa made the venison into summer sausage, brats, bologna, Polish sausage, and dried venison. To me as a young boy, watching Grandpa make sausage was nearly a religious experience. He used secret spices, had a home-made smokehouse only he truly understood, and spent many weeks curing his dried venison. I was fascinated and the love of making sausage and smoked and cured meats was in my blood for life.

John's family opened Hamm's Meat Service in 1978. By then, the deer population had risen dramatically and while there were many hunters, few knew how to process their own deer. What had been a boyhood fascination for John became a career when he attended butchering school and accumulated years of professional experience in the family business (which was sold in 1989 and is now closed).

Today John, his wife Diane, and partner David Mauer operate Wisconsin River Meats in rural Mauston. Close to rushing rivers, bluffs, and wilderness, the fishing here is great and game is abundant. The company's specialty, not surprisingly, is custom deer processing.

"Deer built this place," says David. But deer is not the whole story. Meat cases are filled with products made from Hamm family recipes, some of which date back to Grandpa's time. There are brats, bacon, ham, ring bologna, snack sticks, natural-cased wieners, three types of summer sausage, and landjaeger, a dry, fermented sausage that is their Number 1 seller. "We make a real beef jerky—sliced sirloin tip with a maple-sugar cure," says David. "It's mild and chewy."

Besides smoked and cured products, the company offers fresh, or unprocessed, meats (sold frozen) for wholesale and retail purchase, custom processing of beef and pork, and catering. The Wisconsin River Meats mobile roaster is in demand for local pig roasts, steak fries, and chicken barbecues.

Several additions have enlarged the building since it was built in 1993 and today there are no signs that business will slow down anytime soon. Or the tradition it represents, for that matter. John says his two older children work at the plant, and Kyle, the youngest, "thinks it's what he wants to do when he grows up."

Pizza with Smoked Sausage & Grilled Vegetables
One hearty 14-inch pizza

For a recipe that "cheats" (i.e. uses boxed pizza dough), this is still ten times better than any delivery pizza. Use a baking or "pizza" stone, if you have one. Baking stones are slabs of composite stone that heat evenly and produce a beautifully crisp crust. (Be sure to heat it thoroughly, a minimum of 30 minutes.) You can also use an oiled, heavy-gauge baking sheet. In either case, a wooden peel also comes in handy: it's a thin paddle that slides your pizza in and out of the oven (two large hamburger lifters will work, too).

Toppings:
1 large sweet onion
1 large green bell pepper
1 large red or yellow bell pepper
olive oil
1 1/2 cups pizza sauce
dried oregano
1 cup diced smoked sausage (summer
    sausage, venison sausage, smoked
    bratwurst, etc.)
1 cup shredded low-fat
    mozzarella cheese

Crust:
2 boxes (each 6 1/2 ounces) pizza
    crust mix
2 tablespoons chopped fresh basil
    or rosemary
cornmeal
flour

Heat coals on outdoor grill. Slice onions into thick rounds; cut sweet peppers in half and remove seeds. Lightly coat vegetables with olive oil, grill until nearly tender, then chop coarsely. Meanwhile, heat oven to 425 degrees, with pizza stone inside, if using.

To make crust: Sprinkle cornmeal generously over surface of a wooden peel, or grease a heavy baking sheet. Place crust mix and chopped fresh herbs in bowl. Stir in 1 cup hot tap water until moistened, then beat 30 seconds. Cover and let stand in a warm place (on top the stove is good) 10 minutes. Assemble other topping ingredients.

Turn dough onto a floured surface and knead 1 minute. Press dough into a circle about 8 inches in diameter and transfer to peel or baking sheet. Gently press out into a 14-inch circle (or rectangle of similar size), making the edges thicker than the middle. If using stone, sprinkle cornmeal onto it in the oven. Gently slide crust from peel to stone, or onto baking sheet. Bake 5 minutes. Remove from oven, spread pizza sauce on crust, and sprinkle with oregano to taste. Layer on the sausage, onions, and peppers, then top with cheese. Bake an additional 15-20 minutes, until cheese is bubbly and crust is browned.

Hamm's Lunch Loaf
About 4 1/2 pounds

Deer hunters are always looking for new ways to prepare venison. Here's an easy-to-make luncheon meat adapted from John Hamm's A Sportsmen's Guide to Venison Sausage (Wisconsin River Publications, 1993). If making your own lunch meat sounds odd to you, consider that there are no preservatives or additives in it and that you can control the amount of salt yourself. I found it surprisingly delicious and easy to make. While this version has taken top honors at Wisconsin Association of Meat Processors competitions, John says he sometimes adds hot peppers, garlic, or herbs. If your venison supply is limited, use half beef or pork and half venison, and if your freezer is overflowing with deer meat, the recipe may be doubled.

Even if you don't have venison, this lunch meat can be made with beef or pork or a combination of the two.

John writes, "One problem you will have will be keeping yourself from eating the meat after you add the seasonings and it is nearly done. Hold the gelatin and you can use the same recipe for a delicious venison stew. Serve on potatoes."

> 5 pounds lean venison, beef, or pork (or use a combination), cut into 1-inch cubes
> 1 cup finely chopped onion
> 2 1/2 tablespoons celery salt
> 2 tablespoons salt
> 1 tablespoon ground black pepper
> 1 cup catsup
> 2 1/2 ounces unflavored gelatin

Oil two small loaf pans. Cover venison or other meats with cold water in large, heavy stew pot. Bring to simmer. Partially cover the pot and simmer meat slowly 1 1/2 hours, skimming surface several times in the first 15-20 minutes of cooking. Stir in onion, celery salt, salt, and pepper. Simmer slowly one hour longer. Stir in catsup and cook 15 minutes longer, then drain broth from meat into a bowl. Let stand about 20 minutes, then skim grease from the top of the broth. While broth is standing, "shred" the meat by smashing it with a fork, or, if you prefer a more traditional, marbled effect in the finished product, leave the chunks intact.

Stir 3 cups of the broth back into the meat mixture (extra broth can be used to make soups or stews) and reheat briefly. Mix in gelatin thoroughly. Press mixture into loaf pans; chill thoroughly. Slice meat thinly for deli trays or sandwiches. The lunch meat can be frozen.

Italian-Style Venison Meatloaf
6-8 servings

Cut the fat and increase the flavor with a meatloaf inspired by a meatball recipe from an Italian friend. If you're substituting ground beef, add 10-15 minutes to the cooking time.

> 2 pounds ground venison
> 1/2 cup minced onion
> 1 cup dried breadcrumbs
> 2/3 cup freshly grated, loosely packed parmesan cheese
> 2 teaspoons minced garlic
> 1 cup Italian spaghetti (marinara) sauce, divided
> 1 egg
> salt and pepper to taste

Heat oven to 350 degrees. Oil a baking pan. Lightly mix all ingredients, using only 1/2 cup of the spaghetti sauce. Shape into loaf; place in pan. Spread on remaining sauce. Bake 50-55 minutes.

More Hometown Meat & Fish Flavor

The markets that follow are arranged in alphabetical order by the name of the business. To locate a business by town name, see page 173. Or check the maps on pages *xviii-xxv*. All information is subject to change. Travelers should call or write before visiting to get business hours, directions, and other important details.

52. Andy's Fish Market
51 Green Bay Road
Sturgeon Bay, WI 54235
920-743-2778 or 920-746-0276

•

Andy Johnson's fish market was located on the waterfront in downtown Sturgeon Bay until the town's new marina was built. He's moved up the road now but he still sells his stellar smoked Lake Michigan whitefish and whitefish spread.

53. Bavaria Sausage Kitchen
6317 Nesbitt Road
Madison, WI 53719
608-271-1295 or 608-845-6691

•

As sight-seeing stops go, Madison's majestic State Capitol has nothing on the Voll family's lush sausage kitchen, located on the southwest side of town. Renowned for their bratwurst, ham, and liver sausage, they also make old-world specialties like goose liver sausage, knackwurst, wiesswurst, blood and tongue sausage, and smoky liver pâté. The company uses no artificial coloring, flavors, fillers, or MSG. Besides processed meats and fresh cuts, they offer oven-ready German ethnic entrees like sauerbraten and rouladen, keep a huge cheese counter (containing, among other rarities, 10-year-old ched-

dars), and feature a large variety of imported European foods and gift items.

54. Beck's Fish Market
Highway 35
Genoa, WI 54632
608-689-2302

•

Folks up and down the Mississippi River Valley know about Roger Beck's place located one mile north of Genoa. Here's where they get their fix of locally caught catfish—dressed, smoked, or even fresh or frozen catfish cheeks. They also go for his smoked carp, jerky, and smoked garlic carp fillets.

55. Bernie's Fine Meats
119 N. Franklin St.
Port Washington, WI 53074
414-284-4511

•

Old world recipes, secret spices, and choice meats smoked over hardwood make Bernie's sausages special. Add custom meat cutting and friendly service and you have this old-fashioned meat market and sausage factory. Their summer sausage and hickory-smoked bacon and ham are notable, but if you're feeling adventuresome, go for the Luxemburg mustriepen, a pork, cabbage, and blood sausage that's a favorite with Port Washington locals.

56. BJ's Butcher Shop
P.O. Box 282
1144 Highway 45 South
Eagle River, WI 54521
715-479-4456

•

What distinguishs this meat market from many others is on-the-spot custom cutting. Customers can walk in and order their pork chops, rib-eyes, or T-bones prepared just the way they like. BJ's also offers fresh, plump chickens, venison processing, and a line of exotic frozen meats, including ostrich, emu, buffalo, kangaroo, and lamb.

57. Blau's Saukville Meats
501 E. Green Bay Ave.
Saukville, WI 53080
414-284-0898

•

Located where highways 33 and W meet (or "meat," as Harley Blau says), Saukville Meats offers custom cutting, personalized service, and choice beef, veal, lamb, pork, poultry, and buffalo, plus homemade fresh and smoked sausage, and home-smoked hams and bacon. Customers can order party trays, rent a meat locker, or get their deer processed.

58. Buddha's Sausage Shoppe
1734 Main St.
Green Bay, WI 54302
920-468-5923

•

Buddha's has been a Green Bay tradition since before the Green Bay Packers won their first Super Bowl. Besides being the self-proclaimed "Home of the Golden Brat," the Neuser family makes an astonishing array of excellent sausages, including locally popular Belgian *trippe* (stuffed with pork and cabbage), spicy Louisiana *andouille*, peppery Polish *kielbasa*, Spanish *chorizo*, and an ultra-tender Swedish potato sausage that is the stuff of dreams. Old-fashioned skin-on wieners, the kind that crack lightly and burst with juiciness when you bite into one, are another Buddha's specialty worth dreaming over.

59. Buffalo Farm
800 Western Ave.
County Highway T
Cedarburg, WI 53012
414-375-2006

•

One hundred of the great American beasts graze on 76 acres of land at this combination buffalo farm/petting zoo/party center. The retail store features more than 40 cuts of low-fat, high-protein bison meat and products, including burgers, steaks, brats, and breakfast patties. Visitors can rent the barn, watch a bonfire, pet a buffalo, or take a hayride tour.

60. Butcher Shop of Park Falls
277 N. First St.
Park Falls, WI 54552
715-762-3664

•

Sisters-in-law Karen and Joan Prohaska are owners/operators who process a range of homemade fresh and smoked sausage. Many, like sweet basil Italian sausage, maple pork sausage, and beer-and-onion bratwurst, are from their own recipes. "We're not shy with the spices," says Karen. As a special service to their deer processing customers, the Prohaskas will custom-flavor venison sausage to suit individual tastes.

61. Custom Meats, Inc.
P.O. Box 456;
1300 S. Highway 107
Marathon City, WI 54448
715-443-3734

•

Custom smoking and retail cuts of choice, hormone-free local beef and pork. Try their specialty, mettwurst, a kind of spicy smoked ring bologna.

62. Downsville Meat Processors
N2615 451st St.
Downsville, WI 54735
715-664-8327

•

Six kinds of bratwurst, including sauerkraut brats and "garden" brats (with onion, sweet peppers, and other vegetables), plus a full line of other fresh and smoked sausages, Black Angus beef from their own lot, wild game processing, and locally raised lamb and pork cuts.

63. Ewig Brothers, Inc.
121 S. Wisconsin St.
Port Washington, WI 53074
414-284-223

•

A favorite with the local townsfolk for many years, Ewig's offers smoked and fresh fish, including Lake Michigan chubs, smoked Alaskan salmon, Canadian whitefish and lake trout, and a mixed smoked fish spread.

64. Hoffmann's Meats
W62 N601 Washington Ave.
Cedarburg, WI 53012
414-377-4440

•

David Hoffmann is the fourth generation butcher to own and operate this meat market that opened nearly nine decades ago. He features sausage, mostly German-style varieties, made with top-of-the-line ingredients and natural casings. "Come in for the smell of it."

65. Jim's Meat Market
P.O. Box 25; 411 S. Main St.
Iron River, WI 54847
715-372-8566

•

If you need sustenance for a north-country camping or fishing trip, try Jim's spicy pepperoni sticks, summer sausage, smoked ham, or any of his line of fresh and smoked meats. He also offers custom venison processing.

66. Lodi Sausage Company & Meat Market
150 S. Main St.
Lodi, WI 53555
608-592-3534

•

Nearly every event in Lodi features a Chamber of Commerce-sponsored brat stand with Larry Clark's excellent bratwurst. This "Home of Blue Ribbon Quality Meats" also offers National Champion summer sausage, home-cured spiral hams and bacon, homemade sausages, and complete butchering and processing services.

67. Long's Hillbilly Market
P.O. Box 80; 10386 Main St.
Boulder Junction, WI 54512
715-385-2481

•

Outstanding home-smoked bacon, ham, sausage, bratwurst, and a line of fresh meat cuts. Don't miss the home-made pickled herring. Long's is a grocery store, too.

68. MacFarlane Pheasant Farm, Inc.
2821 South Highway 51
Janesville, WI 53546
800-345-8348

•

Established in 1929, this is one of the largest pheasant farms in the nation. They offer dressed, frozen, and smoked pheasant, plus an array of exotic local and imported meats, including ostrich, alligator, wild boar, elk, rabbit, buffalo, duck, kangaroo, and emu. The retail store also stocks Wisconsin and gourmet mustards, cheese, and other packaged goods.

69. Maplewood Meats
4663 Milltown Road
Green Bay, WI 54313
920-865-7901

•

Maplewood has been family-owned since 1983; they produce a full range of fresh and smoked sausages, bacon, and many fresh cuts from local cattle and hogs. The brats are popular in summertime and their ham is standard during the holidays. They do their own butchering, smoking, and venison processing.

70. Marchant's Foods
9674 Highway 57
Brussels, WI 54204
920-825-1244

•

Home-killed and dressed meats from Marchant's put the best mail order steaks to shame. Don't miss their Belgian *trippe*, a pork-and-cabbage sausage that is outstanding when simmered and then panfried. Trippe (pronounced "trip") is a tradition found only in this part of the state. And if you're really brave, try the sulze, an old-time, coarse-textured lunch meat flavored with vinegar.

71. Northland Turkey Farms, Inc.
W3318 Harlow Road
Chilton, WI 53014
920-849-9344

•

Looking for low-fat turkey products? Visit or order turkey by mail from a family that has been raising turkeys for three generations. More than 50 turkey products are available from an on-the-farm store, including turkey jerky, turkey bacon, turkey salami, smoked turkey, and several kinds of ground turkey.

72. Nueske's Hillcrest Farm Meats
P.O. Box D, Rural Route 2
Highways 29 and 45
Wittenberg, WI 54499-0904
800-382-2266

•

Great grandfather Wilhelm Nueske immigrated to Wittenberg in 1887 and started smoking quality meats over sweet applewood gathered from nearby orchards. Four generations later, the Nueskes are still using his original recipes

Meat market, Palmyra, Wisconsin, c. 1910
State Historical Society of Wisconsin WHi(X3)30742

for curing with brown sugar and honey and smoking over smoldering applewood. Nueske's bacon and ham are renowned throughout Wisconsin.

73. Ray's Butcher Shoppe
4640 W. Loomis Road
Greenfield, WI 53220
414-423-1322
•

A gourmet meat market with old-fashioned quality and service. Try the boneless ham, bacon-wrapped filets, stuffed chicken breasts, and seasoned pork roasts.

74. Ruef's Meat Market
538 First St.
New Glarus, WI 53574
608-527-2554
•

New Glarus' traditional sausage shop since the early 1920s, Ruef's has been owned by Willy Ruef since 1966. Swiss-style meats are the thing here: landjaeger (dried beef and pork snack sticks that come in pairs), kalberwurst (made from veal, whole milk, crackers, and blended spices), veal brats (with a soft texture and mildly spicy flavor), Swiss-style wieners (a mix of beef and pork stuffed into natural casings), and cervelas (finely ground meat with a delicate garlic taste). Mail order within Wisconsin is available.

75. Van Meter's Meats
407 Main St.
Luck, WI 54853
715-472-2141
•

Old-fashioned full-service fresh meat counter specializing in local beef and hogs. Their Danish medister, a fresh, mildly seasoned pork sausage seasoned with allspice and onion, is popular with locals, who enjoy it for breakfast with eggs and fried potatoes. Van Meter's ham and bacon are also favored, but for a real unique treat, try their Norwegian-style head cheese. Containing beef chuck, pork tongue, and pork shoulder, plus nutmeg, cloves, allspice, and ginger, it's leaner and spicier than other head cheeses.

3

Bakeries

3. Bakeries

If I were making the perfect small town, I'd start with Main Street...A block or so from the cafe I'd have a bakery. It would have windows full of cakes and donuts and cookies, and sliding glass doors in the bakery cases, early American wallpaper and a calendar with the hometown high school football schedule on it. Everything would be baked from scratch daily, so as you headed down Main Street you'd catch a whiff of Vienna bread or poppy-seed muffins or kolache, and you'd have to stop in.

—From "Bakeries I Have Known and Loved," by Kit Kiefer, *Wisconsin Trails Magazine*, November/December, 1989.

Historical Flavor

The first breads were small, flat, gritty blobs of flame-baked meal, hardly much of an improvement over the coarse porridge that humankind ate before heat was used to cook grain. Still, primitive families knew a good thing when they saw it, and the discovery of bread—the first systematically prepared food—motivated *homo sapiens* to settle into organized, agricultural communities.

Flat and hard as it was, this early type of bread was enough of a good thing that several thousand years passed before leavening came along. It happened about 3000 B.C. in Egypt's rich Nile Valley, where grain farming was state-controlled and official bakers prepared flatbreads called *ta* in earthen jugs. One day, perhaps, a forgetful slave let a batch of

dough sit out too long and, not wanting to waste the now soured dough, he added it to a fresh batch. The new bread was not only lighter and easier to eat, it was delicious.

Even more tasty were the breads baked in another Egyptian innovation—ovens—which eventually replaced the open-fire method of baking. By the twelfth century B.C. commoners bought *ta* from village vendors, while noblemen chose from dozens of kinds of breads produced by the bakers on their estates.

Both the Jews and the Greeks learned about leavening and ovens from the Egyptians. In Jerusalem a kind of bread "factory" existed, where bakers brought their flour to be baked into breads they later sold at their own shops. In Greece, despite poor soil and a sea-loving heritage, grain cultivation and bread-baking became so important that they were assigned their own powerful goddess, Demeter. The Greeks developed new milling methods that improved bread texture and they invented the bee-hive oven, a closed oven that retained heat and could bake a lot of bread at once. The public bakeries of Athens became famous for the quality and variety of their breads and pastries, which were now being flavored with ingredients like wine, cheese, and honey.

Baking took on even greater sophistication in Rome; here, master bakers were their own bosses and specialized in one of several areas, which included breads, pastries, sweets, and milk-based products. In some cities, *ars pistorica* (the art of baking) gained such respectability that bakers even held public office. The creative bakers of Rome used high quality wheat to produce baked goods lighter in texture and color than ever before. They also introduced the peel oven—it was enclosed in brick for greater heat retention, expelled smoke through chimneys, and was named for the long poles used to handle hot loaves.

As wealthy landowners began to monopolize farms and Rome's population swelled with immigrants from the country-side, the government instigated a public dole. At first free grain was distributed, but eventually the people's allotment came in the form of bread. State-controlled bakeries were inevitable, and as bakers found them-selves more and more tightly regulated, the free artisan nature of the business disap-peared.

Bakeries of antiquity existed only in cities and towns; in rural areas, all baking was done in the home. But whether at home or at the bake shop, milling, or grinding grain, had always been part of the "baking" process. Until the Middle Ages, that is, when baking and milling became separate trades.

Medieval millers used mechanical water mills located along rural waterways, far removed from town bake shops. It seems logical that eliminating the toughest part of a baker's job would foster greater baking finesse and specialization, but this was the Dark Ages and the very opposite was true. As with other artisan crafts of early medieval times, commercial baking took a giant step backwards as economic activity went into serious and lengthy decline. Without vibrant towns and cities, the bak-ing trade couldn't flourish. Few technologi-cal and culinary improvements occurred. To be a baker held little honor. In fact, little about baking itself changed from Roman times, except that dark, coarse-textured products dominated once again (because wheat had become scarce). Only very privi-leged diners enjoyed the elaborate pies and

pastries that court bakers created.

Commercial baking revived when Euro-pean city life reawakened. Bakers were among the first tradespeople to organize into guilds which, although restrictive, gave them a secure monopoly over their trade. Rich regional traditions like British meat pies and a Neapolitan breakfast bread that was the forerunner to Italian pizza devel-oped.

American Pie

Across the Atlantic Ocean, native peo-ples knew nothing of wheat or raised breads. The Incas, Aztecs, and northern tribes cultivated maize and ate flatcakes of ground corn, today called tortillas. Corn grew so easily that its agriculture, at least compared to wheat-growing, was loosely organized; compared to leavened bread, tortillas were an uncomplicated food, made in the home, not by professional bakers.

The transoceanic exchange of wheat- and corn-based baking practices came slowly after the arrival of Columbus, but it came.

Early settlers brought old-world baking traditions to America and, like all diners since the discovery of baking, they had a particular fondness for the breads, cakes, and pastries of their home countries. Homesick families must have felt miser-able about the lack of familiar ingredients like wheat flour, which prevented them from producing their beloved specialties. But they quickly learned to appreciate fast-growing, nutritious corn, and were soon adapting European baking methods to indigenous ingredients. American foods like cornbread and fritters, were the happy result. In turn, native foodstuffs, including chocolate, vanilla, and tomatoes, gradu-ally made their considerable mark on European baking, producing classics like chocolate cake and pizza with tomato sauce.

The tug of culinary traditions was powerful, so despite the bounty they found here American settlers began to plant wheat as soon as possible. And how it thrived in the rich, expansive lands, drawing wave after wave of new settlers who spread ever farther westward. The more the country expanded, the more it fostered regional specialties. Pies, for example, acquired a uniquely American character—Southerners favored molasses-flavored pies, whereas in the northeast maple syrup-sweetened pies, and in the Midwest cream-based pies were popular.

As in other civilizations that came before, commercial baking didn't take hold in the United States until towns sprouted and cities grew. Working class urbanites living in tenements lacked home ovens and the time to bake, so they frequented corner bakeries. The fancier pastries and tortes that bake shops produced were popular with the upper class. Even in small towns, family-operated retail bakeries provided supplementary breads and baked goods to neighborhood families.

But baking remained largely a home craft through most of the 19th century. Home-baked goods were considered superior to bake shop products and typically they were fresher and cheaper than what consumers could get retail.

In the mid-1800s, most bakeries were still one-man shops with little mechanization. Bakers did some delivery to neighbors, but the bulk of their products were sold over the counter to patrons they knew well. There was no need to wrap or identify their goods with labels and no need to advertise. Soon, however, urban populations were growing quickly and people had more money to spare. Changing technology gave bakers more efficient ovens and helpful equipment like dough mixers and dough-shapers. Transportation improvements allowed bakers to deliver products faster and farther away, creating competition that hadn't existed before. By 1900, three-quarters of baked goods were still made in the home, but a factory system had begun to emerge. It was the beginning of the first significant change in baking in hundreds of years.

In fact, baking was the last major type of food processing to move from the home to the factory. When it did move, however, it moved fast. With the rapid spread of mass production and transportation, incredible growth in industrial baking occurred during the early 1900s. During World War I, the Food Administration urged families to buy bread to avoid waste. Consumers began to believe advertising claims that the products from big companies were better than home-baked. Many people came to prefer the more convenient and predictable breads that came wrapped and labeled with a company name.

In 1930, for the first time in history, commercially produced breads and baked goods surpassed home baking. Representing 75 percent of all baked goods, commercial baking became one of the nation's major industries. Except for a temporary Depression-era decline, the large-scale baking industry has dominated in-home baking and small bakeries ever since.

The State of Bread

Throughout Wisconsin's history, no matter how families obtained their baked goods, they had an ever-growing bread list to choose from. Immigrants found an abundance of raw ingredients and rich soils where grains thrived. Native Woodland tribes and every country that sent settlers into the state contributed their specialties. Today, more than its cheese variety, more than its sausage selection, Wisconsin's breads and sweets characterize the notable diversity of its ethnic culture.

Many specialties are identified with a community or region: Cornish pasties from the former lead mine towns of the southwest, fry bread from the reservations, Belgian pies from Kewaunee County, Danish kringle from Racine. Norwegian bakeries sell lefse and horn-shaped *krumkake*, Polish places offer jelly *ponczaks*, and a shop in Milwaukee features Southern delights like peach "fried pies" and pineapple-coconut cake.

The state's agricultural heritage has also sweetened the bakery assortment, with Door County cherry pie, cranberry bread, and the queen of the State Fair, cream puffs. Bakers get creative with local ingredients to produce wild rice bread, maple-glazed doughnuts, and enough apple desserts to fill a book.

The state has every kind of independent bakery. There are ethnic bakeries, health- and earth-conscious establishments, gourmet cheesecake shops, shops that specialize in one or two types of bread, and tiny ma-and-pa places that offer everything from white bread to black-bottom pie. These are the "small guys" and together they represent Wisconsin's gold mine of goodies.

Hometown Bakeries

People love fresh, from-scratch baked goods. Today, families that wouldn't think of making their own sausage or cheese occasionally mix homemade pie dough or bake bread. Home-baking has gone from essential craft to enjoyable hobby.

Ma-and-pa bakeries are a Wisconsin tradition.
State Historical Society of Wisconsin Classified File 6472

And while few buyers get the bulk of their baked goods from small, "scratch" bakeries any longer, many still make the extra trip for special occasions. Most diners recognize that the breads and pastries from independent bake shops are fresher, healthier, more distinctive, and more scrumptious than the highly refined, preservative-laden loaves and cakes found on most grocery shelves. Even supermarkets with in-house bakeries are hard pressed to match the quality and uniqueness of family-operated shops.

We gladly go out of our way for a tiered wedding cake with real buttercream frosting, for those special brat buns for the Fourth of July, or for a crusty loaf of sourdough French to serve when guests are coming to dinner. Small-shop baked goods can be as decadent as custard-filled long Johns or as wholesome as multi-grain bread made from organic flour. They can be as old-fashioned as crullers or as upscale as biscotti. Whatever they are, they are a treat, a small luxury—something that isn't absolutely necessary in our lives, but something we nevertheless must have, if only for the simple, delicious joy of it.

And there are other reasons we must have them. In December, hometown bakeries are at their busiest, churning out *pfeffernüsse*, *bûche de Noël*, *sandbakkels*, sweet potato pie, and the many other heritage specialties that are welcome reminders of our ethnic roots. Supporting a family bakery supports the life and character of a community. In some places, the local bakery serves as a kind of community center, a place where residents bump into each other and catch up on the news. Often a specialty bakery is a draw for tourists, a way for them literally to taste local flavor.

It's a flavor—and an experience—you can't find anywhere else. But you will find it in the jingle of an old-fashioned door-bell as you enter a Main Street bake shop, or in a clerk's Italian accent in a busy Mil-waukee storefront. It's there in the sweet, yeasty smell of Swedish rye bread or the buttery perfume of a double-crust apple pie. In the lilting "hello" and welcoming smile of an across-the-counter neighbor, and in the soul-satisfying taste of a last bite of cheese Danish.

It's in hometown bakeries.

—Please Note

The bakeries that follow are arranged in alphabetical order by the name of the business. Additional bakeries are listed in alphabetical order at the end of the chapter. To locate a bakery by town name, see page 173. Maps are on pages *xviii-xxv*. All information is subject to change. Travelers should call or write before visiting to get business hours, directions, and other important details.

---

76. Bult's Quality Bakery
114 W. North Water St.
New London, WI 54961
920-982-4091
•

Hearty, Healthy Traditions

Bernard Bult was an immigrant from Holland who learned American-style bak-ing in Green Bay before he opened his own place in New London in 1928. Even-tually his son Andrew and daughter-in-law

took over. Now his grandchildren, Jerry Bult and Mary Jo Prahl, run the bakery.

The slender, dark-eyed siblings still use their grandfather's old-fashioned recipes for breads, doughnuts, cookies, and the dessert bars Bernard called "princess slices." But inside the small, red brick storefront, alongside the traditional apple fritters and pinwheel cookies, are the Bults' health-foods: low-fat oatmeal raisin cookies, preservative-free lemon poppy-seed muffins, and a line of breads and buns called "bialy" products that contain no fats, sugars, or cholesterol.

Jerry began adding more nutritious items to the line during the health-con-scious 1980s, when he noticed that one of the bakery's best sellers was a 100-percent whole wheat bread made with honey and molasses instead of sugar. The whole wheat was outselling even white bread.

Today there's a steady demand for both ends of Bult's spectrum.

Bult's Virtually Fat-Free Oatmeal Raisin Cookies
3-4 dozen cookies

1 1/4 cups applesauce
3/4 cup brown sugar
1/2 cup sugar
1 egg
1 teaspoon vanilla extract
1 1/2 cups cake flour
2 teaspoons salt
1 teaspoon baking soda
1 teaspoon cinnamon
1/4 teaspoon nutmeg
3 cups quick-cooking oats
1 cup raisins or dried cherries

Heat oven to 375 degrees. Grease two baking sheets. Mix applesauce, sugars, egg, and vanilla in large bowl. In separate bowl, mix remaining ingredients; stir into apple-sauce mixture. Scoop onto baking sheets; bake 10-11 minutes. Cool on wire racks.

77. Clasen's European Bakery
7610 Donna Drive
Middleton, WI 53563
608-831-2032
●

What's In A Phrase

Neatly typed production sheets list the dozens of whole-grain breads, hard rolls, coffeecakes, cookies, tortes, Danish, and other pastries that are produced daily at Clasen's European Bakery. Clasen's is family-owned but it's a large operation, so checklists like these, and other labor-saving systems, must be steadfastly followed. But at the top of the lists, above the orderly inventory of tasks, are brief phrases in capital letters. "HOLD YOUR-SELVES TO THE HIGHEST STANDARDS," reads one. "DON'T ACCEPT GOOD ENOUGH AS GOOD ENOUGH," says another.

The mottos are like a picture: they say a thousand words about Clasen's, where Bavarian rye bread is crusty and dense, apple streusel coffeecake is all-butter, marzipan torte is light and rich, and chocolate-dipped macaroons melt in your mouth. Bakers prepare fresh, from-scratch products, stock pure butter and real eggs, and use no mixes or artificial preservatives.

This was all standard procedure for the immigrant couple from Germany who opened the Middleton bakery in 1960 and it is standard procedure for their baker daughter, who owns Clasen's today. Michelle Clasen-Wuesthofen inherited a commitment to baking the best. She also trained with the best when she spent four years apprenticing at an award-winning bakery in her parents' homeland.

"It was one of the best places in Germany. The work was real intense, very spe-cific," says blue-eyed Michelle, who does-n't look old enough to be running a cor-poration, but sounds knowing and confi-dent enough to run a country. Michelle started out cutting fruit and eventually worked her way through all aspects of bakery production. "We had weekly rou-tines for each task. I really learned the importance of teamwork."

After her bakery training was complete, Michelle considered apprenticing in the chocolate-making business, too. But despite her innate sense of adventure, she chose to stick with baking and return home. "I think you can only specialize in one thing, can only do one thing well in life," she explains.

Clasen's Bakery practices what Michelle preaches about quality, teamwork, and focus. Take the torte department, for example, where pastry chefs Kim Rosen-berry and Judy Warren produce layered, European-style sponge cakes filled with buttercream and other luscious ingredi-ents. The two-person team is like the proverbial well-oiled machine, cranking out some 60 types of their specialty plus custom orders for weddings and other spe-cial occasions. When one baker is ill, the other one "simply works a little harder." Kim and Judy are so in tune with their work and each other that they fill in each other's sentences. It's hard to keep track of who's talking as they "co-describe" the construction of a Black Forest Whipped Cream Torte:

"The torte is assembled inside a metal ring. The first layer is chocolate sponge cake, then we add a kirsch-flavored syrup. Then comes cherry pie filling, and a layer of vanilla-flavored whipped cream. (It's stabilized with fond neutral, a kind of gelatin used by commercial bakers.) Next is cake again, the kirsch syrup, and some chocolate-flavored whipped cream. Then the torte is frozen to make it firm enough to work with. We remove the ring, using a propane torch to warm the sides. Then the sides are covered with whipped cream. We put chocolate shavings on the sides and in the middle. Then we pipe on whipped cream rosettes and add cherries."

The Black Forest Torte looks and tastes as good as it sounds. And it is just one of the hundreds of delightful creations that fill the aisles in the company's large, spotless store/cafe. Clasen's has the mouthwatering variety of a food court and the culinary excellence of a fine restaurant. That's what happens when you "hold yourselves to the highest standards."

Clasen's Quiche Lorraine with Swiss Cheese
8 servings

Quiche, like croissants, has outlived fads and the food police. It's been filled with everything from arugula to zucchini. It's been de-fatted and de-crusted, reworked and reviled. And just when you think it can't possibly survive, along comes a place like Clasen's to remind us what quiche really is: a classic. This is the real thing, and real men—as well as women and children—love to eat it.

1 cup heavy cream
1/2 cup milk
3 eggs
1/2 teaspoon powdered mustard
1/2 teaspoon salt
1/4 teaspoon pepper
dash of red cayenne pepper
1 1/2 cups (6 ounces) grated
    Wisconsin Swiss cheese
8 slices crisp-cooked bacon, crumbled
unbaked 9-inch pie crust (for
    recipes, see pages 101 and 118)

Heat oven to 375 degrees. Beat heavy cream, milk, eggs, and seasonings in a bowl. Sprinkle cheese and bacon into pie crust. Pour cream mixture over cheese. Bake until firm and lightly browned, 40-45 minutes. Serve warm.

Pear Frangipane Tart
8-10 servings

Pears are an elegant fruit and Clasen's treats them with dignity and class in this sophisticated European-style specialty. Frangipane (pronounced fronz-pahn) is French for a type of puff pastry, but here it refers to frangipane creme, a rum-flavored, flour-thickened custard.

If you use poached pears, you can substitute some of the poaching syrup for the melted apple jelly glaze.

Crust:
1 1/4 cups flour
1/2 teaspoon salt
1/2 cup (1 stick) cold butter, cut
    in small pieces
4-6 tablespoons ice water, divided

Filling:
1/2 cup (1 stick) butter, softened
1/2 cup sugar
1 cup or 1 can (8 ounces) marzipan
    (almond paste)
3 tablespoons rum
1 egg
1 teaspoon almond extract
1 tablespoon flour
8 small pear halves, poached* or
    canned and drained
1/2 cup ground almonds

Glaze:
apple jelly

To make crust: Mix flour and salt in bowl. Cut in butter until it resembles coarse crumbs. Toss in 3 tablespoons ice water with a fork. Toss in additional ice water, one tablespoon at a time, until dough begins to hold together. Turn onto large piece of plastic wrap; pull the wrap around dough to make a tight ball, then flatten to a thick disk. Chill at least two hours.

Heat oven to 350 degrees. Roll out dough on floured surface and line an ungreased 10-inch tart pan with it (use the kind with the removable bottom, if available, or any pan similar in size).

To make filling: Cream butter, sugar, and marzipan with electric mixer. Beat in rum, egg, almond extract, and flour. Spread filling evenly in crust. Slice pears crosswise but keep the slices together in the shape of pear halves. Arrange the sliced halves in a circle on top of filling, elongating them slightly for a fanned effect. Leave a little space in between the halves and a little space in the center of the tart. Sprinkle ground almonds between all the spaces and in the middle of the tart. Bake until golden, about 45 minutes. Cool 10 minutes.

While tart is cooling, gently melt a few tablespoons of apple jelly. Brush melted jelly over partially-cooled tart, including the crust. Cool to room temperature before serving.

To poach fresh pears: Combine 4 cups water with 1 1/3 cups sugar and 1/2 teaspoon vanilla extract; simmer 5 minutes. Peel and halve the pears. Cut out the cores (a grapefruit spoon or melon baller works well). Immerse pear halves in the syrup, cover, and simmer very gently until barely tender, 3-5 minutes. Remove lid; let pears cool in the liquid. Leave them immersed in the liquid until ready to use.

78. Confection Connection
952 W. Main St.
Sun Prairie, WI 53590
608-837-7606

•

Having It All

Here's a short list of what you'll find at Confection Connection: gourmet candies, pastries and baked goods, a lunch restaurant named Diana's, meeting/party room rental, private dinner parties, catering, a mail order business, and cooking classes. You don't really need a list, however, if you live in Sun Prairie. You already know that when it comes to food service, Confection Connection pretty much has it all. And whether you're after a birthday cake or a business lunch, you know who to call: Diana Konkle, the community food pro, the woman who built this culinary mini-empire.

Just don't mention the "pro" part to Diana.

"I'm not really a professional," she argues. "I never went to cooking school." Diana has high, coiffed black hair, erect posture, and impeccable attire. She can recite cookie ingredients by heart and teach plate decorating techniques to 200 people at a time. With customers she's cordial and competent, with students, knowledgeable, and with employees, a role model.

Sounds professional to me.

"It's been a kind of generational evolution," Diana says, meaning the success of her company and her own progress as an entrepreneur. At first, she claims she "wasn't courageous enough for a business." During the 1970s, Diana went from home economics teacher to "mom" to home craftmaker. Her handmade dolls and Christmas ornaments were so popular locally that up to 1000 sold in a day. "But

Diana Konkle excels at hand-decorated cookies and candies at Confection Connection.

I'm a people person. After the kids went to school, I had to talk to someone besides the dolls."

In 1981, on her mother's suggestion, Diana began selling handmade candies and offering candymaking supplies and classes. Thus Confection Connection was born. The Sun Prairie community seemed to take to it—and to Diana—like peanut butter to chocolate.

But soon, as more women worked outside the home, Diana realized that home crafting and candymaking were no longer in vogue. Again following an idea of her mother's, Diana took on a bigger risk and expanded into bakery production. "Homemade pies and such were still a family tradition people wanted. And it was a natural for me to start filling the shelves with what I had grown up with."

Diana had grown up, in fact, on a large farm, doing quantity baking and cooking for the field workers her father employed. Her dad had dreams of being a kind of "king farmer," she says. "He had a sense of adventure, a reaching-for-the-stars attitude. My father gave me the courage to think big and my mother gave me the basic skills and the creative ideas."

Diana made good use of the gifts. The bakery led to a tea room which led to a restaurant which led to catering; meanwhile, she expanded the cooking class schedule and product line, too.

Today, Confection Connection has numerous "signature items"—cinnamon rolls (from a recipe of Diana's grandmother), pies, wedding cakes, and the popular dessert trays that contain an assortment of bars, cookies, and candies. What Diana seems proudest of are her "specialties," whimsical, "hand-painted" candies in seasonal and holiday shapes and colors. The candies are also custom-made for patrons' special occasions. "My customers' home traditions have developed around these candies," she says, beaming. Indeed, in this town, Diana's goodies are often part of the picture no matter what the celebration. "We're a real Sun Prairie tradition."

But does Diana take credit for this? Of course not. "My family has been there, helping in every way," she emphasizes. She says manager Gillian Anderson "makes things efficient" and she couldn't do it without her. Regarding the staff, "I'm not the queen. We work together. We're a very satisfied team."

A team led by a courageous professional who started making dolls and now makes everything from soup to chocolate-dipped nuts.

Jenny Lynns
20-24 confections

Swedish soprano Jenny Lind, who debuted in 1838, was considered the greatest opera singer of her time. I wish I knew how these cereal-based pastries came to be named after her. (It's unlikely she was fond of boxed breakfast cereal: it hadn't been invented yet.) Diana Konkle says the recipe passed around her family for years and was usually prepared in a pan then cut into bars. As for this "drop" version (also newly spelled), she's "a little embarrassed about serving them at the bakery—since they're so easy." All I can say is, "Move over, Rice Krispies Treats."

1 cup light corn syrup
1 cup sugar
1 1/2 cups peanut butter
6 heaping cups lightly toasted rice cereal flakes (Special K cereal is recommended)
1 1/2 cups (about 9 ounces) semi-sweet chocolate chips
for garnish, use any of the following: fresh raspberries, sour cherry balls, maraschino cherries, M&M candies, or jelly beans

Line two large baking sheets with waxed paper. Combine corn syrup and sugar in large, non-metal bowl. Heat in microwave to dissolve sugar, stirring occasionally, 4-5 minutes. (Alternatively, combine corn syrup and sugar in large saucepan and simmer 3-5 minutes.) Stir in peanut butter until well blended. Quickly stir in cereal.

Drop by large spoonfuls onto waxed paper and shape each into a 3-inch round. Make a small indentation or "nest" in the center of each (for the garnish). Let stand until firm.

Melt chocolate chips in double boiler over simmering water or in microwave. Spread bottoms of the confections with a layer of chocolate; return to waxed paper, chocolate side down. Spoon small dabs of the remaining chocolate into the indentations; place garnishes in the chocolate-filled centers. Chilling the confections will quickly set the chocolate but they should be eaten at room temperature.

Snickerdoodles
Makes 4 1/2-5 dozen cookies

This chewy, homespun cookie a la Confection Connection is a Christmas specialty of the Pennsylvania Dutch, who sometimes add walnuts and/or raisins to the dough. The recipe is as old and reliable as the hills.

1 cup vegetable shortening, at room temperature
1 1/2 cups sugar
2 eggs
2 3/4 cups flour
2 teaspoons cream of tartar
1 teaspoon baking soda
1/2 teaspoon salt
for coating: a mixture of 2 tablespoons sugar and 2 teaspoons cinnamon

Cream shortening, sugar, and eggs. Sift together the flour, cream of tartar, baking soda, and salt; stir into sugar mixture. Chill dough.

Heat oven to 400 degrees. Roll chilled dough into balls the size of small shell-on walnuts. Roll each ball in sugar/cinnamon mixture. Place balls 2 inches apart on ungreased baking sheets. Bake until lightly browned but still soft, 7-8 minutes. The cookies will "crack" on top, like gingersnaps. Cool on wire racks or in the pan.

"Basics" Pecan Pie a la Confection Connection
8 servings

The "basics" are a handmade crust, fresh nuts, and real butter. If you want to get fancy, decorate the outer rim of the pie with whole pecans before baking.

4 eggs
1 1/3 cups light corn syrup
2/3 cup light brown sugar
5 tablespoons melted butter, cooled a few minutes
1 teaspoon vanilla extract
1/4 teaspoon salt
1 cup chopped pecans
unbaked 9-inch pie crust (see next recipe or one on page 118)

Heat oven to 350 degrees. Beat eggs, corn syrup, brown sugar, butter, vanilla, and salt until well mixed. Stir in pecans. Pour into pie crust. Bake on center rack until toothpick inserted near center comes out clean, 50-60 minutes, covering pie with aluminum foil about half-way through the baking to prevent excess darkening. Cool completely before serving.

Two-Crust Pie Crust

Makes two single-crust 9-inch pie crusts
(or one double crust)

Whoever coined the phrase "easy as pie" wasn't talking about the crust. Do you mix with a fork or your hands? Do you chill the dough? How much flour to fat? Then there's the question of butter versus shortening, which can spark a debate that keeps two professional bakers busy through a night shift. Here's the all-shortening version from Confection Connection, which, if handled lightly, will produce a flaky crust. Another method (see page 118) uses part butter for flavor.

    2 cups flour
    1 teaspoon salt
    2/3 cup (10 tablespoons) chilled
        vegetable shortening
    5-6 tablespoons ice water

Mix flour and salt. Use a pastry cutter or food processor (with pulse button) to cut in shortening until mixture resembles fine cornmeal. Sprinkle water over mixture a tablespoon at a time as you toss mixture with a fork. Briefly work dough with your fingers and gather it into a ball (use additional water only if necessary). Divide dough in two; place on lightly floured surface. Shape each piece into a thick, flat round and roll out into an 11-inch circle. Arrange rolled crusts in two 9-inch pie pans; roll edges under to form a rim and crimp as desired. Chill crusts before using; they may also be frozen.

> ### 79. Eagle Baking Co.
> **318 N. Wall St.**
> **Eagle River, WI 54521**
> **715-479-1545**
> •

North Woods Pro

The title "Certified Master Baker" is held by just a few dozen people in the United States. Chris Boyd is one of them. Master bakers have years of management experience and must pass rigorous written and practical tests like the ones Chris took at the prestigious Culinary Institute of America in Hyde Park, New York.

What's a culinary pro like Chris doing in the North woods? He says he "wants to take care of the locals." Raised in Eagle River, a town known for its tourism, Chris left to train and gain experience in baking and eventually returned to his hometown to "relax and not work as hard." He decided to open his own bakery, however, after a market study of the area told him that's what locals desired. "Bread and rolls were what they wanted," says Chris, who proceeded to develop recipes for crusty breads like onion-dill, sauerkraut rye, sun-dried tomato, buttercrust, three seed, jalapeño cheddar, and English muffin bread. It's no surprise that his breads are immensely popular with locals, as well as with the droves of visitors who swell Eagle River's population during tourist season. So much for not working so hard.

Eagle Baking Company, the shop Chris and his wife Trudy own and operate, also offers a full line of cakes, pies, doughnuts, and deli sandwiches made from their specialty breads.

A master baker in Eagle River? The North woods never had it so good.

Chris Boyd's English Muffin Bread
2 loaves

Chris Boyd is one of a few dozen people in the U.S. who is a "certified master baker."

Master baker Chris Boyd uses bread flour and old-fashioned cake yeast—a whole two-ounce cake of it—to produce a very yeasty dough that forms the familiar large pores of English muffins. It's an easy bread to make, especially if you have a food processor outfitted with a dough attachment for the mixing. Before baking, says Chris, the dough must be "docked," that is, pierced with holes to release gas. The bread is delicious spread with fresh butter and drizzled with honey.

Unbleached bread flour and cake yeast are available at many larger grocery stores. Look for cake yeast in the refrigerated cases; be sure it is fresh—it should have a freshness date stamped on it—and keep it cold until it is used.

3 3/4 cups unbleached bread flour
1/4 cup sugar
2 ounces cake yeast
2 teaspoons salt
1 1/2 cups warm water
additional bread flour for work surface
cornmeal

Place all ingredients except additional flour and cornmeal in food processor fitted with dough attachment. Using the pulse button, mix until ingredients are combined, 10-15 seconds. Scrape down any unmixed ingredients and mix again, using the pulse button, until dough forms into a ball, about 20 seconds. The dough will be soft and sticky. Turn it onto a well-floured surface and knead it, working in a little additional flour if necessary, until surface is no longer sticky and dough bounces back when pressed lightly, 4-5 minutes. Place dough in large, oiled bowl, cover with plastic wrap, and let rise in very warm place until doubled in bulk, about 1 hour.

Punch down dough, divide in two, cover, and let rise a second time in a warm spot about 20 minutes.

Shape dough into two rounds. Brush loaves all over with water and roll them in cornmeal. Place in pie tins. Using a slender skewer, poke 20-30 holes into the loaves, going in about half-way. Allow bread to rise once more in a warm place, about 30 minutes.

Meanwhile, heat oven to 365 degrees. Bake bread loaves 25 minutes. Cool completely before serving.

Swedish Limpa Bread
2 loaves

Fresh, flavorful, chewy, good bread is the sign of a good bakery no matter where it is located. Here's a classic from Grandma's Swedish Bakery housed in a resort near the northern tip of the Door peninsula (see page 133). Wanda Peterson Mango chronicles family traditions in Grandma's Home Kitchen *(Wan'a Press, 1994), where this recipe was first published. When young Wanda used to slice bread for the family, Grandpa Peterson always reminded her about the old Swedish custom that says you can't marry until you learn how to cut bread straight.*

1 cup milk
1 cup lukewarm water
3 teaspoons (1 1/2 packages) active
    dry yeast
2 tablespoons vegetable shortening,
    softened
3 tablespoons molasses
3 tablespoons brown sugar
2 tablespoons grated orange peel or
    orange marmalade
1 tablespoon honey
1 tablespoon salt
1/2 tablespoon caraway seeds
1/2 teaspoon anise or fennel seeds
1 1/2 cups rye flour
3-3 1/2 cups all-purpose flour

Scald milk. Mix milk and lukewarm water in large mixing bowl and cool to warm temperature (105-110 degrees). Stir in yeast; let stand until yeast begins to bubble, about 10 minutes. Mix in shortening, molasses, brown sugar, orange peel or marmalade, honey, salt, caraway, and anise or fennel. Stir in rye flour; beat well. Add half of the all-purpose flour and beat. Continue to add flour until dough has a satiny look and will not easily absorb any more flour.

Place on floured surface and knead firmly, adding flour as needed, until dough bounces back when pressed, 7-10 minutes. Place dough in oiled bowl, turning it to oil the top, also. Cover with clean cloth; let stand in very warm place until doubled in size, 45-60 minutes.

Turn dough onto floured surface and divide in half. Cover and let stand 10 minutes.

Grease a large, heavy baking sheet. Form dough into two rounds and place the rounds on baking sheet. Make 3 slits, 1/2-inch deep, with sharp knife in top of each loaf. Cover and let rise until doubled, 25-30 minutes.

Heat oven to 375 degrees while dough is rising. Bake bread until crust is light brown and loaf has hollow sound when top is tapped, 35-40 minutes. Cool on racks.

---

80. Earth Crust Bakery
633 Second St.
Stevens Point, WI 54481
715-341-4155
•

Naturally Good

Stevens Point is a Polish town; you can tell from names like Kostka and Dzikoski prominent on trade signs, and from the fact that another bakery in town specializes in jelly *ponczaks* and homemade *kluski* noodles. Despite the old-world influence, however, there's another, very different kind of bakery that's popular with locals.

Earth Crust Bakery's preservative- and additive-free breads and pastries are made from organic flours and natural ingredients. Bakers Denise Brennecke and Claire Kerbel use local products such as honey, pesto, and dairy goods whenever possible. The healthful approach even extends to their power supply—solar panels furnish most of the bakery's electricity.

But the two partners also care about their customers' *mental* health, and that's why their goodies are so mouth-wateringly delicious. The weekly schedule includes items like honey bran bread and whole grain cinnamon rolls. The bakery is housed within the Stevens Point Area Food Cooperative, which celebrated its 25th anniversary in 1997. "We're not considered so funky or hippie anymore," says Denise. "It's surprising how many people have bought into [our style]."

Earth Crust products are available on the co-op's shelves every day. On Thursdays the bakery itself is open for lunch, and regulars flock in for scones, biscotti, fresh vegetable turnovers, puff pastry pizza, and other sweet and savory pastries.

In Stevens Point, thank goodness, there's room for the traditional and the alternative.

Pine Nut Biscotti

Makes 1 1/2-2 dozen

"Regular" ingredients can be used to make this unusual, tender biscotti, but to make it the Earth Crust way, use organic flour, eggs, and lemons as well as turbinado sugar, a coarse-grained, beige-colored crystal containing the molasses portion of sugar. Like all the ingredients used here, it can be purchased at health cooperatives and natural food stores.

2/3 cup pine nuts
4 tablespoons unsalted butter, softened
3/4 cup turbinado sugar or brown sugar
2 eggs
2 tablespoons finely grated lemon zest
    (grate only the yellow part of
    the rind)
2 tablespoons fresh lemon juice
1 3/4 cups unbleached organic
    white flour
1/2 cup unbleached organic whole
    wheat flour
1 1/2 teaspoons baking powder
1/4 teaspoon salt

Heat oven to 350 degrees. Spread pine nuts in a pan and toast in oven until golden brown, 6-10 minutes. Watch closely to prevent burning. Reduce oven heat to 325 degrees. Cool nuts.

Grease a large baking sheet or line it with parchment paper. Cream butter and turbinado sugar in bowl until light-colored and fluffy. Beat in eggs, lemon zest, and lemon juice. Mix flours, baking powder, and salt in separate bowl. Stir flour mixture into butter mixture. Fold in nuts. Using floured hands, shape dough into a log approximately 1 inch high and 14 inches long. Dough will be soft; it's okay to work a little more flour into it if it's too soft to handle. Place on baking sheet and bake 25 minutes. Remove from oven, reduce heat to 300 degrees.

Cool log 10 minutes. Place on cutting board and, using very sharp or serrated knife, carefully slice log into 1/2-inch slices. Arrange slices upright on the baking sheet, return to oven and bake 25-30 minutes longer. Cool thoroughly. Store in air tight container.

81. Eddie's Bake Shop
400 W. Main St.
Merrill, WI 54452
715-536-7463
82.
221 S. Main St.
Medford, WI 54451
715-748-3652

•

Doughnut Dreams

When Barbara and Joe Polak of Maple Hollow (see page 154) lived in an apartment near Eddie's Bake Shop in downtown Merrill, the smell of bakery filled their dreams, for Eddie Miller worked at night. Each morning, says Barbara, "Joe would wake up and wonder, 'Why am I so hungry for doughnuts?!'"

Eddie still works while the rest of the world sleeps, as he has for nearly 50 years, and he still makes central Wisconsin locals hungry for his doughnuts and other goodies. Each night, all night, dressed in a clean, white t-shirt, white cotton shorts, white apron, and white socks and tennis shoes, pausing only for brief coffee breaks, Eddie does what he has loved to do since he was a kid.

"I baked on the farm where I grew up, mostly cakes, pies, oatmeal date bars. I still make all that here, too." He attended baking school in the army and opened his first bakery in 1950.

His nightly routine begins around 9 p.m. when he heats a deep-fat fryer and begins mixing cake batter. Eddie uses long wooden rods that look like giant chopsticks to flip frycakes in the bubbling oil. For his rainbow marble cake he mixes food coloring into the batter with his hands. He slides the cake pans into a rotating oven and pulls huge blobs of yeast-raised dough from a bulging bucket. The blobs will eventually become long Johns, Persians, and filled and glazed doughnuts. But not before he has mixed bread dough, hauled cookies from the oven, washed dishes, and intertwined a multitude of tasks with grace, efficiency, and strength.

Eddie gets assistance—and company—when his wife Betty joins him in the middle of the night. Together they supply products for their Merrill bakery and for one in Medford.

The worst part, says Eddie, is "you live opposite everyone else. When you work nights, you miss your kids' school activities, it's hard to get involved socially."

And the best part? "The work," he says simply.

Apple Hickory Nut Spice Cake

16-24 servings

This simple cake has the same homey feeling as Eddie Miller's bakeries and like them, its apple-spicy aroma may make your neighbors hungry to pay a visit. I adapted this from a cake recipe that used pears instead of apples and enjoy it both ways. It's fairly dense, almost bar-like, and could be spread with a cream cheese frosting or dusted with powdered sugar. Pecans may be substituted for the hickory nuts.

2 cups flour
1 1/4 cups sugar
1 1/2 teaspoons baking soda
1 1/2 teaspoons cinnamon
1/2 teaspoon ground cloves
1/2 teaspoon ground ginger
1/4 teaspoon nutmeg
1/2 teaspoon salt
4 cups peeled, finely diced apples
1/2 cup chopped hickory nuts
1/2 cup (1 stick) butter, melted
2 eggs, beaten
cream cheese frosting or
    powdered sugar

Heat oven to 325 degrees. Grease and flour a 9-by-13-inch baking pan. Sift flour, sugar, baking soda, spices, and salt into a large bowl. Stir in apples, nuts, butter, and eggs until just combined. Spread in pan. Bake 50-60 minutes, until cake springs back when pressed in center. Cool. Frost or sprinkle with powdered sugar.

---

83. Everix Bakery
120 W. Second St.
Fond du Lac, WI 54935
920-921-2250

•

A Legacy From Scratch

The company has three locations in Fond du Lac, but ask a resident where Everix Bakery is and you'll be steered to the proud-looking brick building that stands where Second Street intersects old Military Road, one of the oldest routes in the state. Which is appropriate, since Everix's may be one of the oldest bakeries in the state. Built more than 100 years ago, it was originally a wholesale bakery called Snow's. In 1934 it became a retail-only business when Richard Everix, who hailed from Chilton and whose ancestors had been bakers in Belgium, set up shop in Fond du Lac, where Everix's is now the oldest bakery in town.

It's a local institution for more than its age, however. This is the real thing, a scratch bakery that uses virtually no mixes, bases, or frozen products. You'll find the usual assortment of prod-

Mary Nelson is up to her elbows at Everix Bakery, Fond du Lac.

ucts—doughnuts, breads, pies, cookies, etc.—and you'll find they are done very well. But Everix's also has a range of ethnic, regional, seasonal, and trademark specialties that put the business in another category altogether. There's kolache, a Bohemian fruit-filled pastry. There's semmel rolls and peanut squares, both area favorites. When Colorado Mountain Lion peaches are in season, there's fresh peach coffeecake and cobbler. And there's Everix's signature cake—the Brown-eyed Susan—a doubled-frosted marble cake domed with marshmallow icing and drizzled with caramel frosting.

The person behind this variety and quality is Ellen Everix. In 1982, this trim, tiny woman married Richard Everix, Jr., who had bought the business from his father. Soon after, Ellen took on the heavy load of management at the bakery when her husband fell ill with a vascular disease. Too disabled to bake, Richard wrote the *Richard Everix Formula Book*, a collection of 700 recipes used at the bakery, while Ellen handled the day-to-day operations. They donated the book to the Retail Bakers Association, which in turn funds scholarships with some of the proceeds. Richard died in 1994 and Ellen is still at the helm.

She is very clear about maintaining Everix's reputation for excellence. "That's my name. You have to feel connected when it's your name."

"Our cakes are very good," she specifies quietly and firmly. "Of all the Danish I've eaten wherever I go, we make the best and I don't just say that."

But you don't have to take the word of the owner. Cake decorator Mary Nelson, who at one time managed a grocery store bakery, says: "I was used to seeing things come out of buckets. When I started working [at Everix], I couldn't believe how much they make from scratch here. We do fresh buttercream every day. The fruits are fresh or frozen, not canned. The eclair shells are from scratch. We even roast our own peanuts." She says the angel food cakes are her favorite. "We use fresh egg whites and sift the flour three times."

Dishwasher Mary Jane Luehring agrees: "The angel food is the best. I know because I wash those tins all the time!" Mary Jane is a dark-haired sparkplug who has been hand-scrubbing pots and pans at Everix Bakery for more than a decade. "I got hired at [age] 63. I didn't think they'd hire me—there were lots of applications. I don't know! Ellen didn't think I could lift the Hobart bowls. But I'm 73 and still doing it." She grins and adds, "I flirt with the delivery man, too!"

Ellen smiles as she remembers interviewing Mary Jane. "She came all dressed up, high heels and all." Why did she hire the older woman? "She kept bugging me!" Ellen says this with the same affectionate pride she voices for many other valued employees. She mentions general manager Kristi Smith, two 25-year veterans of the bakery, and the high-schoolers who start out clerking or packaging and become mainstays.

In addition to its long-standing reputation, Everix Bakery endures as an area landmark. The two-story building fills a downtown corner and announces its identity in tall white letters that span the top. Inside, huge, heavy-duty mixing bowls and human-high stacks of battered metal baking sheets stand in high-ceilinged rooms. (According to Ellen, most of the Hobart dough mixers have been around longer than the employees). Natural light and creaking hardwood floors accent the work areas, which are old but clean. And very active. Indeed, if the bakery wasn't in operation 24 hours a day, one could well imagine the building and its contents operating as a living history museum.

Angel Food Cake with Caramel Nut Icing
12 servings

Moist, airy, homemade angel food cake is a rare treat these days, for it does take a certain amount of effort. Once you make it with Everix's outstanding caramel icing, however, you'll be making it again soon.

Separate the eggs when they are cold, but allow plenty of time for the egg whites to come to room temperature before beating them. This will ensure maximum volume. Also, take care that no egg yolk is left in the whites or they won't whip properly. Finally, both the bowl you use to beat the egg whites and the baking tin must be spotlessly clean and dry.

1 1/2 cups sugar, divided
1 teaspoon cream of tartar
1/2 teaspoon salt
1 cup sifted cake flour
12 large egg whites
2 teaspoons vanilla extract

Heat oven to 350 degrees. Sift 1/2 cup of the sugar, cream of tartar, and salt into small bowl. Sift cake flour and remaining 1 cup sugar into separate bowl; do this at least three times, holding the sifter high to incorporate as much air as possible. In a third bowl—it should be large, clean, and dry—beat egg whites at medium speed until foamy. Gradually add sifted sugar/cream of tartar mixture to the whites. Gradually add the vanilla. Raise the speed on the mixer to high and continue beating until mixture holds wet, stiff peaks. Gently fold cake flour mixture into egg whites with a rubber spatula.

Scoop batter into clean, dry 10-inch tube pan (or two loaf pans) and place in oven. Bake until area around the tube of the pan is dry to the touch and cake springs back when pressed lightly in the center, about 50 minutes (less for loaf pans). Invert pan to cool the cake upside down, using cups to prop it up (some pans have legs for this purpose). Cool completely. To remove cake from the pan, gently pull cake from sides, bottom, and center of pan with a fork. Place on serving platter. Spoon warm Caramel Nut Icing (see recipe next page) over top of cake, allowing some to drip over the sides. The icing will set within a few minutes. Serve at room temperature.

Everix Caramel Nut Icing
Makes enough to frost one cake

1/2 cup tightly packed brown sugar
4 tablespoons shortening
1 1/2 tablespoons butter
1/4 cup milk
1/4 teaspoon salt
1 1/4 cups powdered sugar
1/2 teaspoon vanilla extract
2 tablespoons finely chopped
   walnuts

Combine brown sugar, shortening, butter, milk, and salt in saucepan. Bring to rolling boil over medium heat. Turn off heat; cool mixture 5-8 minutes. Stir in powdered sugar and vanilla; beat until no sugar lumps remain. Stir in walnuts. This icing should be used warm (it can be gently reheated) and thinned with additional milk if necessary.

Sweet & Tart Cherry-Orange Sauce
12 servings

Angel food cake is light, absorbent, and sweetly bland; it begs for toppings, of which the possibilities are endless. I developed this one to be as fat-free as angel food cake but to complement it with deep flavor and color. The cherries may be fresh or frozen and thawed.

2 cups pitted tart cherries
2 cups pitted dark sweet
   (or bing) cherries
3 seedless oranges, peels cut off,
   "meat" diced
1 tablespoon orange liqueur (optional)
1/2 - 2/3 cup sugar
2-3 teaspoons arrowroot

Combine all ingredients except arrowroot in bowl. Stir gently until sugar dissolves. Let stand 15-20 minutes. If you've used fresh fruit, you may not have to thicken the juices. If you've used thawed cherries, there will be a lot of juice: it can be thickened by combining arrowroot with some of the juice from the fruit, bringing the mixture to a low simmer in a saucepan, and stirring until thickened. Don't allow it to come to a boil. Thicken further, if desired, with more cherry juice (cherries will continue to give off more juice) and arrowroot. Gently stir cherries and thickened juices together. Cool and chill. To serve, ladle cherry sauce over slices of angel food cake.

**84. Fox Valley
Cheesecake Company**
**100 W. Main St.
Winneconne, WI 54986
920-582-9921**
•

If You Love Cheesecake, Say 'I Do'

You've heard of "38 Flavors"; well, the Fox Valley Cheesecake Company has 39, including piña colada, white chocolate raspberry, cherry cobbler, fudge almond, eggnog, and praline. Fox Valley cheesecakes are preservative-free and are baked daily using only natural dairy products, heavy cream, sweet butter, and Ambrosia chocolate.

Company owner Robin Lucareli, originally from Milwaukee and of Italian descent, says she has a "genetic passion for good food." Her father was a liquor salesman who would take her to elegant restaurants that were on his route; here Robin learned about fine dining and food service operations. Add a fine arts degree (her favorite medium in school was a soft sculpting material) to these earlier influences, and you've got a woman uniquely trained to produce exquisite-tasting, handcrafted, theme cheesecakes.

Robin's wedding customers can choose their dream cake from an album of elaborately decorated cheesecakes, or can hire her to come up with an original design. At the wedding of one fish-loving couple, for example, tall, see-through tubes that held live Siamese fighting fish were part of the arrangement. But you don't have to be getting married to enjoy one of Robin's specialties; the "plain" round ones are available by mail order, from area food stores, and from the corner store in downtown Winneconne.

Says Robin: "We think it's the most elegant way in the world to drink your milk."

Raspberry Glaze
About 2 cups

Robin Lucareli says the recipe for her famous cheesecake is a trade secret, but she does offer the following fruit topping recipe. Try it on Judy's Cheesecake, below, or Angel Food Cake, page 107.

2 cups fresh or frozen raspberries
3/4 cup sugar
1 1/2 tablespoons cornstarch

Mix raspberries, sugar, and cornstarch with 3/4 cup water in saucepan. Cook over medium heat, stirring often, until mixture reaches low boil. Strain through fine mesh strainer, pressing out as much liquid as possible from the seeds. Cool to room temperature and refrigerate. Strain again before each use, adding warm water if consistency is too thick.

Judy's Cheesecake
12-16 servings

When I was little, cheesecakes were jelled, baked in square pans, and usually served with fruit. Today, the fashion is round, very dense, and flavored with everything from espresso beans to pumpkin puree. Still, one of the best cheesecakes I ever tasted was different than either kind: it was a plain, tallish affair that had a bright, lemony flavor and a lighter, slightly cake-like texture I remember to this day, despite it being served to me more than 20 years ago. The baker was friend Judy Johnson, an early culinary influence who, lucky for me, saved the recipe from a Family Circle magazine all these years. It was originally from John Clancy's Baking Book *(Popular Library) and is slightly altered here.*

Both texture and taste seem to be at their best after a day or two of "aging." And some advice: bake this on a cool, dry day. Separate the eggs while they are cold, but allow the whites to come to room temperature before whipping them in a clean, dry bowl.

1 1/3 cups graham cracker crumbs
2 tablespoons plus 1 1/4 cups sugar, divided
3 tablespoons butter, melted
3 packages (8 ounces each) cream cheese, softened
6 eggs, whites separated from yolks
1 pint sour cream
1/2 cup flour
2 teaspoons vanilla extract
grated rind of 1 lemon (grate only the yellow part of the rind)
juice of 1/2 lemon

To make crust: Grease a 9-inch springform pan that is 3 inches deep; place on a large square of aluminum foil and fold foil up round sides of pan. Combine graham cracker crumbs, 2 tablespoons sugar, and melted butter in bowl; mix well. Press three-quarters of the mixture into bottom and partially up the sides of the pan. Chill crust while making filling. Reserve remaining crumb mixture.

Heat oven to 350 degrees. Beat cream cheese in large bowl with electric beaters at medium speed until very soft, about 3 minutes. Gradually beat in remaining 1 1/4 cups sugar until mixture is light and fluffy, about 5 minutes. Beat in egg yolks one at a time. Mix in sour cream, flour, vanilla, grated lemon rind, and lemon juice at low speed.

Using clean, dry beaters, beat egg whites at medium speed until they hold stiff peaks. Using a rubber spatula, gently fold whipped whites into cheese mixture until just blended. Pour into prepared pan. Bake until top is golden and cheesecake is set, about 1 hour and 15 minutes. Turn off oven and let cheesecake cool in oven for one hour. Then remove to a wire rack and let cool to room temperature. Sprinkle remaining crumbs on top. Chill thoroughly (preferably overnight) before serving. Serve plain, with Rasberry Glaze (page 109), or with Sweet and Tart Cherry-Orange sauce (page 108).

---

85. Hometowne Bakery
615 S. Chestnut St.
Platteville, WI 53818
608-348-6655

•

The Gathering Place

Owner-baker Gary Engelke is a tall man with caramel-colored eyes, a brisk manner, and a friendly word for every customer. Having worked in bakeries since he was 14 years old, he knows what his customers like. "Doughnuts," says Gary. "Glazed, raised, apple fritters, and cream-filled long Johns. They sell out everyday." His Hometowne Bakery also has a full line of cookies, coffeecakes, pastries, special occasion cakes, and daily breads (including choices like dill bread, dark rye, and a dense, delicious sourdough).

But you get more than baked goods at Hometowne. Gary thinks of it as a kind of community center, where regulars are encouraged to gather and spend part of their day. "There's the teachers group at 5:00 a.m. and the golfers who come around nine every morning. Also the 'midnight run,' a group of [University of Wisconsin-Platteville] students who show up when the library closes." Gary provides personalized mugs in cherry red and five kinds of serve-yourself coffee so that customers can fill up as often as they like. A glassed-in cake-decorating center offers in-house entertainment and, for rainy days, there's even a drive-up window.

Another Hometowne specialty is the Veggie Pasty, Gary's re-make of the Cornish pasty, a savory, hand-held pie that was daily fare for the immigrant miners who worked in the area during the 19th century. The classic beef-and-potatoes turnover is now served in restaurants throughout the area. Gary's pie is stuffed with fresh vegetables, but for flavor and flaky texture he still makes his super-tender crust the traditional way—with lard.

Hometowne Veggie Pasty
6 extra-large pasties

The pasties served at Hometowne Bakery come with a cheese sauce, but tomato salsa or a sweet-sour chili sauce are also recommended.

Crust:
2 cups all-purpose flour
1 cup cake flour
3 tablespoons buttermilk powder
(optional)

2 teaspoons salt
1 cup (8 ounces) chilled lard, cut
   into small pieces
about 8 tablespoons ice water

Filling:
1 cup finely chopped onion
1 cup finely chopped cauliflower
1 cup finely chopped broccoli
1 cup shredded carrots
1 1/2 cups shredded potatoes
1/2 cup sour cream
1 cup (3-4 ounces) shredded aged
   cheddar cheese
2 tablespoons bottled table spice
   (use the Wisconsin brand called
   Curt's or mix your own combination
   of garlic salt and dried herbs)
salt and pepper to taste

Also:
egg wash: 1 egg mixed with
   3 tablespoons water
topping: cheese sauce, spicy salsa, or
   bottled chili sauce

To make crusts: Mix flours, buttermilk powder, and salt in large bowl; cut in lard until size of small peas. Add ice water one tablespoon at a time while tossing mixture with large fork. Add just enough water to form a fairly damp dough. Dump dough onto large sheet of plastic wrap; use plastic wrap to gather dough into a tight ball. Chill thoroughly, one hour or longer.

To make filling: Combine all ingredients in large bowl.

To form and bake pasties: Divide chilled dough into 6 portions on floured surface. Form portions into balls and roll each one out into a 7-inch circle, using additional flour to prevent sticking. Divide filling among the dough circles, leaving a 1-inch edge all around filling. Fold dough over filling to form half-moons and press top edges securely onto bottom edges all around filling. Crimp to seal tightly. Brush excess flour off pasties. Line a large baking pan with parchment paper or aluminum foil; place pasties on pan. (May be refrigerated at this point until ready to bake.)

To bake pasties: Heat oven to 375 degrees. Brush pasties with egg wash. Bake until golden, 45-50 minutes. Serve piping hot with choice of topping.

---

86. Kathy's On The Square
1701 Dunlap Ave.
Marinette, WI 54143
715-732-1141
•

Dream Works

When Kathy Sohr was considering opening her own bakery, she spoke with the owners of a well-established bakery in Green Bay to get their advice. "Don't do it," she was told. Warned about the tremendous amount of work involved, she went ahead with it anyway.

"It was a dream," she explains, then admits with a wan smile: "But it sometimes becomes a nightmare. Now I tell others 'don't do it!'" Kathy is a tall, resolute woman with red hair and pale blue eyes. She works a minimum of 12 hours a day—during regular business times, that is. During the Christmas season, she has been known to bake 'round the clock, hauling out a twin-size mattress that she wedges between bakery counters and sleeps on for a couple of hours each night.

Kathy was a medical technician and freelance caterer who often thought about opening her own pastry shop when a restoration project in downtown Marinette gave her the opportunity she had been dreaming about. Her husband Fran transformed part of an old warehouse, one of a cluster of buildings being renovated, into an upscale bakery with high ceilings and exposed brick walls. The one-room bakery opened in 1993 but quickly expanded to add a second kitchen, a dining room, and office and storage space.

Kathy badly needed the extra space to keep up with the demand for her cheesecakes, pastries, cakes, and lunch service. "It's all fresh," she says to explain why her products are a hit in the community. "I don't freeze anything. We make our own buttercream frosting. Our cheesecakes are from scratch and we use whole cream cheese, whole eggs, butter, real sour cream."

She and cake decorator Karen Baumgartner may be best known for their special occasion products, including custom-designed, tiered wedding cakes and a wide assortment of Christmas cookies. Karen's decorating is so detailed and realistic that a customer once saved a rose from the top of a cake, thinking the flower was porcelain. "She didn't know [it was frosting] until it melted when she tried to wash it," says Karen.

Wedding cakes are works of art at Kathy's on the Square, Marinette.

Pecan Shortbread Cookies
6 dozen cookies

Six dozen may seem like a lot of cookies to home bakers, but at a commercial bakery, it hardly makes enough to fill a single counter shelf. Still, at Kathy's On The Square, Kathy Sohr hand-rolls and bakes all her cookies in small batches. "I do it like you do in your kitchen," she says. Actually, I think she does it better.

1 1/2 cups (3 sticks) butter, softened
1 cup powdered sugar
2 egg yolks
1 tablespoon vanilla extract
3 cups flour
72 pecan halves

Heat oven to 325 degrees. Using electric beaters, beat butter at medium speed until light and fluffy, about 5 minutes. Add powdered sugar and beat 2 minutes. Beat in egg yolks one at a time. Beat in vanilla. Beat or stir in flour until just blended. Drop by tablespoonful (that's about 3 teaspoons of dough) onto ungreased baking sheets, then roll each spoonful into a ball. Top each cookie with a pecan half, pressing it very lightly into the dough. Bake until cookie bottoms are very light gold in color, 10-12 minutes. Cool in the pans or on a wire rack.

Mexican Wedding Cakes
4-6 dozen cookies

Kathy Sohr's Mexican wedding cakes have crumbly tenderness and real, melt-in-your-mouth butter flavor. "One of my customers told me that she never knew how bad her own cookies were until she tasted mine."

1 cup (2 sticks) butter, softened
2 cups flour
2 cups minced pecans
1/4 cup sugar
1 tablespoon vanilla extract
1 cup powdered sugar

Heat oven to 350 degrees. Place all ingredients except powdered sugar in large bowl. Using electric beaters, mix the ingredients at low speed until blended, then mix at medium speed until mixture is fluffy and clings to the side of the bowl, about 4 minutes. Drop by tablespoonful onto ungreased baking sheets, then roll each spoonful into a ball. Bake until bottoms are light brown, about 10-12 minutes. Cool on pans. Roll cookies in powdered sugar.

Pumpkin Cheesecake with Mocha Top & Bottom
12-14 servings

There is seemingly no end to the possibilities for cheesecake variations at Kathy's On The Square and while this recipe isn't one of hers, it's offered in her spirit of "cheesecake creativity." There will be cracks in this one, but after baking and chilling it, the top is pressed to even out the surface, a smooth glaze is added, and the results are picture-perfect.

5 tablespoons butter, divided
1 1/2 cups finely crushed chocolate
    graham crackers
3 tablespoons finely ground
    coffee beans
3 packages (each 8 ounces) neufchâtel
    or cream cheese, softened
1 cup sugar
5 eggs
2 cups cooked pumpkin puree or 1 can
    (16 ounces) solid pack pumpkin
2 teaspoons vanilla extract
2/3 cup (4 ounces) semi-sweet
    chocolate chips
4 tablespoons hot strong coffee
chocolate-covered coffee beans or
    chocolate-covered raisins

Heat oven to 350 degrees. Melt 3 tablespoons of the butter; combine with crushed grahams and ground coffee. Press into bottom and partially up the sides of a 9-inch springform pan. Bake 10 minutes. Cool thoroughly.

Cream neufchâtel or cream cheese with electric beaters at medium speed several minutes. Beat in sugar 3 minutes. Beat in eggs one at a time. Beat in pumpkin and vanilla. Pour filling into crust. Bake 70-75 minutes, or until instant thermometer inserted in center reads 160 degrees. Cool cheesecake to room temperature then chill thoroughly, preferably overnight.

Melt chocolate chips and remaining 2 tablespoons butter in double boiler. Remove from heat; whisk lightly, then whisk in hot coffee. Cool 10 minutes. Press top of chilled cheesecake to even out surface and "mend" any cracks. Spread chocolate over cheesecake.

Rim the cheesecake with chocolate-covered coffee beans or raisins. Chill to set topping. Run sharp knife around edges of cheesecake to remove from the pan. Serve chilled or at room temperature.

---

87. Krista's Kitchen
947 W. Wisconsin St.
Portage, WI 53901
608-742-0407
•

The Pies Are The Limit

Tour a supermarket or food court and it's obvious what today's consumers want: convenience and choice. Speedy, one-stop shopping with near limitless selection seems to be the order of the day. But limits can be a good thing. Take Krista's Kitchen, for example. This small, state-licensed home bakery in Portage is located blocks from any other business, is open only a few days a week and offers a relatively restricted menu.

There is no handy drive-in or packaged fast food at Krista's. Customers who frequent the bakery, housed in a 165-year-

Krista Bleich bakes luscious, low-fat bread with stone ground, 100 percent whole wheat flour.

old brick home, must take the front walk and pass through a small porch to a living room filled with antique furniture, knick knacks, and a bearskin rug. Through here they enter the kitchen, where Krista Bleich's hand-baked breads and other bakery items, lit by the morning sun, are lined up for sale on wooden tables. Melted butter glistens on loaves of cinnamon-swirl bread. In the air is a warm yeasty smell underscored with melted cheese, coming from trays of whole wheat-cheddar bread that have just been pulled from the oven. Closer to the tables one can see where thick fruit juices have bubbled up through the streusel topping of country-style pies. Fruit-packed muffins and chunky cookies are also on display.

At Krista's Kitchen, the selection is "limited" but the quality is lush. "All of my bakery is made from 100 percent stone ground, whole wheat flour and other whole grains," says Krista, who has kind eyes and curly blond hair. "I am a bit health conscious with my bread-baking and use only non-fat milk products, a minimum of eggs, and a small amount of canola oil when necessary. I bake with natural sweeteners: honey, real maple

syrup, and molasses. I like to use dried fruits and nuts, but when in season, I use whatever is fresh. My cookies, pies, and coffeecakes do contain the 'real thing:' butter, sour cream, brown sugar."

Krista can be downright particular about ingredients and she'll go out of her way to obtain them: she buys aged cheddar from Carr Valley Cheese in LaValle (see page 38) and drives to an Amish general store near Pardeeville for cracked wheat and a special yeast she prefers.

She bakes a few types of breads daily but on the weekend she also offers specialties like her black-and-green-olive bread and buttermilk crescent dinner rolls. Pies and muffins follow the season; in summer they might be filled with fresh peaches or berries; in spring, with rhubarb and maple syrup.

Krista got the bug for baking when she was seven years old and made her first fruit pie with canned blueberry filling and a lard crust. The elderly neighbor lady she served it to was appreciative. "She also told me, but not in a mean way, how I could improve the pie," remembers Krista, who was motivated to try again.

Now Krista's pies are so good they need no improvement. Her little bakery is so well established that she knows most of her customers by name. And business is so strong that she is planning to expand. Within limits, that is. "There is no way that the nature of my business fits the 'strip mall' image. I don't want to move just for the sake of moving.

"I have a small business with old-fashioned ambience. People miss that and want that. And I want to retain as much of that as possible."

Banana Apricot Muffins
12 regular or 6 jumbo muffins

You'll taste the tropics as soon as you bite into these exotic muffins from Krista Bleich. She uses scissors to snip apricots into large pieces for extra-chunky texture. If whole wheat pastry flour isn't available to you, substitute one cup of white flour and up the amount of whole wheat flour to one cup.

2 cups mashed ripe bananas
1/3 cup honey
1/4 cup canola oil
2 tablespoons lemon juice
1 teaspoon vanilla extract
1 1/2 cups whole wheat pastry flour
1/2 cup whole wheat flour
2 teaspoons baking powder
1/2 teaspoon baking soda
1/2 teaspoon salt
2/3 cup coarsely chopped dried apricots
1/2 cup toasted chopped walnuts

Heat oven to 375 degrees; grease a 12-cup muffin tin or line it with paper liners (or use a 6-cup tin to make jumbo muffins). Combine mashed bananas, honey, canola oil, lemon juice, and vanilla in a small bowl. In a large bowl, sift together the flours, baking powder, baking soda, and salt. Stir wet ingredients into dry mixture until just blended. Don't beat or overmix. Fold in apricots and walnuts. Divide evenly among muffin cups. Bake until toothpick inserted in center of muffins comes out clean, 12-15 minutes (18-22 minutes for jumbo muffins). Cool muffins in the pan a few minutes before removing them to a rack.

Maple Rhubarb Pie
8 servings

Krista Bleich fills her country-style pies with seasonal fruits and flavors; this wonderful maple rhubarb pie is one of her specials during the spring and early summer months. You can use fresh or frozen rhubarb, but if you use the latter, do not thaw the fruit before proceeding with the recipe.

5 cups sliced rhubarb (1/2-inch slices)
1/4 cup sugar
2/3 cup pure maple syrup
1 teaspoon vanilla extract
1/4 cup flour
unbaked 9-inch pie crust, well-chilled or frozen (for recipes, see page 101 and 118)

Topping:
1/2 cup flour
1/4 cup sugar
1/4 cup brown sugar
1/3 cup oats
pinch of salt
pinch of cinnamon
4 tablespoons cold butter, cut into small pieces

Heat oven to 425 degrees. Toss rhubarb with the sugar in bowl; let stand 15 minutes. Stir in maple syrup, vanilla, and flour; pour into chilled or frozen pie shell. Place on baking tray lined with aluminum foil; bake 10 minutes. Reduce heat to 350 degrees and bake 10 minutes longer.

Meanwhile, make topping by mixing all ingredients until crumbly in a food processor, using the pulse button, or by hand with a pastry cutter. After pie has baked the first 20 minutes, remove from oven and distribute topping evenly over pie. Continue to bake until topping is golden and there are thick, bubbling juices coming from the pie, another 40-50 minutes. Cool completely before serving. It is delicious served with ice cream, frozen custard, or frozen yogurt.

Krista's Whole Wheat Cheddar Bread

2 loaves

Two Wisconsin specialties in one: the whole grain goodness of Krista Bleich's wheat bread and a three-year-old cheddar from Carr Valley Cheese. (See page 38.) Krista says Carr Valley's is "the best out of all the sharp cheddars I've tried," and recommends downing chunks of the bread with a full-bodied wine.

Krista uses large cubes of cheese, making the loaves rather lumpy and fun to knead, and kind of comical-looking in the final rise. The cheese, which can be cubed smaller if you prefer, melts as the bread bakes, making small pockets of gooey goodness. Leftover bread is best if toasted very lightly or even microwaved to re-soften the cheese.

3 cups unbleached all-purpose flour
2 1/2 cups whole wheat flour
1 package (1/4 ounce) active dry yeast
2 teaspoons salt
2 1/3 cups warm water
2 tablespoons oil
1 tablespoon honey
3/4 pound well-aged cheddar

Mix flours, yeast, and salt in large bowl. Mix warm water, oil, and honey in separate bowl. (Refer to instructions on the package of yeast and use an instant thermometer, if available, to determine the proper temperature of the water.) Stir water mixture into flour; mix well and knead on floured surface, adding additional flour as needed, until dough is springy and not too sticky, 7-10 minutes. Place in oiled bowl, cover with clean cloth, and set in very warm place to rise until doubled in size, 1-1 1/2 hours.

Line a large, heavy baking sheet with parchment paper or foil. Cut cheese into 3/4-inch cubes and knead into dough until well-distributed. Divide dough in half, cover and let rest 10 minutes. Shape dough into two balls, tucking in any cheese that may fall out during the process. Place on baking sheet, cover, and let rise as before until nearly doubled, 30-45 minutes.

Meanwhile, heat oven to 350 degrees. Bake bread 40-45 minutes. Cool before slicing.

> ### 88. Manderfield's Home Bakery
> **237 E. Calumet St.
> Appleton, WI 54915
> 920-731-2181**
> ### 89.
> **811 Old Plank Road
> Menasha, WI 54952
> 920-725-7794**
> •

A Fox Valley Institution

On the day before Appleton's Octoberfest, Manderfield's Home Bakery is in the throes of semmel roll production. The bakers are making thousands of crusty, cornmeal-topped buns, enough to satisfy the throngs of bratwurst and burger lovers who will roam College Avenue during the town's fall celebration. With so many visitors in town, there's also a huge demand for other Manderfield specialties: strawberry and chocolate cream cakes, custard-filled butterballs, fresh breads, iced cake doughnuts, German chocolate cookies, and *placek*, a raisin-and-pecan-studded egg bread. Store clerks race back and forth along the bakery cases trying to keep up with the torrent of customers. In the pastry department, workers form an assembly line to layer and frost the company's signature tortes. And in the breads area, one baker drags giant rolling racks loaded with golden buns out of the ovens as another slaps dough balls onto indented disks and swiftly slides them, one after another, into a squat bun-rolling machine.

For all the flurry and flour in the air there's also a discernable feeling of camaraderie and purpose. And nobody is working harder or faster—or having more fun—than Paul Manderfield. Paul is the third-generation baker who manages this Fox Valley institution; his brother Jerry runs the family's other bakery in Menasha. The Manderfield baking legacy started with grandfather Frank, who baked in several nearby towns and passed his skills on to Dennis, Paul and Jerry's father. Dennis ran Best Bakery in Menasha for 16 years, re-opened it as Manderfield's Home Bakery in Appleton, and is still involved on a part-time basis today.

Paul, who says he "was always interested in baking, more so than the other kids in the family," has a broad, muscular physique, a dark goatee, and dim circles beneath his eyes. As quick and tough as a hockey player, he weaves through the bakery, negotiating dough onto scales, shouting orders over the din, joking with employees, and responding to buzzing timers.

Unlike the stereotypical hockey player with a bad attitude, however, Paul believes that being the best is as much about how you treat people as it is about how good your product is. "We think of ourselves as ladies and gentlemen serving ladies and gentlemen" is the Manderfield motto posted near work stations. Giving retail customers good service is so important to the Manderfields that at one time the family sold its wholesale business in order to give more attention to store customers.

And this kind of respect isn't just for patrons. Try to compliment Paul about how fast he works and he'll respond, "Some of them are faster," referring to his employees, many of whom have been with the company for years. "These people are just great," he says, trying to change the subject. "I give them all the credit in the world." But they will not take it. "Paul is very picky about his product," says Jeanne Mongin, who runs the bakery store. Sure, he's fast but, "If there's one bun that's not right out of 50, Paul will find it."

The friendly banter continues, lightening the workload, as co-workers try to outdo each other giving credit, as thousands of semmel rolls get readied for the weekend, as the Manderfield legacy lives on.

Manderfield's German Chocolate Cookies
4-5 dozen cookies

Be sure to taste these while they are still warm.

2 1/4 cups sugar
1 cup vegetable shortening,
    at room temperature
14 tablespoons margarine,
    at room temperature
1 cup cocoa powder
1 teaspoon vanilla extract
1 teaspoon salt
4 cups flour, divided
1 1/2 cups sweetened coconut
1 cup chopped pecans

Heat oven to 350 degrees. Grease baking sheets or line them with parchment paper. Cream sugar, shortening, margarine, cocoa, vanilla, and salt in a large bowl with electric beaters 3-4 minutes. Gradually beat in 2 cups of the flour at low speed. Beat in the coconut and 1/4 cup water until well mixed, about 2 minutes. Stir in remaining 2 cups flour and the pecans.

Drop or scoop dough onto baking sheets, using 2-2 1/2 tablespoons per cookie and leaving two inches between cookies. Lightly flatten each cookie. Bake 13-14 minutes. Cookies will be soft when they come out of the oven; carefully transfer them to wire racks and let cool.

Creamy Apple Pear Pie
8 servings

From-scratch baking like Manderfield's is the inspiration for recipes entered in Appleton's Applefest Cooking Contest, a feature of the town's annual Octoberfest. This stellar pie, from resident George Thomas, took a first prize in 1997.

prepared dough for double 9-inch
   pie crust (recipe follows)
3/4 cup sugar
1/3 cup flour
1 teaspoon cinnamon
1/4 teaspoon nutmeg
5 medium firm apples
3 large firm pears
3/4 cup whipping or heavy cream
2 tablespoons butter, cut into
   small pieces
cinnamon sugar
French vanilla ice cream or sweetened
   whipped cream

Heat oven to 425 degrees. Divide dough in half and shape each half into a disk. Roll out one disk to line a 9-inch pie pan. Trim to allow a small overhang. Refrigerate rolled crust while you make filling.

Combine sugar, flour, cinnamon, and nutmeg in large bowl. Peel apples and pears, cut them into large chunks, and toss with sugar mixture. Turn mixture into chilled crust. Pour cream over mixture; dot with butter. Roll out second pie crust, place it over fruit, and trim to allow a 3/4-inch overhang. Fold edge of top crust over edge of bottom crust and pinch to make a raised rim. Flute the edges. Vent pie by making several slits with sharp knife in the top. (If you have excess dough, re-roll it, cut out small designs, and decorate the pie.) Bake 15 minutes, then reduce heat to 375 degrees and bake 35-40 minutes longer. Remove from oven and sprinkle with cinnamon sugar. Serve warm or at room temperature with ice cream or whipped cream.

Double Pie Crust
One double or two single 9-inch pie crusts

This is the pie crust recipe I've been using for years. The shortening keeps it tender while the butter provides flavor.

2 1/2 cups flour
1 teaspoon salt
6 tablespoons cold shortening,
   cut into small pieces
5 tablespoons cold butter,
   cut into small pieces
8-9 tablespoons ice water

Mix flour and salt in mixing bowl or food processor work bowl. Using a pastry cutter or the food processor pulse button, cut in shortening and butter until mixture resemble coarse breadcrumbs. (If using food processor, transfer mixture to a bowl at this point.) Sprinkle in ice water, one tablespoon at a time, while you lightly toss mixture with large fork. Stop adding water when mixture holds together in large lumps. Turn dough onto double layer of plastic wrap. Gather wrap securely around dough to form a smooth, tight ball. Chill two or more hours.

To roll out crusts: Handle dough as little as possible during this process. Unwrap dough ball, place on floured surface, and divide it in half. (If chilled dough is too firm, allow it to stand at room temperature 15-20 minutes before working with it.) Press and shape each half into a disk shape. With gentle, even motion, roll out disks from center to form a circle, using a bit more flour to prevent stickiness. Loosen dough from work surface with a flat utensil. Fold each round in quarters, transfer to a 9-inch pie pan, unfold, and crimp edges. Chill crusts before proceeding with pie recipe. May also be frozen.

90. New Richmond Bakery
137 S. Knowles Ave.
New Richmond, WI 54017
715-246-6004

•

Old-Fashioned Favors

Pastries lined up on trays beckon from the front windows of the New Richmond Bakery; inside the small shop more goodies fill the waist-high glass cases. There's a heart-warming array of old-fashioned baked goods here: fruit-filled kolache, Danish, doughnuts, caramel rolls, cinnamon rolls, long Johns, bismarks, date-filled cookies, plain cheesecake. The pudding cakes are irresistible, the maple-glazed apple fritters will make you smile, and the dollar buns will take you back to a time when families sat down together for Sunday afternoon dinner.

Virtually everything here is made from scratch, or as owner Bob Komorouski puts it, "It's a real family bakery." He'd been a baker for more than two dozen years before the time was right for him and his wife Sharon to open a place of their own.

"Our own business is something we've dreamed about since we were married," says Sharon, who has a melodious voice and the kind of prettiness that makes you glad she doesn't spoil it with make-up. The couple bought the business in 1997 from the Garness family, whose traditional Swedish baked goods like *rosettes* and *pizelles* had been mainstays at the bakery for years. Bob's specialties, however, come from recipes he learned from a Czech baker.

Asked how she feels about achieving their dream, Sharon pauses for a moment before responding with a direct "We love it." Then she pauses again and, as if the whole truth must be told, adds, "But as much as we talked about it tying us down,

it's not what I expected. It's hard. The number of hours is hard."

As for the customer response, "They have been great. The people of New Richmond are wonderful. We got offers to help us move. We hear good words about the bakery from them." If she feels welcomed by community members, she also knows that they feel welcome, too. "It's funny how people who come into a bakery are

Sharon Komorouski of New Richmond Bakery enjoys her customers.

cheery. It's not something they have to do. They choose to come here. And they always have a good story to tell me. And then that cheers me up."

Sure enough, in walks a perky lady who begins to talk before the door is closed behind her. It seems her husband wanted to take her deer-hunting. "He's always trying to get me to go," the woman laughs. "This year I just told him the truth. 'I'm so [soft-hearted]. I'd stand where you couldn't see me and *shoo* them away!' Well, it worked. He didn't take me." Sharon chuckles with pleasure and begins to fill a bag as the lady places her order.

Peach Upside Down Cake
8 servings

The past lingers in the present at down-home bakeries like the New Richmond Bakery, as it can at home when you crank up the oven, plug in the coffeepot, and enjoy something sweet and old-fashioned. I've long lost track of the source of this endearing dessert, but it is the kind of keepsake food that draws us to small-town bakeries. Serve it with sweetened whipped cream or peach ice cream.

1/2 cup packed light brown sugar
6 tablespoons softened butter, divided
3 cups peeled fresh peaches, tossed
    with 3 tablespoons sugar (or use
    thawed, drained peaches without
    adding sugar), divided
1/3 cup milk
1 tablespoon lemon juice
1 teaspoon vanilla extract
1 1/4 cups cake flour
1/2 teaspoon baking powder
1/2 teaspoon baking soda
1/4 teaspoon salt
1/4 cup white sugar
2 eggs

Heat oven to 325 degrees. Cream brown sugar and 4 tablespoons butter in bowl. Spread into bottom of ungreased 9 1/2- or 10-inch glass pie plate. Arrange 2 cups peaches in spiral pattern over mixture.

Finely chop remaining peaches; combine with milk, lemon juice, and vanilla. Sift cake flour, baking powder, baking soda, and salt into second bowl. Cream remaining 2 tablespoons butter with white sugar in third bowl; beat in eggs. Stir milk and flour mixtures alternately into third bowl. Spread mixture over peaches. Bake until toothpick inserted in center comes out clean, 40-50 minutes. Cool 15 minutes. Run knife around edges of cake, place serving plate over cake and invert cake onto plate. Serve warm or at room temperature.

---

91. O & H Danish Bakery
1841 Douglas Ave.
Racine, WI 53402
414-637-8895

•

4006 Durand Ave.
Racine, WI 53405
414-554-1311
For mail order: 800-227-6665

•

Crazy for Kringle

Sheboygan has brats and Monroe has cheese, but few towns have as close an identification with a food as Racine, the kringle capital of the nation. Each year local bakeries produce millions of the flaky, multi-layered pastries, supplying a formidable local demand as well as shipping to kringle-lovers nationwide.

Kringle, like a good portion of the town's population, is a result of Danish immigration since the 1800s. And like the descendants of early settlers, kringle has changed over the decades, adapting to American ways while retaining its Danish flavor. Once a huge, pretzel-shaped affair that was often filled with almond paste, today's kringle is smaller, flatter, and oval-shaped. And the fillings vary widely.

At O & H Danish Bakery on Douglas Avenue, one of several Racine bake shops that make kringle, a list of filling types is painted on a wooden paddle near the bakery cases. It reads like the contents of a lush gift basket: almond, apple, apricot, blueberry, cheese, cherry, chocolate, date, pecan, pineapple, prune, raspberry, strawberry, cranberry. Such variety is one of the reasons Racine natives often cite O & H as the town's ultimate bakery. Other reasons include the melt-in-your-mouth texture and freshness of O & H kringle and the extraordinary array of from-scratch European and American baked goods they offer.

Ray Oleson, center, and sons, Dale and Eric, turn out scrumptious Danish kringle at O & H bakery, Racine

Eric Olesen, part of a trio of brothers who operate this third-generation business, says it all started with his grandfather, Christian Olesen, who came to Racine from Denmark when he was 14 years old. Christian became a baker and worked in a number of shops before teaming up with Harvey Holtz to open the appropriately named O & H Bakery. Christian's son Ray started working at the bakery at age 16, took it over as an adult, and, according to his son, is the driving force behind the company's great success. Eric says his mother, Myrna, a talented, self-taught cake decorator, has also been instrumental. "She's the bakery's biggest critic, a constructive critic of how we can improve, and she's nurtured the creative drive in the family."

At O & H, says Eric, the emphasis always has been on customer satisfaction; its most important customers still are the locals who frequent the company's two Racine locations. "We do no wholesale [because] what we enjoy is being able to hand our customers the product, knowing that we made it the best that we could, and seeing the smiles on their faces."

Even their mail order business, which averages two thousand kringle a week during the first 11 months of the year and 15,000 each week during December, takes something of a back seat to store sales. "At Christmas, we determine the level of mail orders we can take, and then we won't take more," says Eric. "Our first priority is quality and capacity for the store."

O & H Danish Kringle
Two kringles, 10-12 pieces each

A home-size version of the renowned kringle from O & H Bakery is a satisfying project for a lazy weekend day. The number of steps may look daunting, but the dough is easy to work with and each step is carefully described and quite do-able. The finished pastry keeps for several days. Kringle is a Christmas morning tradition in Danish-American homes, but it needn't be Christmas, nor need you be Danish to treasure it.

Dough:
1 1/2 sticks (3/4 cup butter), softened
1 package (2 ounces) cake yeast
1/4 cup warm water
1/4 cup lukewarm milk
1/4 cup sugar
1/2 teaspoon salt
1/2 teaspoon lemon extract
1 egg
2 cups sifted all-purpose flour

Butterscotch filling:
1 cup brown sugar
1/3 cup butter, softened
pinch of salt
pinch of cinnamon
1/2 egg white

Other:
chopped nuts, fruit, or jam
1 1/2 cups powdered sugar

To make dough: Trace or mark an 8-inch square in pencil on each of two pieces of waxed paper. Divide softened butter in half and spread each half evenly over the marked squares. Chill to harden the butter.

While butter is chilling, break up yeast, place in large bowl, and stir in 1/4 cup warm water until yeast is dissolved. Add the 1/4 cup lukewarm milk, sugar, salt, lemon extract, and egg; mix well. Stir in flour until dough is smooth.

Turn dough (it will be soft and sticky) onto well-floured surface. Sprinkle with flour and knead it very lightly and briefly, about 3-4 turns. Roll out dough to an 8-by-12-inch rectangle with floured rolling pin. Place one of the chilled butter squares over the bottom two-thirds of dough; peel off waxed paper. Fold the top, uncovered third of dough over the middle third, then fold the remaining third over the top of the fold. Now, working from the right side of the dough rectangle (instead of the top), again fold one end over the middle third of dough, and fold remaining third over the fold, making a square of nine layers. Flour lightly and wrap in waxed paper. Chill 30 minutes.

Roll out dough again to an 8-by-12-inch rectangle. Place second square of chilled butter over dough as before and again do the folds as described above, to make a square of 18 layers. Flour lightly, wrap in waxed paper, and chill 2 hours.

Meanwhile, make butterscotch filling by mixing ingredients until smooth. Line two baking pans with parchment paper or aluminum foil.

After dough has chilled a second time, cut it in half. On floured surface, lightly roll out each piece to a 20-by-6-inch rectangle. Spread half of the butterscotch filling lengthwise down the middle third of each rectangle, then spread your choice of nuts, fruit, or jam over the filling. Fold one of the long edges to the center of filling. Moisten other long edge and fold over the top to completely cover filling. Press along seam to seal well. Place each folded rectangle, seam side up, on a prepared baking sheet and form into oval shape, pressing ends of kringle together to close the circle. Flatten kringles with your hand, cover with light cloth or plastic wrap, and let rise in warm

(70-degree) place for 1 hour.

Heat oven to 350 degrees before dough completes its rising. Bake kringles until golden brown, 25-30 minutes. Cool in pans on wire racks.

Combine powdered sugar with 2 tablespoons water; beat until smooth. Spread icing over cooled kringles. It's also nice to decorate the kringles with chopped nuts or fruit.

O & H Cranberry Slices
24-30 bars

Clearly easier to make than kringle, and with no scrimping on quality ingredients, here are O & H's buttery cranberry bars. Use fresh or frozen cranberries.

2 eggs
2 cups sugar
15 tablespoons butter, melted
2 cups cake flour
12 ounces (about 3 cups) cranberries
3/4 cup finely chopped pecans

Heat oven to 350 degrees. Generously grease a 9-by-13 inch or similarly sized baking pan. In a large bowl, beat eggs with electric beaters on medium speed until frothy. Beat in sugar gradually. Lower speed and beat in melted butter. Stir in flour, cranberries, and pecans. Press mixture into prepared pan; bake until toothpick inserted near center comes out clean, 40-45 minutes. Cool on wire rack and cut into bars.

92. Pauc's Bakery
127 N. Main St.
Amherst, WI 54406
715-824-3760
•

The Little Bakery That Could

Some "family-run" businesses are merely owned or managed by actual family members, but at the little bakery on Amherst's main street Connie and Mike Pauc do it all themselves. "Mike's the real baker," says Connie. His from-scratch assortment of pies, muffins, breads, rolls, and cookies are baked in a brick hearth oven that is more than 100 years old. Specialties like Granny Loaf, an iced, loaf-shaped coffeecake, and *"Ferragossa,"* Italian-style vegetable-cheese bread, are always in demand. Connie runs the store,

Connie and Mike Pauc keep customers happy in Amherst.

where a stenciled staircase leads to an old projection room; the building has housed a bakery since 1927, but before that it was a theater.

How do they handle the busy times, or if one of them is ill? "Sometimes my mother will help," says Connie. "We usually have to close if one of us gets sick. But if Mike gets sick, then we're shot!"

Pauc's Old-Fashioned Almond Cookies
8-10 dozen small cookies

These simple cookies are the kind moms used to bake for after-school snacking. Get 'em while they're warm and fresh.

1 cup (2 sticks) butter, softened
1 1/4 cups brown sugar
1 egg
1 1/2 teaspoons vanilla extract
2/3 cup sliced almonds
3 scant cups flour
1 teaspoon baking soda
1 teaspoon salt
for garnish: sugar and additional
    sliced almonds

Heat oven to 325 degrees. Lightly grease two baking sheets. Cream butter and brown sugar in large bowl until light and fluffy. Mix in egg and vanilla until smooth. Lightly crush the almonds, then combine them with the flour, baking soda, and salt. Stir flour mixture into butter mixture until well-combined. (If dough is very soft, chill it for 20-30 minutes before rolling it out.)

Roll out dough on floured surface to 1/4-inch thickness. Use a cookie cutter to cut dough into half-dollar-size rounds (or cut them larger, if desired). Place rounds on prepared cookie sheets. Lightly press a few sliced almonds into tops of cookies and sprinkle with sugar. Bake 10-11 minutes.

93. Peter Sciortino's Bakery
1101 E. Brady St.
Milwaukee, WI 53202
414-272-4623
•

Successful Failure

Missing an exam: it's the fear of college students and the recurring nightmare of many graduates. But for Guiseppe Vella, it was the doorway to success.

Guiseppe, who is in his early twenties, has been working at Sciortino's Bakery since, as he puts it, he was "very young." Owned and operated by Peter Sciortino from 1946 to 1997, the shop specializes in classic Italian baked goods and is located on bustling Brady Street near downtown Milwaukee. In late 1995, while Guiseppe was in college studying pharmacy—and baking part-time at Sciortino's—he got a call from his boss asking him to come in and help out with the Christmas rush. "I was supposed to be studying for an exam, but I came in and made cookies with him," says Guiseppe, a dark-haired man with a sparse goatee. "Mr. Sciortino asked me, 'So, you gonna fail?' and I said 'yeah.' And that's when he asked me if I'd be interested in taking over the bakery."

At first, Guiseppe didn't believe it was a real offer. "I always thought that if he would sell, I'd love it, but I never asked 'cause I thought he'd pass it on to his grandchildren." Guiseppe's parents didn't believe it, either. "They thought I was lying because I missed the exam."

But the offer was real, so Guiseppe left school to work closely with the aging owner and learn his secrets. He mastered the art of making Italian bread with shatteringly crisp crusts and *cannoli* with creamy, chocolate-and-ricotta-cheese filling. He learned to produce tender *biscotti*, a type of Sicilian cheesecake called *casatini*, and dozens of Italian cookies like glazed cocoa-flavored *tutus* and almond-filled *pipatelli*.

"Mr. Sciortino polished me up," says Guiseppe, and although he's still not quite sure why he was the chosen one, it's clear that Sciortino chose well. Guiseppe has both an aptitude and a passion for baking plus a confidence that the bakery can continue to live up to its excellent, long-held reputation. He and two co-workers, his sister Maria and brother Luigi, became official owners in January of 1997. But, as Guiseppe points out, "Everything's the same: the name, the recipes, many of the employees."

Still, not quite everything is the same, for Guiseppe and his siblings have done so well since taking over that business is growing. One rather large new order, for

Guiseppe, Maria, and Luigi bake delicious Italian specialties at Peter Sciortino's Bakery in Milwaukee.

example, is the 18,000 cannoli baked for Milwaukee's Festa Italiana, the largest annual Italian festival in America.

All in all, as Sciortino's customers will agree, it's a good thing Guiseppe missed his exam.

Tutus
About 6 dozen cookies

A tutu is a small, ball-shaped chocolate cookie flavored with cinnamon and glazed with a lemony icing. During the Christmas season at Sciortino's, the Vellas bring in extra help to hand-roll tutus in batches that yield more than 3000 cookies at a time. No wonder this is Guiseppe's response when you ask him about his future as a baker: "I'm not going anywhere," he says. "This is my life."

    1 1/4 cups sugar
    1 cup vegetable shortening, at
        room temperature
    1/2 cup cocoa powder
    1 egg
    1 cup lukewarm water
    1/2 teaspoon baking powder, divided
    1/4 teaspoon cinnamon
    1/4 teaspoon vanilla extract
    5 cups flour

Glaze:
    3 1/2 cups powdered sugar
    1/2 teaspoon lemon extract

Place sugar, shortening, cocoa powder, and egg in large bowl. Beat with electric beaters at medium-high speed, scraping down sides occasionally, until creamy, about 3 minutes. Lower speed and mix in lukewarm water, 1/4 teaspoon of the baking powder, the cinnamon, and vanilla. Raise speed once again to medium and beat mixture 2 minutes. In separate bowl, mix flour with remaining 1/4 teaspoon of baking powder; stir this gradually into creamed mixture. Turn dough onto lightly floured surface and knead it until all the flour is thoroughly incorporated and a fairly soft dough has formed.

Grease two large baking sheets or line them with parchment paper.

Roll small handfuls of the dough into 1-inch-wide "ropes" then cut the ropes into 1-inch pieces. Roll the pieces between the palm of one hand and a work surface into smooth balls about the size of a walnut. (If dough is too soft or sticky, lightly flour the work surface as needed.) Place balls on prepared baking sheets. Let cookies stand 1/2 hour before baking.

Heat oven to 390 degrees. Bake tutus 12-14 minutes. Cool on pans.

Make a glaze by beating powdered sugar with 1/2 cup water and lemon extract in a small, deep bowl. Place wire racks on newspaper sheets or paper towels. Immerse tutus in the glaze, a few at a time. As you remove each one, let it hang over the bowl for a moment to allow excess glaze to drip off. Place dipped tutus on racks (a bit more glaze will drip off onto the paper); let stand until glaze is set.

---

94. Spooner Bake Shoppe
217 Walnut St.
Spooner, WI 54801
715-635-2643
•

Small Batches, Big Rewards

Phil Markgren started working for the family business when he was 12 years old. Today, the fine, upturned lines around Phil's brown eyes and his pleased, relaxed manner indicate a career's worth of on-the-job enjoyment. Dressed in baker's whites and a spotlessly clean baseball cap, Phil is proud to tell you about the Spooner Bake Shoppe's history and continuing success. It's a familiar story: baking experience that spans three generations, an undeviating commitment to freshness and quality, and hands-on, day-in/day-out family involvement.

The bakery is located up north, way up north, in fact, where county forests out-acre private lands and two-lane highways snake around sky-blue lakes. Spooner, like many towns in Wisconsin's rugged Indian Head Country, is small but very active during tourist season. "You see solid Minnesota plates coming into town on Friday; on Sunday it's the same going out of town," says Phil, who has ruddy cheeks and a blonde-red, gray-flecked beard. But he points out that Spooner is not as "touristy" as other places. "We have a 'regular tourist' trade, the ones with lake homes. They're here for the whole season. And once they come [to the bake shop], they seem to come back all the time." Indeed, whether it's seasonal residents, short-term visitors, or year-round locals, everybody returns to the Spooner Bake Shoppe.

Members of the Markgren family—Phil, his brother, wife, children, and grandchildren—work hard to keep the bakery supplied with homemade cinnamon rolls, a variety of Danish-dough products, and other items that have been popular since Phil's parents bought the bakery in 1952. Luscious pies made with lard crusts, special occasion cakes (expertly decorated by Phil's daughter Kim Fox), old-fashioned cake doughnuts, and all sizes of buns are all part of the "basic line."

But new items are also always in demand and that's okay with Phil. He says he's always trying to come up with different ideas, like the Wild Rice Bread that now outsells all his variety breads, including Cranberry Walnut Wild Rice Bread, Cheddar Loaf, and something he calls Dakota Bread, a honey-sweetened multi-grain loaf that won a prize in a Minnesota contest. (Phil's entries are frequent winners at the Upper Midwest Bakers Convention, held annually in Bloomington.) Phil also developed Jack Pine Bread, made of whole wheat flour, cornmeal, oatmeal, bran, molasses, and honey, to celebrate the hardy north country locals, who laughingly refer to themselves as "Jack Pine Savages."

Cookies from the Spooner Bake Shoppe are "all-scratch, no preservatives, and always fresh," says Phil. "We make smaller batches every day or every other day; that's the reason we sell so many." The bakery also has a line of candy—fudge, divinity, peanut brittle, cashew brittle, and coconut brittle—all of which Phil makes himself.

What with all the products and customers, things get very hectic at the bakery. As for Phil: "I like it busy. It's really fun when there's a million things going on. I like coming to work in the morning. I like the challenge of being on top of everything." He grins and the fine wrinkles near his eyes spread like open palms. "I like seeing it all come together."

Wild Rice Bread
2 medium-sized loaves

Created by Phil Markgren of the Spooner Bake Shoppe, this bread showcases one of the region's natural resources. It's the kind of bread you'll want to swipe with whipped butter and make a whole meal out of. Home cooks may not stock all the types of flour and grain called for, but they are readily available; or you could substitute more all-purpose or whole wheat flour for the rye flour or cornmeal. Make sure the wild rice is thoroughly cooked and, if desired, chop it before mixing it in with the other ingredients to produce a more even-textured bread. I like the effect of a loaf studded with whole grains, however.

2 1/2 cups all-purpose flour
3/4 cup whole wheat flour
1/2 cup oats (regular or quick)
3 tablespoons rye flour
3 tablespoons yellow cornmeal
1 tablespoon salt
1 ounce (1/2 package) cake yeast
1 1/4 cups warm water
3 tablespoons honey
3 tablespoons shortening, melted and
   cooled to lukewarm
3/4 cup cooked wild rice, at room
   temperature

For top of loaves:
1 egg beaten with 1 tablespoon water
additional whole wheat flour

Mix all-purpose flour, whole wheat flour, oats, rye flour, cornmeal, and salt in large bowl. Soften yeast in the warm water in medium bowl; stir in honey and shortening. Stir in wild rice. Stir wild rice mixture into flour mixture until thoroughly mixed. Turn onto floured surface and knead until dough is stretchy and has lost much of its stickiness, 7-10 minutes. Place in large, lightly oiled bowl, cover with plastic wrap and let rise in very warm place 1-1 1/2 hours.

Punch down dough, divide in two, and form into round loaves. Brush tops with beaten egg mixture and roll them in whole wheat flour. Place loaves in 8-inch pie pans. Lightly slash tops 3-4 times with a sharp knife. Cover and let rise again in very warm place until indentation remains when you lightly poke the bread, about 45 minutes.

Heat oven to 400 degrees while bread is rising. Bake bread 35-40 minutes. Remove from pans and cool completely on wire racks.

Date-Filled Cookies

About 4 dozen cookies

These are a specialty of many bakeries in northern Wisconsin, including the Spooner Bake Shoppe. The cookie is typically folded over a sweetened date filling into a half-moon; sometimes cranberries, cherries, or other fruits are used. The recipe here is from my mother-in-law, Marion Block, who sandwiches the filling between two slices of rolled dough, the way her grandmother used to do. You can tell it's an old recipe from the use of cream of tartar, which, in combination with baking soda, was used as a leavener before baking powder came on the market.

Cookie dough:
1/2 cup shortening, at room
   temperature
2 cups brown sugar
2 eggs
1 teaspoon vanilla extract
3 1/3 cups flour
1 teaspoon baking soda
1 teaspoon cream of tartar
1/2 teaspoon salt

Filling:
1 pound finely chopped dates
1/2 cup brown sugar

To make dough: Cream shortening and brown sugar. Beat in eggs and vanilla. Sift flour, baking soda, cream of tartar, and salt together; stir into sugar mixture until well combined. Form dough into two cylinders, each about 1 1/2 inches in diameter and 12 inches long. Wrap in waxed paper and chill thoroughly.

To make filling: Combine dates, brown sugar, and 1/2 cup water in saucepan. Cook over low heat, stirring often, until dates are soft and mixture is thick, 10-15 minutes. Cool to room temperature.

To bake cookies: Heat oven to 350 degrees. Grease two large baking sheets or line them with parchment paper. Slice dough rolls into 1/4-inch-thick slices.

Place half the slices on baking sheets. Place 1 teaspoon filling on each slice. Allow the remaining slices to come to room temperature (so they become supple), then place them over the filling-topped bottom slices. Press edges of top slices lightly onto bottom slices (no need to overlap them; the edges of the bottom slices can jut out a bit). This will partially seal the cookies; they will seal more as they bake. Bake 8-9 minutes. Cool on wire racks.

---

95. Tom's Pastry Shoppe
409 Milwaukee St.
(Highway 42)
Kewaunee, WI 54215
920-388-2533

96. Wautlet's
412 Steele St.
Algoma, WI 54201
920-487-3829

•

The Taste of Memories

Whenever I'm in Tom's Pastry Shoppe or Wautlet's Bakery, I never doubt the power of food. The two bakeries located in neighboring towns along Lake Michigan can instantly transport me back to my childhood, when goodies with funny names like kolache, Belgian pie, peanut squares, and knee caps were familiar and beloved specialties in my family circle.

Growing up in Green Bay, we were surrounded by rich pockets of ethnic settlement. My father was Belgian, descended from Walloons who settled in the lower part of Wisconsin's "thumb." My mother was Polish; her people populated an area on the other side of the Bay. To the southeast, right along the big lake, were the Czechoslovakians, called Bohemians back then. German, Native American, Danish, Dutch, and many other ethnic influences were not far, either.

The varied heritage of the area is still evident in its landscape and architecture. Polish roadside shrines and Belgian barns, for example, are visual reminders of the region's unique history. But there is no better way to experience the cultural past than to do it the way my family did—by tasting it. And the ethnic bakeries in Kewaunee and Algoma are ideal places for this.

Both places feature the foods I associate with the special occasions of my youth. They have caraway rye bread and iced long Johns just like the ones my grandmother made and cooled on a big ironing board when she visited once a week. Both establishments feature Belgian pies, made with yeast-raised crust, fruit filling, and a cottage cheese topping; we ate these at community picnics and family gatherings. And they carry knee caps, which look a lot like their name, small, bumpy pastries doused in powdered sugar and filled in the concave center with whipped cream. Bohemian knee caps were once a regular feature at supper club weddings in the area, always the first to disappear from platters that also contained brownies and other dessert bars.

At Tom's you'll find *buhuite* (pronounced bu-ta), the Czech triangular pastries filled with poppy seeds or prunes. At Wautlet's there are peanut squares; I've never been able to confirm just what nationality these are and only once have I seen them outside the Lake Michigan region. They are yummy rectangular pieces of white cake dipped in thin frosting and crushed peanuts. The cornmeal-topped German hard rolls called semmel buns, tiny Czechoslovakian *kolache* filled with fruit, cheese Danish, and Door County cherry pies are just a few other choices to

Dorothy Belleau introduces her customers to kolache at Tom's Pastry Shoppe.

try at these hotbeds of heritage.

Tom and Dorothy Belleau own and operate Tom's Pastry Shoppe in Kewaunee; Jim and Sue Belleau run Wautlet's in Algoma, and yes, there is a connection with the names: Tom and Jim are brothers. Their father Mose is a French Canadian American who learned to bake in Oconto. When he opened the Pastry Shoppe in Kewaunee in the 1940s, he had to master new skills in order to satisfy his culturally diverse customers. Thus his sons grew up baking a world of specialties. Tom eventually took over the Pastry Shoppe; Jim owned two other bakeries before buying Wautlet's in 1980.

As time has passed, most folks are several generations removed from their ethnic heritage, but food is still a great way to connect with the past. And Wautlet's and Tom's Pastry Shoppe are two places where old-world goodies can still be savored, no matter what your heritage.

Knee Caps
Makes about 3 dozen small pastries

I didn't know that a home-size recipe for knee caps existed until my sister Judy Ann passed this one along to me. She got it from an elderly friend, Grace Quinlan, who first tasted the yeast-raised, deep-fried pastries at a Bohemian tavern near Maribel, where she grew up. "My two aunts worked there; they got the secrets and passed them on," says Grace. "Knee caps were always served at big weddings." The few places that still serve them today, like Tom's Pastry Shoppe and Wautlet's Bakery, dip them in powdered sugar and fill the centers with whipped cream. Grace and Judy Ann, however, favor a fruit filling and small dabs of whipped topping.

1/4 cup sugar
3 tablespoons shortening or butter
1/4 teaspoon salt
3/4 cup milk
1 1/4 ounces cake yeast
1/4 cup warm water
1 egg, lightly beaten
3 cups flour
lard, shortening, or vegetable oil
    for deep-frying
powdered sugar
blueberry or cherry pie filling
    (optional)
whipped cream

Place sugar, shortening or butter, and salt in large bowl. Bring milk to boil in small saucepan. Stir hot milk into the sugar mixture until shortening melts; cool to lukewarm.

Meanwhile, soften yeast in the warm water. Stir in beaten egg. Stir yeast/egg mixture into milk mixture. Mix in half the flour and beat thoroughly. Add remaining flour and mix well. Cover dough with towel and let rise in warm place until double in size, about 45 minutes.

Place dough on floured surface, flour it lightly, and knead

very briefly. Roll out to 1/3-inch-thick. Cut into 2- or 2 1/2-inch rounds with cookie cutter. Gather scraps, re-roll, and cut again. Allow dough rounds to rise a second time while you heat lard, shortening, or oil in deep, heavy pot. Test the heat of the fat by dropping a small piece of dough in it; the dough should begin to puff and "bubble" immediately (the temperature should be between 350 and 365 degrees).

Just before frying the pastries, make a large, deep indentation in the middle of each (for the filling) with your thumb. Drop the rounds into the oil with the indentation side down. Fry only a few at a time; do not crowd the pot. Turn them over as soon as one side is golden brown (this will only take a moment!) and fry until second side is golden brown and pastry is puffed. (If they darken too quickly, reduce the heat.) Suspend finished pastries briefly over pot to allow excess oil to drip off. Drain on paper towels, again with indentation side down. Cool completely.

When ready to serve, roll or toss knee caps in powdered sugar (they should be generously covered). Fill centers with dabs of pie filling and/or whipped cream.

Wautlet's Peanut Squares
Makes 28 servings

Peanut squares aren't really square, they're rectangular; maybe that's why some folks call them peanut bars instead. Few people seem to have heard of them, but when I served one to a friend who grew up in Mayville, she gave a squeal and said, "Ooh, peanut squares! They remind me of church suppers and potlucks!"

Jim Belleau of Wautlet's Bakery chuckles at how popular they are, given how easy he says they are to make. Maybe for a life-long baker they're easy. The recipe involves making a white cake and icing, roasting peanuts, and double-dipping the cake pieces; still, the results are absolutely worth it. Jim's cake recipe uses specialty ingredients available only commercially,

so here is the delicious, dependable white cake from the 1975 Joy of Cooking. *The rest of the recipe is pure Wautlet's.*

You can roast the peanuts before or after baking the cake. As for the egg whites, separate them from the yolks when the eggs are cold, then allow them to come to room temperature before whipping.

Cake:
3 1/2 cups sifted cake flour
4 teaspoons baking powder
1/2 teaspoon salt
1 cup (2 sticks) butter, softened
2 cups sifted sugar
1 cup milk
1 teaspoon vanilla extract
7 egg whites, at room temperature

Icing:
1 cup hot water
1/3 cup light corn syrup
1/2 teaspoon vanilla extract
1/2 teaspoon salt
5 1/2 to 6 cups powdered sugar

Topping:
4 1/2 cups (about 1 1/2 pounds) raw
    Spanish peanuts

To make cake: Heat oven to 375 degrees. Grease a 9-by-13-inch baking pan that is at least 2 inches deep. Sift before measuring the cake flour, then sift it two more times with the baking powder and salt. Cream butter in large bowl, add sifted sugar gradually, and cream mixture until very light. Stir flour mixture and milk alternately into butter/sugar mixture, stirring the batter well after each addition. Beat in vanilla.

In a clean, dry bowl, whip egg whites until stiff but not dry. Fold them gently into the cake batter. Spread batter in prepared pan. Bake until toothpick inserted in center comes out clean, 30-40 minutes. Cool completely.

To make icing: Combine hot water, corn syrup, vanilla, and salt in deep bowl.

Add just enough powdered sugar to make a very thin icing. To prepare peanut topping, roast peanuts in 300-degree oven, tossing occasionally, about 45 minutes. Cool thoroughly. Grind peanuts to a very fine mince in food processor or blender. Place in a bowl.

To prepare peanut squares: Trim the cake by slicing a thin layer off the four sides. Cut cake into 1-by-3-inch pieces. Dip each piece in icing, allow excess to drip off, then roll cake in the ground peanuts.

Bob Weber makes daily bread and lots of other goodies.

---

97. Weber's Bakery
**161 S. Main St.
Lodi, WI 53555
608-592-4115**
•

Trial By Fire

Baker Bob Weber is a towering man with a deep voice and thinning hair. On a steamy summer afternoon, with eyes red from weariness, Bob pauses in his work to sip a cup of coffee and tell a story about his father, who opened Weber's in Lodi in 1921.

"My dad had come over on the boat from Switzerland, but first worked in a bakery in Madison. One day, the owner there started making a batch of molasses gingersnaps—they were something special. Nobody knew how to make them; the recipe was in the guy's head. Well, a fire started in the basement just when he was scaling the [ingredients]. During the fire, when everyone else left, my dad ran to scope out the scales. He had 30 seconds to figure out the recipe. [He did it by read-

ing] the scale weights.

"One day the next week the owner was sick. So my dad made the gingersnaps. When the owner came back to work, he said, "Who made these cookies?" Well, he found out and he never spoke to my father again.

"That bakery in Madison is long-closed, but we are still making those gingersnaps at Weber's!"

Weber's also makes a lot of other bakery goods, including caramel-covered doughnuts, pumpkin fry cakes with cream cheese frosting, holiday pear bread, Susie the Duck-shaped butter cookies, and homemade egg noodles. Several of his products have taken first place in an annual Wisconsin Bakers Association contest.

Wisconsin writer Kit Kiefer once wrote that a town with a good bakery is bound to be full of solid citizens, honest cops, and happy children. If that's the case, then Lodi must be a fine place indeed.

Date Nut Macaroons
3-4 dozen

Unlike his father's ex-boss, Bob Weber doesn't mind sharing recipes. Here's one he says is easy enough to make at home. With no flour, these chewy macaroons are more confection than cookie. They will puff in the oven, then slump again as they cool.

    4 cups powdered sugar
    2 cups lightly packed sweetened
        coconut flakes
    4 large egg whites
    3/4 cup finely chopped dates
    2/3 cup finely chopped walnuts
    1 teaspoon vanilla extract
    1/2 teaspoon salt

Heat oven to 325 degrees. Generously grease and flour baking sheets or line them with parchment paper. Mix all ingredients well with a wooden spoon in bowl. Beat mixture with electric beaters at medium speed 4 minutes. Drop by tablespoonful onto baking sheets, leaving at least one inch between cookies. Bake until golden brown, 15-17 minutes. Cool macaroons on the pans.

More Hometown Bakery Flavor

The bakeries that follow are arranged in alphabetical order by the name of the business. To locate a bakery by town name, see page 173. Maps are also available on pages *xviii-xxv*. All information is subject to change. Travelers should call or write before visiting to get business hours, directions, and other important details.

98. Cadott Bakery
334 Main St.
Cadott, WI 54727
715-289-4288
•

This third-generation bakery produces all-scratch breads, doughnuts, and just about every kind of pie you can think of. Holiday specialties include rosettes, orange pound cake, stollen, and hand-decorated Christmas cookies.

99. Cynthia's, Ltd.
310 East Walworth Ave.
Delevan, WI 53115
414-740-0994
•

Owner Cynthia Hellen says the "Ltd." in her bakery's name stands for "lots to do." That's because besides the whipped cream tortes, European breads, old-world pastries, and 40 kinds of gourmet cheesecake she makes, she'll also tackle any special order you might have. "Lots of places have a limited selection, but here, if you want it, I'll make it," says Cynthia.

100. Fosdal Home Bakery
243 E. Main St.
Stoughton, WI 53589
608-873-3073
•

Homemade Norwegian specialties, including fancy-shaped butter cookies like *krumkake* (horn-shaped), *sandbakkel* (cup-shaped), *berlina kranser* (loop-shaped), and *rosettes* (flower-shaped).

101. Gourmet Garage
P.O. Box 1226, Highway 13 South
Bayfield, WI 54814
715-779-5365

•

Homemade pies, cakes, tortes, cheese-cakes, cookies, breads, pizzas, and wedding cakes, plus authentic Cornish pasties from an old-country recipe. Also featuring traditional *lefse* and Scandinavian holiday specialties.

102. Grand Dad's Bakery
28 E. Jackson St.
Hartford, WI 53027
414-673-5600

•

Specialties include doughnuts, cookies, Danish coffeecake, pastries, and fine homemade candies, up to 400 types of baked goods throughout the year. Also known for beautifully decorated cakes, wedding cakes, tortes, and cheesecakes.

103. Grandma's Swedish Bakery
Wagon Trail Resort
1041 Highway ZZ
Ellison Bay, WI 54210
920-854-2385

•

The Peterson family has operated Grandma's Swedish Bakery (part of Door County's Wagon Trail Resort) since 1970, but their old-world recipes for pecan rolls, cardamom coffee cake, and Swedish rye go back generations. See Swedish Limpa Bread, page 102.

104. Iron River Baking Co.
P.O. Box 66, Highway 2
Iron River, WI 54847
715-372-8860

•

The perfect place for a coffee break when you're traveling in the northern-most region of the state. In fact, don't drive through Iron River without stopping here for homemade Danish, doughnuts, breads, luscious coffeecake, and more.

105. Joyce's Old Country Cheesecakes
P.O. Box 211,
323 S. 7th St.
Eagle River, WI 54521
715-479-3394

•

Visitors invariably cry "oo-ooh!" when they walk into Joyce's and see handmade, gourmet cheesecakes and specialty cakes that look and taste like a fantasy. Prepared with all natural ingredients, the cheese-cake comes in varieties like rum raisin, German chocolate, peppermint pattie, turtle, and fruit-topped.

106. Leroy's Bakery
630 S. Main St.
Rice Lake, WI 54868
715-234-3066

•

Date-filled cookies, ginger creams, macaroons, spritz, caramel loaf bread, bread sticks, sweet rolls, garlic toast, coconut custard pie, banana cream pie, eclairs to die for, and window-side booths in which to relax and enjoy it all.

107. Linda's Bakery
W3436 Highway 16
West Salem, WI 54669
608-786-1818

•

Features decorated specialty cakes plus an array of breads, dinner rolls, bagels, pies, cupcakes, cookies, and assorted sweets. Owner Linda Meeker is a recipient of the Wisconsin Women Entrepreneurs' Woman of the Year Award.

108. McCoy's Cake & Pie Shop
4925 W. Fond du Lac Ave.
Milwaukee, WI 53216
414-871-9363
•

Knock-your-socks-off Southern baking comes out of this mother-and-son operation, open since 1983. Mamie and Chris Waters bake from-scratch cakes (including fudge, caramel, pineapple-coconut) and pies (like sweet potato, egg custard, coconut custard, pecan, chocolate custard), as well as hand-held apple or peach "fried pies," and custom-made specialty cakes. The recipes are family traditions passed down from Mamie's mother in Mississippi.

109. Natural Ovens of Manitowoc
4300 County Trunk CR
Manitowoc, WI 54221
920-758-2550 or 800-772-0730
•

One of Wisconsin's best known health bakeries produces low-fat, nutritious breads, muffins, cookies, and bagels. The not-so-secret ingredient is roast, ground fortified flaxseed, rich in omega-3, an essential fatty acid. Natural Ovens was founded by biochemist Paul Stitt, who saw a need for fresh, preservative-free whole grain foods in the Midwest. His healthful, flavorful products, made without dairy foods or refined sugars, include items such as "Happiness Bread," a cinnamon raisin pecan bread, and "Brainy Bagels," so wholesome that area students say it helps them learn better.

110. Nature's Bakery
1019 Williamson St.
Madison, WI 53703
608-257-3649
•

Worker-owned and -operated since 1970, Nature's Bakery produces whole-grain breads and baked goods using 100% organic grains; they use other organically grown local ingredients whenever possible. Nature's healthy breads, buns, granolas, cookies, muffins, scones, and vegetarian entrees are sold at grocery stores throughout the area, and are also available direct from the bakery located on funky Williamson Street on Madison's diverse east side.

111. New Glarus Bakery & Tea Room
534 First St.
New Glarus, WI 53574
608-527-2916
•

A small-town, from-scratch bakery known for crunchy hearth breads, cakes, cookies and doughnuts. They really shine at Christmas when Swiss, German, and Norwegian holiday treats are featured, including spicy *pfeffernüsse*, cookies, nut horns, and their famous stollen.

112. Not By Bread Alone
900 S. Jackson St.
Green Bay, WI 54301
920-432-0373
•

Filled breads, desserts, wedding cakes, catering, and to-go soups, salads, and entrees. The signature "Not By Bread Alone" is a lusty Italian bread with a baked-in filling of pesto, sun-dried tomatoes, artichoke hearts, and cheese. Located on the near east side of Green Bay in a pleasant urban neighborhood.

113. Old World Bake Shop
422 Second St.
Hudson, WI 54016
715-386-6239
•

Known in the Hudson area for French bread, muffins, organic whole wheat bread, and a wide array of old-fashioned European-style pastries. Their specialty breads include tomato-herb and "Cobblestone," a cinnamon bread sprinkled with doughnut crumbs. This is a place where customers can call in a special order in the morning and have a fresh cake or pie by dinnertime.

114. Quality Bakery
154 N. Iowa St.
Dodgeville, WI 53533
608-935-3812
•

Family-owned since 1928, Quality Bakery features Cornish specialties like saffron breads and buns, English tea biscuits, and the hand-held meat-and-potato pies called pasties. These are foods that have been popular in the Dodgeville region since immigrants arrived to mine the lead-rich hills in the early 1800s.

115. Quality Bakery
406 Main St.
Marathon City, WI 54448
715-443-2502
•

This is a friendly, ma-and-pa kind of place with mouth-watering items like caramel pecan Danish coffeecake, sticky buns, bismarks, marble twists, and hand-dropped cookies. Try their "Zorba roll," an onion roll stuffed with green onions and colby cheese. "We're not quantity, we're quality," says Cindy Wood, whose husband Lyle is the baker. "We love our work."

116. Town Hall Bakery
6225 Highway 57
Jacksonport, WI 54235
920-823-2116
•

Baker Krista Olson works magic in an historic building located across the street from Lake Michigan. The hall, these days decked out in rose-colored walls and eclectic art work, was deeded to the town by a turn-of-the-century patrician on the condition that alcohol never be served there. But who needs liquor when you can have fresh pear cake, peanut blossom cookies, fruit tarts with homemade lemon curd, raspberry almond scones, Door County cherry crisp, or any of Krista's outstanding selections? Top-quality ingredients, skilled baking, and an artist's philosophy of food and living make Krista's products shine. This is one of the most soul-satisfying bakeries in the state.

117. Village Bakery
P.O. Box 37
505 Water St.,
Princeton, WI 54968
920-295-8851
•

An old-timey spot on the main drag that features home-baked goods. The crullers (pronounced "crawlers" here) are light and excellent with a crusty glaze.

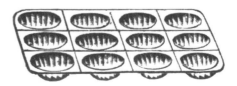

⪽4⪼
Miscellaneous Markets

4. Miscellaneous Markets

Two spinsters lived on Garfield Avenue [in Milwaukee]. They were candy makers, and you could buy the most delicious candy at their shop. They had big flat trays in glass-covered cases. They specialized in a three-layer caramel: a top dark chocolate layer, a middle white layer, and a bottom light tan caramel layer. Time and time again I was sent to buy a small bag of them. Wish I could have some of them right now! There was another small candy store down on Cass Street. The owner made such powerful cinnamon balls that when you put one between your gums and cheek it felt it would burn a hole to the outside.

—From *It Was Fun Being Young*, by Walter E. Schutz (Karl Publishing Company, 1988)

Historical Flavor

Old-world candies, pure maple syrup, dried cherries, home-canned pickles and jams, ethnic foods, frozen custard, sorghum syrup, honey mints—these are some of the hometown products that independent producers sell from in-home shops, retail stores, and small factories. Some places are as tiny as a shed, others as large as a three-story warehouse, but each one offers one-of-a-kind quality foods and a direct relationship with their customers. Each one also reflects something of the state's history, a rich legacy of agricultural, ethnic, and other cultural influences.

Sweet as Candy

Chocolate is native to the Americas, but we can credit our European heritage for getting us addicted to chocolate candy.

The cacao bean first grew in the tropical lowlands of southern Mexico and Central America. Pre-Columbian Americans drank a chocolate drink, but it wasn't the sweet, creamy hot cocoa we know today. The energizing beverage Montezuma gulped down daily was spicy and grainy-textured. Indeed, neither sugar nor milk were added to chocolate, nor were the means to make it smooth discovered until after Europeans got hold of it.

Chocolate processing improved slowly but surely as it spread across Europe. At first chocolate lovers mainly consumed it as a liquid. By the time immigrants were streaming into Wisconsin, however, chocolate cakes and pastries were popular, and solid (or "eating") chocolate was available.

The first retail chocolate-candy shop in the United States opened on the East Coast in 1860. By the early 1900s, the manufacture of chocolate had become big business. Germans and Americans were eating more chocolate than anyone else. European, and eventually, American factories supplied the coating chocolate that small-scale candy-makers melted down and used in hand-dipped specialties. Soon, practically every town in America had a local sweet shop that lured chocoholics and other "sweet-tooths."

Almost everybody loves chocolate, but Wisconsinites have inherited a special appreciation for hand-dipped chocolates—and other fine candies—from their European ancestors. Nowhere is this more true than in the Fox Valley, where small, independent candy stores still churn out top-notch confections in town after town (some, in fact, can barely keep up with demand). Perhaps candy-making thrives in this area because of the concentration of German-, Belgian-, and Dutch-Americans—people who all have a history of loving and knowing chocolate. Certainly there are an unusual number of shops that have been in a family for generations, and certainly loyalties have developed. In towns with more than one candy business, in fact, chocolate lovers have been known to display fierce devotion to their favorite clusters, creams, and caramels, and to their favorite shop. Whatever the reason, the Fox Valley is a veritable hotbed of fine chocolate. Anyone who visits a family-run shop can taste some of the very best of our past.

Institute and the State Historical Society of Wisconsin give credit to Two Rivers, Wisconsin. Here, at a small soda fountain in 1881, a customer asked the owner to put some chocolate syrup on his order of ice cream. The concoction seemed odd and at first it was only offered on Sundays (the likely origin of its name). But sundaes

Ice cream parlor on 10th Street in Manitowoc.
State Historical Society of Wisconsin WHi(X3)39301

We All Scream for Ice Cream

In early America, wealthy colonists bought frozen desserts at fancy confectioneries, but most citizens rarely tasted ice cream. As 19th-century technological advances made ice cream easier to make and more affordable, the urban masses also began to enjoy it regularly. By the late 1800s, specialties like ice cream sodas and sundaes were the rage; the temperance movement was in full swing and ice cream parlors offered a sociable alternative to saloons and strong drink.

Although several towns around the country claim to be the birthplace of the ice cream sundae, both the Smithsonian

quickly took off and soon everything from fresh fruit to marshmallows topped ice cream.

Ice cream, and ice cream parlors, have come a long way since the sundae was invented. In the 20th century large plants began to manufacture ice cream in many flavors and forms. Cars created a whole new culture of roadside stands that pushed ice cream to new heights of popularity. Ice cream cones, ice cream sandwiches, and ice cream bars made it ever more convenient to enjoy a cold sweet. Chain stores replaced many of the independent shops.

The latest phenomenon, in Wisconsin and around the country, is premium ice cream. One premium type, however, has been a particular favorite in Milwaukee and eastern Wisconsin for some time.

Smooth, egg-enriched frozen custard is the draw at custard stands that still experience out-the-door lines on sultry summer days. Custard stands became centers for teenage activity during the 1950s and '60s, but the area's passion for quality ice cream could possibly date even further back, to a time when a bustling ice-harvesting industry and the availability of fresh cream from nearby dairy farms made ice cream manufacturing viable. Then, perhaps, as the region's urban customer base grew, a tradition took root.

While few businesses make their own product any longer, small, independent ice cream shops and stands thrive in many towns. Ice cream isn't an American invention, but it has acquired a uniquely American character over its history. Once a treat only for the aristocratic, ice cream is America's democratic dessert, and ice cream shops are one of the sweetest aspects of American culture.

Land of Milk & Honey

Ancient and widespread, honey was humankind's principal sweetener for most of history. Contrary to popular belief, wild bees existed in the New World before Europeans arrived. Aztec and Maya peoples, in fact, ate honey gathered from domesticated hives.

The Pilgrims imported European bees because they were much more productive than American bees. When some of these foreigners escaped their keepers, they started a steady spread westward, filling hollow trees with golden nectar and providing native Indians with an unexpected and delicious treat. But the luxury had its dark side for the tribes, as they discovered what soon followed the bees: white settlement.

Wisconsin's open prairielands were like a gigantic apiary for honey bees, and immigrants brought beekeeping know-how from their homelands, creating an ideal situation for the honey industry. Early pioneers simply gathered the bounty from hollow trees, but gradually farmers kept bees for both honey and crop pollination. By 1875 commercial beekeeping was in full swing—professional apiarists like Adam Grimm of rural Jefferson had large beekeeping operations that were no longer mere sidelines to other farm business. Beekeepers met to share their knowledge and formed the Wisconsin State Beekeepers Association.

Beekeeping grew to become Wisconsin's fifth largest industry, but faced a sharp decline when a bee disease called foulbrood became widespread by 1914. Stringent regulation put things back on track: a 1920 report said there were 8,000 beekeepers in the state, and by 1929 Wisconsin's bee production was second only to California nationwide.

There was no such thing as "honey shops," as it were, but honey was, and still is, often available direct from the source. Five generations of the Diehnelt family (see page 148), have produced and direct-marketed honey in eastern Wisconsin. Today, independent producers continue to sell their honey at farm stands and in small retail outlets.

Honey retains a wholesome, old-fashioned image, but these days it's also making inroads on the gourmet scene, most notably through specialty products like honey spreads and honey candies.

Liquid Gold

Many of the products featured in this book came from European food traditions, but there is a native specialty that was consumed here long before the first white explorers arrived. Maple sugar, one of the area's first commercial foods, was sold by Woodland Indians to foreign travelers, who must have been cheered to taste something so sweet and delectable among the strange vegetables and tough meats they were offered.

Natives also taught settlers how to draw the sap from certain trees and boil it down to make syrup and sugar. This sparked the beginning of a small but meaningful industry for the state, an industry that is part of the identity of Wisconsin's North woods and gives many dairy farms a profitable sideline business. Maple syrup commands gourmet prices today, but you can be sure of getting the real thing—100 percent pure Wisconsin maple syrup—if you buy from one of the small producers who dot the state and sell their liquid gold from home stands or shops.

Small Successes

Independent food producers sell their specialties from small markets all around the state. Some hark back to the memorable flavors of earlier times to offer old-time goodies like sorghum syrup and home-canned pickles. Others, such as a dried cherry manufacturer in Door County, share new ways to enjoy local crops. Ethnic markets let owners (and customers) preserve their cultural heritage, and for some shoppers, they feed a taste for adventure.

Wherever specialty shops exist and whatever they produce, the food comes from the heart.

—Please Note

The featured businesses that follow are arranged in alphabetical order by the name of the business. Additional businesses are listed in alphabetical order at the end of the chapter. To locate a business by town name, see page 173. Maps are also available on pages *xviii-xxv*. All information is subject to change. Travelers should call or write before visiting to get business hours, directions, and other important details.

---

118. Baraboo Candy Co.
P.O. Box 63
E10891 Co-Op Lane
Baraboo, WI 53913
800-967-1690 or 608-356-7425
•

Home of the Cow Pie

No one seems to remember exactly how or when it happened. Dennis Roney, proud maker of the famous Cow Pie, says the candy was "discovered" in the mid-1980s, before he bought the business called Wiscandy and renamed it the Baraboo Candy Company. Legend has it that one day when some Jumbos—oversized pieces of turtle candy—were coming down a factory conveyor, a worker noticed one with particular contours. "It looks just like a cow pie," she exclaimed, and everyone snickered. At that moment, according to Dennis, "the light bulb went on and they went with it."

"It's a gag gift but people are surprised at the quality," says Dennis. The Cow Pie is made with real Wisconsin butter and milk, choice Ambrosia-brand chocolate, and pecans. Still, the confection is best known for its amusing resemblance to the brown mounds farmers and hikers are careful to avoid.

Wisconsinites love a good laugh and they know a good thing when they see one. So they love the Cow Pie, which is both a good thing and a good laugh.

Entrepreneur Dennis Roney and his wife Lennis have been operating the Baraboo Candy Company, and continuously adding to its line, since 1992. "I got into it because I thought candy was a 'fun food,' recession-proof. But I was wrong in some ways. [The business] is very competitive. There's lots of hard work." The fun part for him is the development and promotion of new products, including the naming of

Baraboo Candy Company

them: goodies like Udderfingers, chocolate-dipped toffee sprinkled with almonds, and Chewy Gooey Pretzel Sticks, salty rods dipped in caramel, toasted nuts, and either milk chocolate or white confectioners' coating. There's also Moo Chews, Monte Caramels, and Green Bay Puddles. "It's like cooking pasta: you keep throwing stuff up there until something sticks," says Dennis. In all, Baraboo Candy carries about 300 products that "stick," some the company makes from scratch and some they simply distribute.

Dennis, who moved up from Chicago, marvels about two things he's learned since living in Wisconsin and running a business that features state icons. "One, the loyalty Wisconsin has as a state is impressive. There's this strong unifying bond. Residents are really behind the Packers and the Badgers." He's also discovered more about people outside Wisconsin. "They think we all own cows!" There's a certain fascination with our farm animals. "People just love to collect pigs and cows," declares Dennis in happy wonder. Indeed, more than half of his company's wholesale business comes from outside Wisconsin.

The sweet, mood-enhancing smell of melting chocolate permeates the factory, which looks something like "Willy Wonka." There are huge, glimmering copper bowls in monster mixers, barrels that

dispense milk and cream, and a giant tempering machine which melts 1200 pounds of chocolate at a time. Machines do some of the work, but they can't do it alone. Gloved, hair-netted workers in white jackets hand-form and weigh the Cow Pies, which are then doused in chocolate and sent for a 10-minute ride through a temperature-controlled tunnel to dry properly. Across the room, great swatches of firm, fragrant caramel are machine-pressed, then hand-measured and hand-cut. On the other end of the room, a crew of senior citizens count and package Moo Chews, keeping up with a steady supply of the mini-treats that parade off a conveyor.

Baraboo Candy Company confections are sold in stores throughout the region, but to get the freshest products (plus an eye-popping, mouth-watering shopping spree through the candy store), customers visit the factory store located just north of Baraboo on Highway 12. Mail order is also available.

Chocolate Toffee Apples
6 servings

Use crisp, semi-tart apples like McIntosh or Empires for this recipe. Granny Smiths are too hard.

6 medium apples
6 wooden skewers or tongue depressors
1 package (3 ounces) Udderfingers candy or other butter toffee
1 cup (6 ounces) semi-sweet chocolate chips
1 tablespoon vegetable shortening

Line a large plate with waxed paper. Rinse and dry apples thoroughly. Insert skewers. Finely grind toffee in food processor or crush in heavy plastic bag with blunt object.

Melt chocolate chips and vegetable shortening in double boiler over simmering water. Stir until smooth and remove from heat. Dip and twirl each apple in the chocolate, tilting the pan to entirely coat apple. Hold apple over pan for a moment or two to allow excess chocolate to drip off. Sprinkle ground toffee over apple and place apple on waxed paper-covered plate. Chill to set the chocolate.

---

119. Bea's Ho-made Products
763 Highway 42
Gills Rock, WI 54210
920-854-2268
•

Busy Bea's

In Grandma's time a cook had to juggle many tasks. Early morning was a time of getting ready: selecting and scrubbing produce from the garden, slicing and salting vegetables, sorting canning jars, and mixing pie crust and bread dough. Throughout the day the work got harder and hotter: pitting cherries and simmering fruit on the stove-top, boiling jars to sterilize them, filling pies, and baking bread. Grandma would finish the afternoon clean-up just in time to start the evening meal. After the supper dishes were stacked, she sat down to make plans for the next day. Grandma's work was never done, so it always had to be organized. And despite a complicated schedule, she didn't cut corners. Her pickles and jams tasted like a summer day, her whole-grain breads and fruit-laden pies were simply the best.

Not many people cook like this any-

more, but they do at Bea's Ho-Made Products. Located on an 1884 homestead near the tip of the Door County peninsula, the company makes jams, jellies, sauces, and pickles the old-fashioned way—from scratch, with quality ingredients and no preservatives or artificial colors. And with, no doubt, the organizational skill of a dozen grandmas.

The operation opened in the 1960s when the Landins—Bea, Bob, Linda, and Lori—began selling home-grown produce and chopped cherry jam from a roadside picnic table. Soon the Landins found themselves with a booming home-canning business. Bea's Ho-Made Products grew steadily through the decade; each year the family added new items to meet an ever-growing demand. Today, Bea's line numbers around 130 products, including such goodies as three-bean salad, piccalilli, hot garlic dills, sweet cucumber chips, and a list of fruit preserves that reads like poetry.

Bea and Bob have retired and turned over ownership to their daughters, but they are still "floaters" during the busy summer months at the canning kitchen. One of the daughters, owner-operator Lori Walch, handles the retail store. The bulk of the business is managed by a year-round "grandma" named J. David Manson who has been with Bea's for 15 years. "I do the ordering, planning, scheduling, food processing. I handle the money and the personnel," says David, with an oh-it's-nothing tone in his voice. "Basically, I make sure the grass gets cut and the light bulbs get changed."

David's nonchalant manner and deadpan humor belie his skill as the heart of the processing operation. He pulls out a worn notebook filled with scribbled numbers, each page tracking the company's annual output of a different product. "This tells me how much to make each year," he says. Grandma didn't need a computer and neither does David.

Still, Grandma only had to can during the harvest season and David processes all year long. During summer, his crew is kept busy pickling cucumbers. ("Oh, it's wild. We barely keep up with the crop," says David drolly.) Therefore, most of the fruit preserves are processed in winter, from frozen fruit. He buys as much local produce as possible. All the cherries come from Door County and the cucumbers are Wisconsin-grown. "Some years, depending on the crops, I'm able to get raspberries and other crops from nearby, too."

Bea's products are found at markets throughout Door County, including at their own busy retail store in Gills Rock. Visiting Bea's, where wall-to-wall shelves are packed with a sun-lit kaleidoscope of beckoning goodies, is like stepping through a closet door into a fantasy world. Here there are also fresh-baked pies and warm-from-the-oven pastries for which shoppers have learned to arrive early, or else they will have disappeared. And don't forget to pause at the viewing window to watch the canning elves in action. For those who can't make it to Gills Rock, Bea's offers mail order.

I'll bet Grandma didn't do that.

Bea's Zucchini & Onion Pickles
6 pints

Kitchen pantries were once well-stocked with canned pickles, jams, and sauces, but not many cooks today have the time for more than a few seasonal favorites. If you have a garden, you'll want to include these bread-and-butter zucchini pickles in your annual canning schedule; they'll help you keep up with the vegetable's infamous fertility. And as for the rest of your pantry, well, thank goodness for Bea's.

Note: This recipe assumes basic canning knowledge. If you have never canned pickles before, learn the basics from the latest edition of a reliable guide like Putting Food By, *by Janet Greene, et al.(Penguin Books, 1991).*

5 pounds small zucchini
2 pounds onions
1/4 cup salt
1 quart white vinegar
2 cups sugar
2 teaspoons celery seed
2 teaspoons turmeric
1 teaspoon dry mustard
6 clean, hot, pint size canning jars
   with lid assemblies

Slice zucchini and onions 1/4-inch thick. Mix with salt and let stand at room temperature 3-4 hours (or refrigerate overnight). Drain well but do not rinse. Combine vinegar, sugar, celery seed, turmeric, and mustard in large, non-reactive kettle; stir well, bring to boil. Add drained vegetables; return to boil and cook, stirring often, until zucchini starts turning pale yellow, 5-10 minutes. Pack into clean, hot jars, leaving 1/2-inch headroom. Wipe rims with clean, damp cloth; secure lids. Process in hot-water bath 5 minutes. Cool. Check lids; refrigerate any that have not sealed properly.

Door County Barbecue Sauce
About 2 1/2 cups

This is a glaze for grilled chicken or Cornish game hens. It also makes a spunky, low-fat dip for pretzels.

1 tablespoon olive oil
1/2 cup minced onion
1 tablespoon minced garlic, mashed
   with flat of knife to a paste
1 tablespoon Dijon mustard
1 jar (5 ounces) Bea's Cherry Jelly (or
   substitute 1/2 cup of another brand)
1 can (15 ounces) tomato sauce
1/2 teaspoon hot pepper sauce (or
   more if you like it hot)
1/2 teaspoon ground pepper
1/4 teaspoon liquid smoke

Heat olive oil in small, heavy saucepan over low heat. Add onion and garlic and cook, stirring often, until onions are translucent, 8-10 minutes. Stir in remaining ingredients until well blended. Simmer gently, stirring often, until reduced and thickened, 15-20 minutes. Adjust seasonings to taste.

Asparagus Dillys
1 quart

When there's no time for canning but you still want homemade goodness, refrigerator pickles are the answer. And don't stop with cucumbers and beans—try asparagus, whose inherent elegance makes even plebeian pickles sophisticated. Peeling the stalks helps the asparagus absorb flavor and makes a particularly handsome presentation.

    1 teaspoon dill seed
    1 teaspoon dill weed
    2 medium cloves garlic, thin-sliced
    1-2 jalapeño peppers, seeded and
       thin-sliced
    1 pound asparagus
    1 1/2 cups cider vinegar
    5 teaspoons coarse kosher salt

Place dill seed, dill weed, garlic, and peppers in clean one-quart canning jar. Trim asparagus to fit height of jar and peel them. Pack asparagus, tips up, into jar. Bring vinegar, salt, and 1 1/2 cups water to boil in non-reactive saucepan. Pour hot liquid over asparagus, cover tightly with fitted lid, and cool to room temperature. Refrigerate at least two weeks to develop flavor.

120. Cherry De-Lite
Country Ovens, Ltd.
P.O. Box 195 229 Main St.
Forestville, WI 54213
920-856-6767 or 800-544-1002
•

Life Is Just a Bowl of Dried Cherries

Door County dairy farmers Mike and Kathy Johnson were looking for a way to diversify their 125-year-old family business. They considered "everything from growing mushrooms in the basement to broccoli," says Kathy, but when someone suggested drying cherries, a famous local crop, they decided to give it a try. Kathy used a $15 home dehydrator for the first test and the results got raves.

The company they named Country Ovens, Ltd. began processing "Cherry De-lite" dried cherries in 1987. At first just four people did all the work, but today the business is big enough to have its own factory/retail store and to sell the little red wrinkled fruits via mail order and at roadside stands and shops throughout the peninsula.

Only fancy, Grade A tart cherries from Door County are used for these flavor-filled goodies. Country Ovens slow-thaws the pitted, sugared cherries then drains off the juice (which is used to make products like syrup and wine) and spreads the fruit on large trays. The trays get stacked on wheeled carts, 16 of which are loaded into a custom-made oven that can dehydrate 7,000 pounds of cherries at a time. Stored airtight in cartons, the fruit is packed, sealed, labeled, boxed—all by hand. It takes eight pounds of fresh cherries to make one pound of dried.

The product is fat-free, chock full of Vitamin A, and 100 percent natural—that means no artificial color or preservatives are added. The meaty, sweet-tart fruits are a delicious substitute for raisins in cookies, cakes, and other sweets and they are just as compelling in salads and other savory dishes. But they may be best of all as an out-of-hand snack. Stored airtight, Cherry De-lites keep well for months. Once someone in your house tastes them, however, they won't last that long.

Cherry De-lite Fruit Relish
About 2 cups

Try this fruit relish—it's out-and-out excellent. The folks at Country Ovens recommend serving it with turkey, chicken, or pork. Like chutney, it is also superb with curry dishes. Some people simply layer it with cream cheese on crackers. My favorite is adding the ruby relish to a smoked turkey sandwich on light rye with thin slices of Swiss cheese.

Try to locate a thin-skinned orange and lemon for this recipe and use a very sharp knife to slice them as thinly as you can.

1 orange
1 lemon
3/4 cup dried cherries
3/4 cup dried cranberries
2 cups brown sugar
1/2 teaspoon each ground
    cinnamon, nutmeg, and cloves
1/2 stick cinnamon
1/2 cup apple cider vinegar

Wash and dry orange and lemon. Slice off and discard their ends. Cut both fruits in half lengthwise, cut out cores and remove all seeds. Slice orange and lemon halves paper-thin. Combine all ingredients in heavy saucepan. Bring to simmer and cook over low heat, stirring frequently, until fruit is very soft and mixture is thick, 30-45 minutes. Cool. Serve chilled.

Dried Cherry Waldorf Salad
6 servings

Green Bay resident Ann Galbraith Miller took first place in a Wisconsin Trails *magazine cooking contest with this remake of a classic Waldorf salad.*

4 large apples (use both sweet and tart)
lemon juice
1/3 cup dried Door County cherries
2-3 stalks celery, sliced
1 cup fruit-flavored yogurt or 1 cup
    plain yogurt mixed with maple syrup
    and cinnamon to taste
1/2 cup chopped roasted almonds
fresh berries, sliced star fruit, or
    kiwi for garnish

Cut apples into 1/2-inch chunks; toss with lemon juice to prevent browning. Combine with dried cherries, celery, and yogurt. Chill. Just before serving, sprinkle with almonds and top with fruit garnish.

Chocolate Cherry Bundt Cake
16 servings

No one I've served this dessert to has been able to guess the secret ingredient. That's because zucchini (yes, zucchini!) adds denseness and moisture without affecting the cake's considerably rich chocolate-cherry flavor. If you don't have a Bundt pan, the cake can also be successfully baked in an angel food cake tin (but be generous with the butter and flour when you prepare the pan). Serve with cherry vanilla ice cream or frozen yogurt.

3 eggs
3/4 cup white sugar
3/4 cup brown sugar
2 teaspoons cherry extract
1/2 cup canola oil
2 cups flour
1/3 cup unsweetened cocoa
1 teaspoon baking powder
1 teaspoon baking soda
1/2 teaspoon salt
3/4 cup low-fat milk
2 heaping cups grated zucchini
1/2 cup coarsely chopped
    dried cherries*
powdered sugar

Heat oven to 350 degrees. Grease and flour a 12-cup bundt pan. Beat eggs with electric mixer at medium speed in large bowl 2 minutes. Gradually add the sugars and cherry extract and beat until thick, about 2 minutes. Beat in oil.

In separate bowl, sift flour, cocoa, baking powder, baking soda, and salt. Alternately stir flour mixture and milk into egg mixture. Fold in zucchini and chopped dried cherries. Pour into prepared pan. Bake until toothpick inserted near center comes out clean, 45-55 minutes (do not overbake!). Cool cake in pan about 15 minutes, then invert onto rack and cool completely. Dust with powdered sugar before serving. Note: This cake freezes well.

To prevent sticking while you are chopping dried cherries, sprinkle them first with a little flour.

121. Honey Acres, Inc.
Highway 67 North
Ashippun, WI 53003
920-474-4411
•

Honey Of A Heritage

When 19th-century immigrants came to Wisconsin, they found an ideal place to carry on the food customs of their homelands, some of which went on to become culinary signatures of the state. Germans found ample wildlife and grazing lands for domesticated animals and used their butchering skills to make sausages. The clear waters and cold weather near Lake Michigan made beer brewers happy. Swiss and other European dairy farmers learned that the region's rich soil would sustain feed crops for cows, which allowed cheesemaking to flourish.

It was the same for beekeeper Christian Friederich (C.F.) Diehnelt of Rosswien, Germany, who came across in 1852 to discover the abundant fresh clover and wildflowers of southeastern Wisconsin's meadowlands. Soon he built an apiary and began selling honey. And while honey didn't make it to icon status statewide, it certainly dominates the lives of C.F.'s descendants, who are still in the honey business five generations later.

The company, once called Linden Apiary, passed from father to son to grandson and was moved from Milwaukee to Menomonee Falls, where in 1930 it was renamed Honey Acres. In 1980, a larger plant opened in rural Ashippun; today C.F.'s great grandson Walter is master beekeeper and the immigrant's great-great grandson Eugene Brueggeman is president of a business that's been in the family since early statehood.

On a breezy day near the end of September, production at

Packing honey at Honey Acres, Ashippun.

Honey Acres is winding down for the season, which lasts from about July 1 through October 1. During the warm months the bees feed on clover, wildflowers, basswood, and buckwheat, producing an array of honey that ranges from pale-colored and mellow-flavored to red-tinged and robust.

Honey Acres bees may rest during winter, but the business doesn't. During the season, when nectar-laden frames are pulled from the hives they are sent to the factory. First, the waxy capping is scraped off. The honey is extracted from the frames by the power of centrifugal motion, piped into a truck-sized tank, then piped into barrels where it is held until it's scheduled for the bottling machine.

Since honey can crystallize as it stands, the barrels are gently warmed and the contents strained just before bottling. "It's a year-round operation," says Eugene, who also buys honey on the open market to bottle and sell. The fall months are particularly busy as the factory gears up for the "gift-box holidays," and all year long there's a demand from places like Harrod's of London for their specialty products.

Although only a portion of the honey bottled by Honey Acres is produced from their own hives, only Honey Acres honey is used to make certain specialty products. These include honey mints (sweet, smooth pure honey centers covered with dark chocolate and flavored with mint oil), honey bears (soft, chewy confections in the shape of tiny bears), honey mustards, and honey cremes (sweet, fruit-flavored spreads for breads, bagels, and muffins).

You can find these items and more at the factory two miles north of Ashippun on Highway 67, where a gift shop stocks Honey Acres products (also available by mail order). The building also houses the entertaining Honey of a Museum, with its educational video about bees and beekeeping, a close-up view of the activity in a real bee tree, and colorful, informative displays.

Honey Carrot Soup
5-6 servings

Carrots have a natural sweetness that's highlighted with honey in a soup adapted from "Cooking with Honey," a booklet from the folks at Honey Acres. I added the mint because I think it also has an affinity for carrots. The color of this soup is a beautiful melon-orange. Low-salt canned chicken broth may be substituted for homemade.

1 pound young carrots, thinly sliced
1 cup chopped onions
2-3 cups chicken broth
2 tablespoons honey
1 cup milk or half-and-half
salt and pepper
sour cream or yogurt
chopped fresh mint or parsley

Combine carrots, onions, and enough chicken broth to barely cover vegetables in soup pot. Bring to low simmer, cover, and cook until vegetables are very tender, about 15 minutes. Puree in blender or food processor until smooth. Return to pot; add honey and milk. Season to taste with salt and pepper. Heat gently and thoroughly. Garnish each bowl with a dollop of sour cream or yogurt and chopped fresh mint.

Sweet Potato Salad
6-8 servings

The sweet potato is another naturally sweet vegetable that honey complements. But don't think of this as a "sweet" salad; it's really a savory side dish that goes well with spicy main courses like jerk chicken or blackened catfish.

3 pounds sweet potatoes, peeled and
    cut into chunks (about 8 cups)
4 tablespoons apple cider vinegar
3 tablespoons honey
finely grated zest of 1 lemon (grate only
    the yellow portion of the rind)
2 tablespoons lemon juice
1 tablespoon brown mustard
salt and pepper
3 tablespoons corn oil
1 small sweet red pepper,
    finely chopped
3 slender green onions, finely chopped

Place sweet potato chunks in pot; cover with water and bring to simmer. Cook until barely tender, 8-10 minutes. Meanwhile, mix vinegar, honey, lemon zest, lemon juice, mustard, and salt and pepper to taste in large bowl. Whisk in corn oil. When sweet potatoes are done, drain well and gently toss with dressing (which will be absorbed). Stir in sweet red pepper and green onion. Let stand at room temperature 1 hour or in refrigerator several hours, stirring occasionally. Serve at room temperature.

Sweet & Spicy Bean Salad
6-8 servings

The flavor of a little honey is distinct enough to stand up to a spicy bean salad without over-sweetening the vegetables. If you have home-cooked dried beans instead of canned, all the better.

1/2 pound green beans, cut into
    1-inch pieces
1 can (16 ounces) "chili hot" beans,
    drained
1 can (15 ounces) garbanzo beans,
    drained
1/2 cup finely chopped sweet onion
6 tablespoons apple cider vinegar
3 tablespoons honey
2 jalapeño peppers, seeded and
    finely minced
pepper to taste

Bring large pot of water to boil; add green beans and boil under partially tender, about 3 minutes. Drain. Toss still-hot beans with remaining ingredients. Marinade several hours or overnight in refrigerator, tossing occasionally. Serve at room temperature.

122. Kaap's Old World Chocolates

1921 S. Webster St.
Green Bay, WI 54301
920-430-9041
Mail order 888-430-9043

•

Making Candy, Making Memories

Mention Kaap's chocolates to a Green Bay resident and it's like bringing out a treasured photo album: the response will be small cries of delight and fond reminiscing. Carl and Carol Johanski knew this when they decided to buy the landmark business that has been part of Titletown for more than 85 years. Indeed, like loyalty to the Packers and deep-fried bay perch on Friday nights, Kaap's candy is part of the very fabric of Green Bay life. "People come in with their stories about Kaap's every day," says Carl, who revived this cherished hometown tradition when he re-opened Kaap's Old World Chocolates in 1996.

Having grown up in Green Bay, I have stories of my own about Kaap's, which was once a restaurant as well as a candy kitchen. When I was sixteen and selling women's sportswear at Nau's department store, Green Bay's downtown was a bustle of unique, locally-owned businesses. I had my pick of spots for a lunch break. Usually all I could afford was a bowl of Chili John's or a sandwich from Schweger Drug, but once every few weeks, I'd splurge and go to Kaap's for a grown-up plate lunch and a couple of caramels to go. Later, during my college years, a bag of Kaap's candy could help me through a tiresome study session or a break-up with a boyfriend. And all through my growing-up years, Christmas wasn't just about Santa Claus and midnight Mass; it often meant Kaap's

angel food candy and Tom and Jerry mix.

Back then, the store was still operated by its original owner, Otto Kaap, a musician and self-taught candymaker who built the business from a small candy kitchen into a bakery/bar/German restaurant complex famous for its charming atmosphere and high-quality food and service.

Otto was a bald, gangly gentleman with large ears, wisps of white hair, and a thin, turned-down mouth. He worked the front register in a dark suit and bow tie, making a rather dour contrast to the display cases crammed with sweets that flanked him. In truth, Otto scared me a bit. But I would have braved the bogeyman for Kaap's legendary chocolate creams. Or caramels. Or truffles. Or dipped fruits and nuts.

Variety, hands-on preparation, and top-notch ingredients characterized Kaap's candies then as they do now. After Otto died in 1974, Horst Stemke, his brother Walter, and Erich Dietrich operated Kaap's restaurant until, with the razing of the building to make way for an urban mall, it was closed in 1980. Stemke continued to offer a limited line of Kaap's candies until Carl Johanski, in the midst of a career change, approached him about buying the business. "I always thought Kaap's had the best candy," says Carl, "And I do love chocolate." Today, Carl uses Otto's original recipes, equipment, and in a couple of cases, employees, to produce a full line of Kaap's old-fashioned, hand-dipped confections.

Green Bay is very happy about that. Carl describes the mad rush for chocolate that occurred when he re-opened the business on Webster Street in the fall of 1996: "The whole thing was just a blur. Despite being around candy all the time, I never ate, I lost 15 pounds. I made candy day and night. If there had been another day before Christmas, I don't know what we would have done...we were out of candy!" During the week between Christmas and New Year's, "it took several employees all day just to keep up with the Tom and Jerry mix. It has a lot of powdered sugar in it. The women were white from head to toe."

Two staff members are Lucretia Luedeman, dipping expert, and Mary Tahlier, the prime packer. Both were on the staff at the original Kaap's, Carl notes, emphasizing his intent to change as little as possible from the way things were done in Otto's day. "We make the true cream, the way it used to be—soft-centered, so that when you bite into it, it should run down your chin a bit." Kaap's holiday specialties still include chocolate eggs for Easter and angel food candy at Christmas time.

The only changes they've made are to improve something, says Carl, like adding real maple syrup to the maple creams and offering angel food throughout the winter months.

And, perhaps, creating sweet, new memories for the folks of Green Bay.

Angel Food Candy
About 100 pieces (enough for several homemade Christmas gifts)

The art of candymaking is almost a lost one, which is one reason to be grateful for places like Kaap's. But there's a joyful satisfaction in preparing your own batch of sweets, too, not the least of which has to do with the reactions you'll get. This is an Allen family recipe.

For successful candymaking, you'll need the right equipment and the right weather. Pick a clear, dry day, for humid weather can throw temperature readings off. Be sure you've got an accurate candy thermometer. Use a large pan; many candies boil or foam up significantly as they cook so you'll need plenty of room. The pan also should be heavy enough so the heat is distributed evenly and the bottom doesn't scorch. Stir the mixture with a long wooden spoon; a metal spoon will get too hot to handle. Finally, for cleanup, use very hot or boiling water to melt away any sticky mess.

2 cups firmly packed light brown sugar
2 cups light corn syrup
4 teaspoons baking soda
about 3 pounds baking chocolate,
    chopped

Generously butter a large pan (at least 10-by-14 inches). Combine brown sugar and corn syrup in 4-quart, heavy saucepan. Bring to boil and cook over medium heat, stirring constantly, until mixture reaches crack stage—290 degrees on a candy thermometer. This will take 30-40 minutes. As soon as it reaches the right temperature, turn off heat, add baking soda, and quickly beat mixture with wooden spoon briefly but thoroughly (mixture will foam up considerably). Quickly pour mixture into the buttered pan. Allow the mass of candy to cool long enough to handle it, then remove from pan.

Now allow candy to cool and harden completely. Angel food candy is done correctly when it is foamy but brittle. It should crunch lightly when you bite it and then melt in your mouth with a smoky-sweet flavor. Break the candy mass into irregular pieces (use a blunt object for this).

Melt chocolate in double boiler (you may have to do this in batches). Using tongs, dip candy pieces into chocolate to coat them completely; place on waxed paper. Refrigerate candy to set the chocolate. Store airtight in a cool, dry place.

> **123. The Kosher Market**
> **Kosher Meat Klub**
> **4731 W. Burleigh St.**
> **Milwaukee, WI 53210**
> **414-449-5980**
> •

Where Everything Is Kosher

Like other immigrant groups in the early 20th century, Jews became more and more Americanized as they tried out new dishes like macaroni and cheese and new products like canned tomatoes. Still, few food companies knew how to promote their products to the large Jewish population who followed *kashrut*, the set of dietary laws that stem from the Hebrew Bible. According to Joan Nathan in *Jewish Cooking in America* (Alfred A. Knopf, 1994), one of the first packaged foods to be rabbi-approved and promoted as kosher was Maxwell House coffee. Soon the H. J. Heinz Company was producing vegetarian baked beans specifically for the kosher market, and a Jewish baker named Charley Lubin began selling a line of frozen cheesecakes that he named after his daughter, Sara Lee.

Today there are thousands of canned, packaged, and frozen kosher goods—so many, in fact, that entire stores are devoted to them. In Wisconsin, the place to go is The Kosher Market in Milwaukee. Everything here, from crackers to bottled salad dressings, is kosher.

But The Kosher Market doesn't sell just packaged goods. People regularly come from all over the state to make selections from the meat cases, where they find the "Rabbinical Supervision" label on ground beef, veal patties, calves liver, beef rib steaks, and a variety of meats. You can even buy a kosher Thanksgiving turkey here.

People like Lori Greenberg of Madison get a shipment of meats each week for the Sabbath. Once a year she makes a special trip to Milwaukee. "I rent a van and fill it with everything I need for the entire Passover week: canned matzo soup, bottled gefilte fish, boxed cake products, everything with the special Passover label."

Marcia and Dovid Eisenbach opened the store in 1977. "It was a kosher club originally," says Marcia. "When we opened it was very small, a little store with a few shelves." Now, in addition to the rabbi-approved groceries and meats, the business also produces specialty items and operates an active catering service from their kosher kitchen. Prepared foods like chopped liver are popular, as are several kinds of kugel, including potato, Jerusalem, salt and pepper, and sweet kugel.

As Joan Nathan points out, many Americans feel that the kosher symbol on food labels is synonymous with better and safer. "Of the 6,500,000 people who purposely buy kosher foods, only 1,500,000 are kashrut-observing Jews," she says. So whether you are Jewish, Muslim, vegetarian, a Seventh-Day Adventist, or a "regular" grocery shopper, you'll find what you need at The Kosher Market.

Sweet Noodle Kugel

12 or more servings

This is a simple, plainly delicious kugel from Marcia Eisenbach of The Kosher Market. If you must jazz it up, add raisins or a butter-crumb topping.

1 pound medium or wide noodles
4 eggs
1 cup sugar
1 teaspoon cinnamon
2 tablespoons margarine, melted
1 can (8 ounces) crushed pineapple, drained

Heat oven to 350 degrees. Grease a 9-by-13-inch baking pan. Boil noodles until tender in boiling, salted water; drain. Mix well with remaining ingredients and spread in prepared pan. Bake until liquid has set and surface is partially browned, 40-50 minutes.

Day-After-Thanksgiving Turkey Noodle Soup
Any number of servings

What's the secret to really good soup? The stock, of course. There's no substitute for fragrant, long-simmered homemade broth, in this case made from a leftover holiday bird (or an everyday bird, for that matter). It seemed silly to give measurements here, for turkey soup is a feel-as-you-go kind of thing, a preparation that comes more from the heart than the head. No two batches are alike, nor should they be; vary the flavorings and vegetables as you will.

Broth:
large turkey carcass, preferably with
    a little meat still clinging to
    the bones
onion skins and ends
carrot peelings and ends
celery leaves and cores
a few peppercorns
bay leaf

Soup:
butter
chopped onion
chopped celery
chopped carrot
dried parsley, sage, and rosemary
optional: other vegetables such as
    corn, chopped beans, sliced
    mushrooms, etc.
broth
chopped cooked (leftover) turkey meat
egg noodles
salt and pepper

Break up turkey carcass and place in large stock pot with remaining broth ingredients. Cover with cold water and bring to a very slow simmer over medium heat. Reduce heat to low; slowly simmer stock, without letting it boil, several hours. Strain through cheesecloth into large bowl. Refrigerate overnight.

Heat a little butter in soup pot, add onion, celery, and carrots. Cook over medium heat until vegetables are softened. Stir in herbs and other vegetables, if using. Skim congealed fat from surface of chilled broth. Pour broth into soup pot, add chopped turkey meat, and bring to slow simmer. Cook gently until vegetables are very tender, 15-20 minutes. Add noodles and cook until tender. Season soup to taste with salt and pepper.

---

124. Maple Hollow
W1887 Robinson Drive
Merrill, WI 54452-9543
715-536-7251
•

Mastering the Art of Maple Syrup

Before Barbara Polak moved from California to Wisconsin, she had never made maple syrup. But when she married Joe Polak, Barbara became part of a family that has maple syrup flowing in its veins. The Polaks have nearly 110 years of experience in the business, beginning with Joe's immigrant grandfather, whose 19th-century orchard and sawmill enterprise added maple syrup making to its line; continuing with Joe's dad, who expanded the syrup venture; and passing to Joe himself, who as a maple sugaring equipment dealer and former president of the Wisconsin Maple Producers Association, is something of a leader in Wisconsin's maple syrup industry today.

And Barbara? She seems to have absorbed all 110 years of experience into her own veins. When she gives a tour of Polak's Maple Hollow and describes the intricacies of maple syrup processing—from the depiction of a tubing system that snakes through an 80-acre expanse of maple trees to a definition of their specialty maple cream—it's clear that this California girl walks the maple syrup walk and talks the maple syrup talk.

The tubes, she explains, send sap to a pumping station which moves the sap into stainless steel vats. At the syrup house, a cherry-red building that looks like a playhouse on the outside and a mad scientist's laboratory on the inside, a "reverse osmosis machine" removes most of the moisture in the sap before it goes to an evaporator. "This saves a lot of wood," says Barbara. "We use the removed water in the yard or for cleaning."

After evaporation, the sap is now syrup and is held in hot-sealed drums so that the Polaks can bottle year-round. In the canning room, "we reheat the syrup in a 60-gallon steam kettle and check its density. Too thick and we add water, too thin and we boil it some more." Next the syrup takes a trip through the filter press, then is kept hot—for sterilization purposes—in a water-jacketed tank until it is syphoned into bottles. The bottle covers are screwed on by hand. Labeling and shipping are also done by hand.

During tapping season, Barbara explains, cooler temperatures produce the amber-colored, delicate product that some say has the truest maple flavor. Warmer temperatures can cause the sap to darken and develop a heartier tasting syrup.

Besides syrup, the Polaks make maple candy, maple cream, and maple sugar. The cream is pure maple syrup cooked to a taffy-like substance then whipped to an ultra-smooth, golden-white spread. It is rich but fat-free, delicious on toast, bagels, or muffins. Barbara recommends maple cream as a cookie frosting, cake or candy filling, or doughnut glaze. She sprinkles maple sugar granules—another offspring of pure syrup—on foods like cereal and squash. "Use it in recipes as you would white or brown sugar," Barbara advises. "It gives true maple flavor without changing the texture of the dish."

Trust her, she's knows what's she talking about.

Muddled Maple Old-Fashioned
1 serving

Recipes for old-fashioneds usually call for whiskey, but ask for the drink in a Wisconsin bar, and you're likely to get one made with brandy. Less likely but just as "Wisconsin" is this version flavored with sweet maple syrup.

1 orange wedge
1 teaspoon maraschino cherry juice
2 teaspoons maple syrup
4 dashes bitters
1 1/2 ounces brandy, bourbon, or whiskey
sour or sweet soda
maraschino cherry and orange slice

Mash orange wedge, cherry juice, and maple syrup with a fork in a 12-ounce rocks glass. Fill with ice. Add bitters and liquor. Pour in soda to fill glass. Stir vigorously. Garnish with cherry and orange slice.

Maple Glazed Onions

3 servings

Give onions the maple syrup treatment in this culinary equivalent of making a silk purse out of a sow's ear.

16-20 small onions (1 pound total)
1 1/2 tablespoons butter
salt
2 tablespoons maple syrup
1/4 cup chicken stock or apple cider
1 tablespoon apple cider vinegar
freshly ground black pepper

Drop onions (skin-on) into a pot of boiling water. Parboil 4 minutes; drain and let cool. Trim off ends with a sharp knife, leaving a little of the root ends on. Slip off skins. Cut a 1/4-inch-deep "X" in root end of each onion.

Melt butter over medium-low heat in a skillet large enough to hold onions in a single layer. Add onions; sprinkle lightly with salt. Cook 12 to 15 minutes, shaking pan frequently to prevent sticking. Pour in maple syrup and continue to cook, shaking pan, 2 to 3 minutes. Add stock or cider, vinegar, and pepper to taste. Raise heat and bring liquid to hard simmer. Cook until reduced to a syrupy glaze, again shaking pan often. Can be held at this point, then gently reheated.

Sugarbush Gingersnaps

5 dozen cookies

Pure maple syrup, maple sugar, and fresh ginger root make these treats snap with flavor. If maple sugar isn't available, use all white sugar (1 cup total). Maple cream, an ideal frosting for the cookies, may separate if stored in the cupboard. To correct this, beat until smooth. For best results, keep maple cream chilled; bring to room temperature to spread it.

Maple sugar and maple cream are available at specialty stores and by mail order from Maple Hollow and other producers.

4 tablespoons (1/4 cup) butter,
   softened
3/4 cup white sugar
1/4 cup maple sugar
1 egg
1/4 cup maple syrup
1 1/2 tablespoons apple cider vinegar
1 teaspoon vanilla extract
1 1/2 teaspoons grated
   peeled ginger root
2 cups plus 2 tablespoons
   all-purpose flour
3/4 teaspoon baking soda
1 teaspoon ground ginger
1 teaspoon ground cinnamon
1/4 teaspoon ground cloves
bottled maple cream

Cream butter and sugars thoroughly in a large bowl. Beat in egg. Stir in syrup, vinegar, vanilla, and grated ginger root. Sift flour, baking soda, ground ginger, cinnamon, and cloves in a separate bowl. Stir dry mixture into wet mixture until a soft dough forms.

Roll dough into four logs, each about 1 1/2 inches in diameter. (Use flour on hands to prevent sticking.) Wrap in wax paper and freeze until firm, two or more hours.

Heat oven to 375 degrees. Grease cookie sheets. Slice 1/4-inch rounds from logs and place 1 1/2 inches apart on cookie sheets. Bake 9-10 minutes. Cool on wire racks. Frost with maple cream.

> ### 125. Mercado El Rey
> **1023 S. Cesar Chavez Drive**
> **(16th St.)**
> **Milwaukee, WI 53204**
> **414-643-1640**
> •
> **El Rey Plaza**
> **3524 W. Burnham St.**
> **Milwaukee, WI 53215**
> **414-643-1616**
> •

Viva El Rey

At Mercado El Rey, a Mexican food market on Milwaukee's south side, the variety is astounding. Down the produce aisles, jam-packed mounds form a long, multi-colored mountain of fresh fruits and vegetables. Here you'll find *camotes dulces* (sweet potatoes) as big as footballs, smooth-skinned emerald *aguacates* (avocados), spiky *nopalitos* (cactus), blackened *platanos* (plantains), and shiny, plump *chiles* so gorgeous they'll bring tears to your eyes without even being tasted. Above the produce bins festive *piñatas* dangle from a wire; like dancing gods in a cartoon heaven, the colorful tigers, snowmen, Mickey Mouses, and Cookie Monsters seem to glorify the bounty below.

Grocery shelves are lined with imported products: canned *jugos* (fruit juices), packaged *galletas* (cookies), dried beans, dried chilies, exotic spices, and favored brands of soda.

Brightly lit refrigerated cases yield not just one, but several kinds of *chorizo*—a spicy sausage tinted and flavored with burnt-red *achiote* (annato seeds). There are Mexican deli salads, *pico de gallo* (fresh tomato salsa), and dairy products like crumbly *queso rancherito* and thick, rich *crema fresca casera*, manufactured from quality Wisconsin cows.

For all this variety, the real splendor at Mercado El Rey is the line of foods produced in-house and sold from small shops located within the larger store. The El Rey *panaderia* (bakery) churns out traditional Mexican baked goods, including pumpkin-filled *empanadas*; pinwheel-shaped *molletes*, frosted egg-bread pastries; and *bolillos*, the crusty, torpedo-shaped hard rolls that pervade central and southern Mexico. A *carneria* (meat market) yields everything from *chuleta* (steaks) to *menudo* (the stomach lining of a cow). Fresh El Rey tortillas, often still moist and warm from the press, sell by the caseful, or you can enjoy them in one of the menu items featured at El Rey's restaurant.

And finally, there's the deli counter, located in a back corner of the store, where shoppers have more bewildering choices. What shall it be? *Papas rellenas* (stuffed potatoes) or *flautas* (stuffed, deep-fried corn tortillas)? *Arroz con gandules* (rice with pigeon peas) or *ensalada de nopalitos* (cactus salad)? And what about the *chicharron*, great, wickedly delicious slabs of fried pork rind? Whatever you do, don't miss the *tamales*, that very special, very labor-intensive Mexican specialty of stuffed *masa* (corn dough) steamed in fragrant corn husks. Individual bean- and chicken-filled tamales are available at the deli counter, but the ones filled with shredded pork are so popular that they are sold by the dozen from a self-serve warming oven near the front of the store.

It all started on February 15, 1978, when brothers Beto and Ernesto Villarreal (pronounced VEE-yah-ray-AHL) and their wives, two sisters named Kris and Olivia, opened a small store on 16th Street in the heart of Milwaukee's Latino community. "At first we all kept our regular jobs, but one by one we all left as the business grew," says Olivia, a trim, gracious woman who describes herself as the company's books-and-numbers person. "We had no idea how far this would go," she says.

In fact, it went very far, as small food markets go. Today the El Rey enterprise

*Olivia Villarreal and Idalia Mercado in the panaderia
at Mercado El Rey in Milwaukee*

includes three grocery stores, a tortilla factory, all of the two Villarreal couples' children, and 175 profit-sharing employees. The business serves a large Latino population as well as many other shoppers in the Milwaukee area.

How did they do it? Olivia gives much credit to their banker, who guided them through sensible expansion. "It was like he was our parent," she says. "He taught us to take little steps, but he made sure we were secure." And she admits that she and her partners have worked and studied hard to make the business a success. "We weren't born yesterday. We have degrees. We each have our areas [of expertise]. The first five years we didn't take a vacation."

But more than anything else, says Olivia, it was their faith in God that helped. "We were *given* this," she emphasizes. "We worked, but we were given the opportunity. We'd be stupid to think we did it ourselves."

And because the Villarreals have had help, they believe it is their responsibility to help others, too.

The business, for example, is more than a place to shop. Customers who speak little

or no English can cash checks or pay utility bills with ease at a service counter. The in-house markets are designed to encourage a sense of community. It might be more cost-effective to sell pre-cut, shrink-wrapped meats, for example, but Olivia sees a value in the over-the-counter camaraderie at the carneria. "This is a social thing," she notes. "They may be lined up ten deep, but they don't care, they want to catch up with each other."

"You have to act as if God is watching you," Olivia goes on. "We've been blessed and we're proud of what we've done, but you have to think about the people."

It's clear that the folks at Mercado El Rey do think about people, from the way they share their blessings with employees and customers, to how they provide Latino families with a rich and precious taste of the homeland.

Tamales El Rey
25-35 tamales

Tamales are a Christmas tradition in Mexico, South Texas, and the Latino homes of Wisconsin. Like many holiday ethnic specialties that require elaborate preparation, they encourage family or friends to gather together and share tasks, making the process as nourishing as the results. "Everybody is up to their elbows in masa," says Olivia Villarreal of Mercado El Rey. "Then you clean up and everybody gets all dressed up. After Midnight Mass, we come back and eat and eat. The 24th [of December] is the most important. The 25th is a day of rest!"

The instructions are adapted from recipes by a Villarreal aunt, Tia Criselda. "Usually if the tamale is being filled with chicken, turkey, or seafood, the masa is left white," notes Tia Criselda. "If it is being filled with pork, venison, or beef, the masa is colored with chili powder or ancho or guajillo chilies."

Tomatillos are small, green tomato-like fruits with papery husks. Tostadas are crispy, flat taco shells. You can find these and other specialty ingredients at Latino markets like Mercado El Rey or on the ethnic foods shelves at supermarkets.

> 1/2 pound dried corn husks (about 50 total)
> 2/3 cup lard, softened
> 4 cups *masa harina de maiz* (corn masa mix)
> 1 tablespoon salt
> 1/2 tablespoon baking powder
> about 3 cups chicken, beef, or pork stock
> 1/3 cup melted lard
> optional: 3 tablespoons chili powder or 3 dried ancho or guajillo chilies that have been seeded and cleaned then boiled and pureed with 1/2 cup water
> 1 recipe tamale filling: Chicken & Green Sauce or Pork and Red Sauce, next page
> pico de gallo (chopped fresh tomato salsa or bottled salsa)

Soak corn husks in hot water at least one hour, separating them from each other as they soften. Weight the soaking husks with heavy objects to keep them submerged.

To make masa dough: Beat softened lard with wooden spoon in large bowl until fluffy, 3-5 minutes. Mix masa harina, salt, and baking powder in separate bowl. Mix masa harina alternately with meat stock into beaten lard until dough is soft and spreadable. Beat in melted lard and, if desired, the chili powder or pureed chilies.

Drain corn husks. They should be a bit bigger than a spread-out hand; if not, overlap two of them to make 1 tamale. (Reserve enough soaked husks to line the pot in which they will be steamed.)

To form each tamale: Place 2-3 tablespoons masa dough in center of spread-out husk. Flatten masa so that it covers an area about 3 inches wide by 5 inches long (leave at least 3 inches at the bottom, pointed end of corn husk unspread with masa, and about 1 inch at the wide, top end unspread with masa). Spread 1-2 tablespoons filling down center of masa. Bring the two sides of the husk up and press them lightly together so that the masa forms a seal around the filling. Keep holding the two sides of husk together as you fold them over and around the tamale. Now fold the pointed end about 3 inches up and over the "seam." Continue filling and folding all the tamales.

To cook tamales: Place water to a two-inch depth in bottom of large pot fitted with steam basket. Cover bottom of steam basket with reserved husks. Arrange tamales in steam basket with folded side down and tamales slightly inclined so that filling won't slide out of the open end. If you have any corn husks left, use them to cover the tamales. Place pot on high heat and bring water to boil. Lower heat, cover pot tightly, and steam tamales 1-1 1/4 hours. Tamales are done when masa doesn't stick to corn husks when unrolled. Serve with pico de gallo. Tamales may be frozen and resteamed or reheated in microwave oven.

Chicken & Green Sauce Tamale Filling
(Tamales Verdes de Pollo)

4-6 fresh *serrano* chilies, stems removed
13 ounces (12-15 medium) fresh
   tomatillos, husks removed
1 clove garlic
1/2 cup chicken stock
1/2 cup chopped cilantro (fresh
   coriander)
1 tablespoon vegetable oil
1/4 cup chopped onion
2 chicken breasts (each 8 ounces),
   cooked and shredded with a fork
salt
additional chicken stock, if needed

Place serrano chilies in medium saucepan; add water to fill half the pan. Bring to strong simmer and cook 4-5 minutes. Add tomatillos; cook 4-5 minutes longer. Drain; transfer chilies and tomatillos to blender or food processor. Add garlic and chicken stock; puree. Add cilantro and process briefly.

Heat oil in large skillet, add onion, and saute until translucent. Stir in tomatillo puree; cook over medium-high heat, stirring often, 5-6 minutes. Reduce heat to low, stir in shredded chicken, cover, and cook 5 minutes. Add salt to taste. If filling is too thick, thin with additional chicken stock. Cool; set aside until ready to fill tamales.

Pork & Red Sauce Tamale Filling
(Tamales Rojos de Puerco)

2-4 dried *ancho* or *guajillo* chilies,
   rinsed and seeds removed
1 clove garlic
1/2 cup pork or beef broth (or
   substitute liquid used to soak
   chilies)
1 tablespoon vegetable oil
1/4 cup chopped onion
1 pound pork tenderloin, cooked and
   shredded with a fork
1/2 teaspoon ground cumin
salt
additional pork or beef broth, if needed

Place chilies in small saucepan, cover with water, bring to simmer, and cook 15 minutes. Drain. Scrape "flesh" from the chili "skins." Discard skins and place flesh in blender or food processor. Add garlic and broth; puree.

Heat oil in large skillet, add onion, and saute until translucent. Add the chili puree and cook over medium-high heat, stirring often, 3-5 minutes. Reduce the heat to low, stir in the shredded pork, cover, and cook 5 minutes. Season with cumin and salt to taste. If filling is too thick, thin with additional broth. Cool; set aside until ready to fill tamales.

Cactus Salad Tostadas
(Ensalada de Nopalitos)
6 servings

A cup of cooked baby shrimp may be added to this El Rey specialty.

1 can (26 ounces) sliced tender cactus
1 cup diced tomatoes
1/2 cup chopped onions
1/2 cup chopped cilantro
   (fresh coriander)
1 can (7 ounces) sliced green pickled
   jalapeño peppers
1 teaspoon crushed oregano leaves
1 package (5 ounces) *rancherito* cheese
   crumbled
6 tostada shells

Rinse and drain cactus well. Combine with tomatoes, onions, and cilantro in bowl. Strain juice from pickled jalapeños into tomato mixture; add oregano and half the cheese and stir gently. Cover and marinate in refrigerator at least 1 hour.

To serve, divide salad among the tostadas and garnish with remaining cheese and sliced jalapeños .

---

126. Mississippi Brittle, Ltd
1232 Caledonia St.
La Crosse, WI 54603
608-796-1792 or 800-647-2785
•

Brittle and Beyond

"I don't make peanut brittle," says Sara Weihaupt. "You can get that anywhere." What the dark-eyed entrepreneur does make is Mississippi Brittle, a dense, buttery confection crammed with whole pecans. It's a lusciously delicious candy made without preservatives or additives, reason enough for its popularity at regional gift shops and food stores. But Sara has several more reasons for considering her brittle something special.

First, it comes from a secret recipe passed to her through her family's generations. She makes it the old-fashioned way, on the stove-top, without machines or pre-mixed ingredients, using a keen eye, plenty of real Wisconsin butter, and, as Sara puts it, "Grandma's pinch of this and a

pinch of that."

Sara is a young widow whose black hair is just beginning to turn gray at the temples. She decided to manufacture her favorite family treat after moving to La Crosse in the late 1980s. She came here because her terminally ill husband wanted to spend his last years enjoying the area where he had grown up, a region of bluffs and riverways that Sara also appreciated because of its similarity to her native Pennsylvania. While caring for her husband, Sara realized she also had to think about her own future.

"At first, my only plan was to get through it, but eventually it occurred to me: what am I going to do with the rest of my life?" She was crossing a bridge on the Mississippi River one sunny summer day when the idea to make candy hit her.

"I thought, my God! The candy! Of course!" What had just occurred to her was that the territory she had come to love had no regionally identified product like the beer and cheese in other parts of the state. In that moment Sara recognized that her family's excellent brittle, which she dubbed Mississippi Brittle, was worthy of such status. And she set out to make it happen.

Born in a time of crisis, Mississippi

Sara Weihaupt makes a dense, buttery brittle crammed with goodies at Mississippi Brittle, La Crosse.

Brittle is what sustained Sara through difficult years. Her company now produces several types of brittle products besides their signature pecan brittle, including Mississippi Mix, with whole cashews, almonds, and pecans, and Crantastic Gourmet Brittle, with dried cranberries.

Wholesale accounts have spread Mississippi Brittle throughout the region. The company's retail store, located in La Crosse's quaint Old Towne North neighborhood, is a stop on the local convention bureau's tour. And when visitors ask for a taste of local flavor, natives have plenty of reasons for saying Mississippi Brittle is something special.

Apple Brittle Crisp
6-8 servings

Apples from La Crosse area orchards and Sara Weihaupt's luscious brittle are two regional products featured in this updated classic. Use tart, crisp apples, preferably something local and in season, or mix two or more varieties for more dimension. Jonathans, Macouns, Empires, Cortlands, and McIntosh are several possibilities.

    2 pounds medium apples (6-8 total)
    1/4 cup white sugar
    1 tablespoon fresh lemon juice
    1 cup rolled oats
    3/4 cup firmly packed brown sugar
    1/4 cup flour
    1/2 teaspoon salt
    1/4 teaspoon cinnamon
    5 tablespoons cold butter, cut into
       small pieces
    4-6 ounces Mississippi Brittle or
       other high-quality brittle candy
    whipped cream or ice cream

Heat oven to 375 degrees. Butter an 8-by-12-inch baking dish. Peel and thickly slice the apples. Toss with white sugar and lemon juice; spread in prepared dish. Combine oats, brown sugar, flour, salt, and cinnamon in bowl. Cut in butter with pastry cutter until mixture resembles coarse meal (or you may do this in a food processor using pulse button). Place the brittle in a heavy-duty plastic bag and pound it with a blunt object until brittle is broken up into fine pieces. Toss brittle with oat mixture; sprinkle evenly over apples. Bake until fruit is tender and bubbly and topping is golden brown, 30-40 minutes. Serve warm or at room temperature with whipped cream or ice cream.

---

127. Northern Wisconsin Maid Sugarbush
W8052 Maple Ridge Road
Park Falls, WI 54552
715-762-4796
•

Straight From The Heart

"Take a delicious break from the digital, microwaved, synthetic food of modern day America," reads the brochure from Northern Wisconsin Maid Sugarbush. "Try something as primitive, primeval, and direct from Mother Nature as pure Wisconsin maple syrup." Reading this, I understood what it is about maple syrup that we love so much: it stirs something in us, something genuine and fundamental. We *recognize* the sweet rich flavor from deep within ourselves.

And naturally, we want to share the experience. Maybe that's why Rosemary and John Slack, owners of 200 acres of maple trees near Park Falls, have been in the maple syrup business for more than 30 years. They may use machinery—vacuum-pumped tubes instead of buckets, and wood-fired evaporators instead of boiling pots—but their products are still 100 percent maple-pure and naturally good. They do all their own tapping, processing, bottling, and labeling, making maple syrup, maple candy, maple fudge, and maple butter to supply groceries and gift stores within a 100-mile radius of town.

The Slacks also make products from another natural wonder, wild berries. John gathers wild strawberries, raspberries, and blackberries, which the couple processes into jam. Their goods are available for sale 24 hours a day at the tiny log Sugar Cabin they built across the driveway from their house. The couple's policy here is as generous and guileless as their products. "Come in!" says the hand-printed sign near the entrance. "Help yourself, the light is behind the door, everything is priced. Leave payment on the counter. If you need help, please come to the house. Thank you and have a good day! John and Rosie Slack."

Golden Maple Gingerbread
8-12 servings

This is "blonde" gingerbread, pale in color but not in flavor. The cake is dense, moist, and mapley rich and the fresh ginger leaves a tingle on the tongue. It is very easy to make and as soon as you taste it, you'll be making plans to make it again. Use regular or no-fat sour cream.

2 cups flour
1 teaspoon baking soda
1 teaspoon ground ginger
1/2 teaspoon salt
1 egg, beaten
1 cup sour cream
1 cup maple syrup
1 teaspoon finely minced fresh ginger
powdered sugar

Heat oven to 325 degrees. Grease and flour an 8-by-8-inch baking pan. Sift flour, baking soda, ground ginger, and salt into large bowl. Combine egg, sour cream, maple syrup, and fresh ginger in separate bowl, then stir into flour mixture. Pour into prepared pan and bake until toothpick inserted near center comes out clean, 30-35 minutes. Serve warm or at room temperature with maple-sweetened whipped cream or maple nut ice cream.

Smoked Pork Chops with Maple Mustard Sauce
4 servings

Maple syrup is outstanding with smoked meats, especially when accented by spunky mustard. Use a Dijon-style mustard or try one flavored with honey, cranberries, horseradish, or—guess what—maple syrup. The chops can also be cooked on the grill.

2 teaspoons butter
1/4 cup minced onion
1/3 cup plus 2 tablespoons maple syrup, divided
1/3 cup apple cider vinegar
2 tablespoons flavored mustard, divided
2 teaspoons Worcestershire sauce
1/2 teaspoon liquid smoke (optional)
4 smoked pork chops, at least 3/4-inch thick

Melt butter in small skillet over medium-low heat. Add onions and saute until translucent. Stir in 1/3 cup maple syrup, vinegar, 1 tablespoon mustard, Worcestershire sauce, and liquid smoke, if using. Whisk until smooth. Simmer 6 to 8 minutes, stirring often. Keep warm.

Line broiler pan with aluminum foil; heat broiler. Trim excess fat from pork chops. Combine remaining 2 tablespoons maple syrup and 1 tablespoon mustard; brush half the mixture on one side of chops. Broil meat, plain side down, 4 to 5 minutes. Turn chops, brush with remaining mixture, and broil until heated through, 4 to 5 minutes. Serve with the warm sauce.

---

128. Rolling Meadows Sorghum Mill & Brooms
N9030 Little Elkhart Road
Elkhart Lake, WI 53020
920-876-2182
•

How Sweet It Is

If you're middle-aged or younger, it's quite possible you've never tasted sorghum syrup. But this old-time sweetener was once so popular that Wisconsin produced hundreds of thousands of gallons annually. In farm kitchens, the dark, molasses-like syrup topped pancakes, flavored pies and cookies, and seasoned baked beans. Country doctors prescribed it for iron-deficient patients. The sorghum industry faded when cane sugar became cheaper; these days there's only a handful of producers in the state.

Two of them are Richard and Cheryl Wittgreve, who raise sorghum, broom corn, and other crops on their farm north of Elkhart Lake. They decided to grow sorghum when Richard, who fondly remembered eating sorghum syrup as a youth in Iowa, couldn't locate any in Wisconsin. Their first press was an antique sorghum press the couple found in Iowa and restored. "Our first attempt at making sorghum was by placing a large canner pan on top of some blocks and building a fire under it!" says Cheryl, a fine-featured woman with strawberry-blond hair and wire-rim glasses. "The juice is green, green. The first time I saw it, I thought, no thanks, you keep it. But it smelled good."

Now they use a large three-roller press, have a custom-built, room-size processing pan, and, instead of a making few gallons for personal consumption, average hundreds of gallons a year. In fact, according to the Wittgreves, Rolling Meadows is the largest working sorghum mill in Wisconsin.

While modern technology aids the process, sorghum processing requires a certain faith. For one thing, there's the crop itself. Sorghum, an elegantly tall cane whose tops turns a stunning burnt red when fully ripe, grows best in warmer climates. Though the couple uses an early maturing seed, the threat of an early frost is always present. They must take great care to cut and bundle the cane before a killing frost comes, or else an entire crop can be lost, which has happened to the Wittgreves several times.

Then there's that green juice, which is extracted from the cane, filtered through straw, pumped to the cook room, held for a time in tanks to settle out starches and impurities, boiled until a menacing-looking scum rises (and is discarded), and finally bottled.

Who would believe that a thin, kelly-green liquid full of tiny bits of stalk could become a thick, fragrant, delicious syrup? Sorghum, while similar to molasses, is milder, and has no strong after-bite, says Cheryl. Compared to molasses, she thinks it blends better with other flavors, providing more sweetness and less sharpness. Cheryl says sorghum will keep in the cupboard for at least a year; should it happen to "sugar off," it can be reconstituted simply by heating it.

The Wittgreves sell bottled sorghum from their farm store and offer sorghum-processing and broom-making tours between late August and October. (They urge travelers to call ahead before visiting.)

"Years ago I would have thought my husband was crazy if he had told me what we would be doing today," writes Cheryl in a Rolling Meadows brochure. "But realizing that sorghum is one of the oldest natural sweeteners and watching the trend toward more natural and healthy eating today makes us proud to be part of preserving this American heritage. It's a lot of work, but it's also a lot of fun."

Sorghum Butter Flowers
24-32 flowers

An easy, elegant way to make a brunch or coffee break special.

1/2 cup (1 stick) unsalted butter, softened
2 tablespoons sorghum syrup

Beat butter and sorghum with wooden spoon until creamy and light. Transfer to a pastry bag fitted with a small star tip. Pipe sorghum butter "flowers" onto pan lined with waxed paper. Chill to set. Place flowers on serving plate lined with paper doily. Serve with pancakes, waffles, French toast, or coffeecake.

Coleslaw with Granny Smith Apple & Green Onion
6 servings

A touch of sorghum sweetness mellows the tart apple and lemon accents in this coleslaw, which is best when very fresh. Try this one with fried fish and boiled new potatoes or tuck the coleslaw into a fish fillet sandwich.

4 cups shredded cabbage
1/2 cup shredded or chopped carrot
4 tablespoons minced green onion
2 tablespoons fresh lemon juice
1 tablespoon sorghum syrup
1 tablespoon olive oil
1 Granny Smith apple, peeled and finely chopped
salt and pepper

Toss all ingredients except salt and pepper. Chill 30 minutes, season to taste with salt and pepper, and serve.

Pecan Mustard Chicken
4 servings

Here's a baked, "breaded" chicken breast that puts packaged breadings to shame. Walnuts or hickory nuts could replace the pecans. Serve with spinach salad and rice pilaf or dill-lemon linguine.

4 boneless, skinless chicken breasts (each 6-8 ounces)
3 tablespoons Dijon mustard
1 1/2 tablespoons sorghum syrup
1 tablespoon olive oil
salt and pepper
1 cup minced pecans

Heat oven to 375 degrees. Grease a baking pan or line it with parchment paper or aluminum foil. Place chicken breasts on wax paper on a work surface; remove and discard any small pieces of fat. With the heel of your hand, pound and flatten each breast. Whisk mustard, sorghum, and olive oil together in bowl. Stir in salt and pepper to taste. Spread minced nuts in shallow pan. Brush mustard mixture evenly all over chicken, then lightly press each breast into the nuts on both sides. Place chicken on baking pan; bake 20 minutes. Turn each breast over and bake until done, about 10 minutes longer.

Heat oven to 350 degrees. Grease and flour an 8-by-12-inch or 9-by-13-inch baking pan. Sift flour, cocoa powder, baking powder, baking soda, and salt into large bowl. Using a wooden spoon or electric beaters, thoroughly mash the bananas in a second bowl. Beat in the remaining ingredients (except frosting). Stir wet ingredients into dry; pour into baking pan. Bake until toothpick inserted in center comes out clean, 18-25 minutes, depending on the size of the pan. Do not overbake. Cool completely before frosting.

Banana Chocolate Cake
16-24 servings

Home bakers like Richard Wittgreve's aunt, whose recipe was the inspiration for this one, would sweeten chocolate cake with sweet-tart sorghum when sugar was scarce during World War II. Lard and buttermilk are two other old-time ingredients in this dense, moist cake. I added bananas, whose flavor really comes through when you use very ripe fruit.

For an old-fashioned frosting, combine powdered sugar with cocoa powder and beat in a little milk until desired consistency is reached.

2 cups flour
6 tablespoons unsweetened
   cocoa powder
1 1/2 teaspoons baking powder
1/2 teaspoon baking soda
1/4 teaspoon salt
3 very ripe medium-large bananas
1 scant cup sorghum syrup
1/2 cup buttermilk
2 tablespoons lard or
   vegetable shortening, melted and
   cooled to room temperature
1 egg, beaten
1 teaspoon vanilla extract
chocolate frosting

129. Uncle Harry's Frozen Custard & Ice Cream
100 S. Jefferson St.
Waterford, WI 53185
414-534-4757
•

What the Country Needs

If you try to use a straw to sip a malt from Uncle Harry's Frozen Custard & Ice Cream shop in Waterford, prepare to give your cheeks a workout, because their thick shakes and malt are made with frozen custard, not ice cream. "That's premium custard," says owner/operator Jim Clappier, meaning it has extra eggs and a higher butterfat content than regular custard. (As if any frozen custard could be called "regular.") If you are a chocolate malt aficionado, as I am, you'll find theirs as thick and smooth as a new down blanket and as malty and satisfying as, well, the chocolate malt of your dreams.

Uncle Harry's is a small shop in a small town but it is big with locals. On a brisk November weekday just before 11 a. m.

students begin to cluster around picnic tables outside the entrance. As soon as the door is unlocked, the queue-up begins in front of the ice cream counter. In summer, when the shop's take-a-number device goes into high gear, many of those same students are on the other side of the counter scooping ice cream for the hordes.

The building first housed a Sinclair gas station complete with hydraulic pumps and the green dinosaur logo. After additional years as a White Flash service station, it was transformed, fittingly enough, into an old-fashioned ice cream shop and named Uncle Harry's, after the original owner.

Jim and Ginny Clappier came along in 1994, when a company buy-out had just left Jim without a job at the department store he had managed for years. The Clappiers, who lived along the Fox River about a mile from the shop and already were fans of Uncle Harry's, were in the market for a small business when a *Milwaukee Journal* want ad caught their eye. It described an ice cream shop for sale in their area. "I wonder if that could be Uncle Harry's?" they thought, and called right away.

After purchasing the business, the Clappiers worked with the previous owners to learn how to make 69 flavors of Uncle Harry's ice cream and custard. Then they studied at the University of Wisconsin's famed Babcock Hall Dairy and were soon inventing flavors of their own. Jim says Ginny is the creative force behind concoctions like Turtle Temptation, a kind of sundae-in-a-cone, and All-American Cherry, with vanilla ice cream, maraschino cherries, and blueberry swirls for a patriotic red, white, and blue effect.

The Clappiers' products have won 16 awards at the State Fair, in consumer contests where the contestants are anonymous. "What makes us unique?" says Jim, and lists several things: "The ice cream is hand-dipped, not soft-serve. The many flavors. The custard in our malts. The homemade waffle cones. Real fruit purees. Natural ingredients."

Yes, many things make Uncle Harry's unique, including things Jim Clappier doesn't list—the milk comes from Wisconsin cows, the ice cream and custard are made on premise—but if only one thing could be named, it would be quality. As a sign near the shop entrance says: "We have what the country needs. A good ice cream cone."

Peanut Butter Cup Ice Cream Pie
8-10 servings

Ice cream pies are simple to make and can be varied with quality ingredients like premium frozen custard or ice cream and candy or cookie fillings. At Uncle Harry's, you'll find inspiration in creations like Peppermint Stick or Brandy Cherry Chip Pie. Or, one of my favorite binges, Peanut Butter Cup Pie. Here's one inspired by the goodies at Uncle Harry's.

1 1/2 cups finely crushed chocolate grahams
5 tablespoons melted butter
1 pint chocolate ice cream or frozen custard
1 pint peanut butter or vanilla ice cream
1 heaping cup (about 6 ounces) finely chopped chocolate-covered peanut butter cups (chill the candy for easier chopping)

Heat oven to 350 degrees. Grease a 10-inch pie pan. Mix crushed chocolate grahams with melted butter; press evenly into bottom and sides of prepared pie pan. Bake 10 minutes, cool to room temperature, then freeze 1/2 hour.

Soften ice cream in refrigerator until spreadable but not melting, 40-60 minutes. Working quickly, spread the chocolate ice cream in the frozen pie shell. Sprinkle on half the chopped peanut butter cups. Spread peanut butter (or vanilla) ice cream over the chopped candy, then sprinkle remaining candy over ice cream. Cover with plastic wrap and freeze pie until firm, two or more hours.

To serve, soften pie in refrigerator 20-30 minutes. Cut into pieces and serve immediately.

More Hometown Specialty Flavor

The businesses that follow are arranged in alphabetical order by the name of the business. To locate a business by town name, see page 173. Maps are on pages *xviii-xxv.* All information is subject to change. Travelers should call or write before visiting to get business hours, directions, and other important details.

130. A & W Maple Crest
Route 3, Highway DD
Richland Center, WI 53581
608-647-4015
•

Naturally organic maple syrup made the old-fashioned way. Medium and dark grades are sold directly from the farm or shipped by mail order. Tours during maple season in March and April.

131. Beerntsen's Candies, Inc.
200 N. Broadway St.
Green Bay, WI 54303
920-437-4400 or 888-986-6937
•

Beerntsen's has been called one of the most beautiful candy stores in the United States. Photographs, fixtures, and even some furniture from the 1920s grace candy cases filled with more than 125 kinds of confections. Caramels, creams, angel food candy, peanut brittle, bon bons, and more are all made from scratch with the highest quality ingredients.

Henry Beerntsen started it all in 1925, passed the candy baton to his son Melvin in 1960, and now grandson Mark is leading the pack. "The only thing that has changed is our address," says Mark. "All the recipes are the same."

132. Beerntsen Confectionery, Inc.
108 N. 8th St.
Manitowoc, WI 54220
920-684-9616
•

Another branch of the Beerntsen family, another handsome store, and another candy-making dynasty. The Manitowoc Beerntsen's was founded in 1932 by Joseph Beernsten; his grandson Tom is now owner and full-time candy-maker. Carefully preserved black walnut booths and arches are as gorgeous as the company's turtles, butter almond toffee, and other renowned hand-dipped confections. "We do all our own chocolate work and we make our own ice cream," says Tom. "When you order a sundae, everything is homemade: the ice cream, the marshmallow cream, the hot fudge sauce." Beerntsen's of Manitowoc also offers light lunches.

Jorden's Confectionery, 12th & Garfield, Milwaukee, 1901
State Historical Society of Wisconsin WHi(X3)45116

133. The Chocolate Caper
113 S. Main St.
Oregon, WI 53575
608-835-9294

•

"Chocolate so good, it shouldn't be legal" is Claude and Ellen Marendaz's slogan and I couldn't have said it better myself. Swiss-inspired confections made from top-quality chocolate, fresh-from-the-farm nut butters, and other ingredients. Their line includes creamy Swiss pralines, chocolate-dipped dried apricots, peanut butter cups with raspberry jam, and exquisite truffles. Mail order available as weather permits.

134. Freese's Candy Shoppe
7312 W. Greenfield Ave.
West Allis, WI 53214
414-453-5353

•

Since 1928, Freese's has been supplying the Milwaukee area with old-world confections like fairy food (also known as angel food) dipped in milk or dark chocolate, creams, cherry cordials, English butter toffee, and nut clusters.

135. Grandma's Candy, Cakes & Confections
P.O. Box 105
1022 Main St.
Oconto, WI 54153
920-834-4923

•

"The more you make from scratch, the more you're in demand," says owner Joanne Dufek. She's in demand a lot, with hand-dipped chocolate candies, toffee made in copper kettles, fresh roasted nuts, from-scratch pastries, and wedding and novelty cakes.

136. Guth Candies
415 E. Main St.
Waupun, WI 53963
920-324-5031

•

Fresh ingredients, small batches, and original recipes perfected for nearly 75 years make Guth's Candies a Waupun institution. Their line of fine chocolates includes turtles, melt-aways, almond rocca, creams, English toffee, truffles, fruit clusters, and whimsical chocolate images.

137. Maple Syrup Ranch
P.O. Box 353
N3534 Highway 63 North
Shell Lake, WI 54871
715-468-2251

•

For 35 years Rollie Schaeffer made maple syrup strictly for home use and gifts, but when he retired, says his wife Margo, he decided to make "really nice maple syrup big-time." Now the couple employs seven people during tapping season, sells grade A medium amber syrup in various sizes, and offers free tours year-round. Margo also makes maple-hazelnut candy and cornshuck dolls.

138. Oaks Candy Corner
1200 Oregon St.
Oshkosh, WI 54901
920-231-3660

•

Family-owned candy business since 1890. Hand-dipped chocolates, "melty bars" (large melt-aways), "snappers" (turtles), creams, caramels, and much more. Don't miss the "oysters," an Oaks original made of vanilla cream centers rolled in chocolate and rolled again in crushed peanut. At Christmas, they make seven kinds of candy canes; at Easter, it's chocolate Easter bunnies and cream-filled eggs.

139. Rural Route 1 Popcorn
11623 Highway 80 North
Livingston, WI 53554
608-943-8283 or 800-828-8115

•

The folks at Rural Route 1 had been harvesting seed corn for five generations when the government offered to pay them not to grow seed corn on part of their land. When they tried planting a few acres of popcorn in that section, they were surprised to discover that the land was uniquely suited to the crop. At first, the company sold only pop-your-own kernels but now microwave popcorn and popped popcorn in 16 flavors are available, too. Visit their gift shop/popcorn store for free samples of their products, including cheese-corn, cashew chocolate popcorn, and K'nuckle, a white fudge popcorn with whole almonds. Mail order is also available.

140. Slack's, Inc.
W12153 Slack Road
Lodi, WI 53555
608-592-4804

•

Located off County Trunk V about 1/2 mile from Gibraltar Rock and 2 miles from the ferry at Merrimac, Slack's has been producing home-canned goodies for nearly 45 years. More than 50 varieties of jams, jellies, relishes, butters, and salsa are available year round.

141. Uncle Tom's Newport School Candies
703 Europe Bay Road
Ellison Bay, WI 54210
920-854-4538

•

Homemade peanut brittle, fudge, and pancake mix. Seasonal hours. Mail order available.

Beekeeper
State Historical Society of Wisconsin Classified File 54817

142. Vande Walle's Candies, Inc.
400 N. Mall Drive
Appleton, WI 54915
920-738-7799 or 800-738-1020

•

Don Vande Walle used to have a bakery in Shawano, and when several of his sons wanted the business to get into candy-making, he expanded and opened a store in Appleton. Today he heads a multi-faceted family-business that specializes in chocolate candies, European-style cakes and pastries, breads, and homemade ice cream. Virtually everything—some 170 products—is made from scratch, including turtles, melt-aways, cherry cordials, truffles, angel food candy, ice cream, whipped cream tortes, and bagels. "Your candy should be fresh and in excellent condition," reads their brochure. "If not, we will replace it free."

143. Willow Creek Apiaries
6185 Highways 35 and 61
Potosi, WI 53820
608-763-2063

•

The third generation of a beekeeping family operates this honey and cheese gift shop, offering pure Wisconsin honey and several flavors of creamed honey spread they produce and bottle themselves.

For Further Reading

In researching this book I used many sources, including publications from state and local historical societies, state agricultural publications, magazine and newspaper articles, interviews with proprietors of the businesses highlighted in this book as well as with experts, and a number of books. Here are some of the best sources if you want more information about the subjects covered in this book. Most are available through your local bookstore or library.

Allen, Terese. *Wisconsin Food Festivals.* Amherst, Wis.: Amherst Press, 1995.

Apps, Jerry. *Cheese: The Making of a Wisconsin Tradition.* Amherst, Wis: Amherst Press, 1998.

Chenel, Laura, and Linda Siegfriend. *American Country Cheese: Cooking with America's Specialty and Farmstead Cheeses.* California: Aris Books, 1989.

Hachten, Harva. *The Flavor of Wisconsin.* Madison: The State Historical Society of Wisconsin, 1981.

Holmes, Fred. *Old World Wisconsin: Around Europe in the Badger State.* Minocqua: Heartland Press, 1944.

Shafer, Mary A. *Wisconsin: The Way We Were.* Minocqua: Heartland Press, 1993.

Risjord, Norman K. *Wisconsin: The Story of the Badger State.* Madison: Wisconsin Trails, 1995.

"Wisconsin Specialty Food Shops," "Wisconsin Specialty Meats, Fish & Poultry: Buyer's Guide to Products and Services," and "Guide to Wisconsin Cheese Factory Outlets and Tours" are all free publications available from the Marketing Division of the Wisconsin Department of Agriculture, Trade and Consumer Protection, Box 8911, Madison, WI 53708.

Wisconsin Trails Magazine often has features about local markets and local food businesses.

Markets and Stores Listed by Town Name

*Indicates a featured business

Index

To locate a recipe by type of menu item (appetizer, soup, main course, dessert, etc.), see pages *xiv-xvii*. To locate a business by town name, see pages 173-175.